The International Theory of Leonard Woolf

The Palgrave Macmillan Series on the History of International Thought seeks to publish the best work in this growing and increasingly important field of academic inquiry. Its scholarly monographs cover three types of work: (i) exploration of the intellectual impact of individual thinkers, from key disciplinary figures to neglected ones; (ii) examination of the origin, evolution, and contemporary relevance of specific schools or traditions of international thought; and (iii) analysis of the evolution of particular ideas and concepts in the field. Both classical (pre 1919) and modern (post 1919) thought are covered. Its books are written to be accessible to audiences in International Relations, International History, Political Theory, and Sociology.

Series Editor
Peter Wilson, London School of Economics and Political Science

Advisory Board
Jack Donnelly, University of Denver
Fred Halliday, London School of Economics and Political Science
David Long, Carleton University
Hidemi Suganami, University of Keele

Also in the Series
Internationalism and Nationalism in European Political Thought
    by Carsten Holbraad

The International Theory of Leonard Woolf:
A Study in Twentieth-Century Idealism

Peter Wilson

THE INTERNATIONAL THEORY OF LEONARD WOOLF
© Peter Wilson, 2003

All rights reserved. No part of this book may be used or reproduced in any manner whatsoever without written permission except in the case of brief quotations embodied in critical articles or reviews.

First published 2003 by
PALGRAVE MACMILLAN™
175 Fifth Avenue, New York, N.Y. 10010 and
Houndmills, Basingstoke, Hampshire, England RG21 6XS.
Companies and representatives throughout the world.

PALGRAVE MACMILLAN is the global academic imprint of the Palgrave Macmillan division of St. Martin's Press, LLC and of Palgrave Macmillan Ltd. Macmillan® is a registered trademark in the United States, United Kingdom and other countries. Palgrave is a registered trademark in the European Union and other countries.

ISBN 0-312-29473-5 hardback

Library of Congress Cataloging-in-Publication Data
Wilson, Peter (Peter Colin)
The international theory of Leonard Woolf: a study in twentieth-century idealism/by Peter Wilson.
   p. cm.—(Palgrave series in the history of international thought)
  Includes bibliographical references.
  ISBN 0-312-29473-5
   1. International relations—Philosophy. 2. Idealism—History—20th century. 3. World politics—1919–1932. 4. Woolf, Leonard, 1880–1969—Contributions in international relations. I. Title. II. Series.

JZ1305.W55 2003
327.1'092—dc21
                                          2003043375

A catalogue record for this book is available from the British Library.

Design by Newgen Imaging Systems (P) Ltd., Chennai, India.

First edition: August, 2003
10 9 8 7 6 5 4 3 2 1

Printed in the United States of America.

Transferred to Digital Printing 2007

Contents

Preface	vi
List of Abbreviations	xi
Leonard Sidney Woolf: A Chronology of his Life and Works, 1880–1969	xii
Chapter 1 Fabian, Internationalist, and "Interwar Idealist"	1
Chapter 2 What is Idealism?	11
Chapter 3 International Government: An Exposition	23
Chapter 4 International Government: Analysis and Assessment	53
Chapter 5 Imperialism: An Exposition	83
Chapter 6 Imperialism: Analysis and Assessment	115
Chapter 7 Liberal Internationalism, Anticapitalism, and Consumers' Co-operation: Toward a Nonstate, Nonmarket Approach to International Economic Organization	143
Chapter 8 The Idealist Counterattack: Mr. Woolf versus Professor Carr	177
Chapter 9 Woolf's Legacy: Ideals, Reason, and Historical Change	209
Notes	219
Bibliography	251
Index	265

Preface

This book attempts to add to a growing body of literature that casts doubt on the conventional image of interwar international thought. It does so through a detailed analysis of a neglected figure in the field of International Relations (IR), Leonard Woolf. Since the publication of E. H. Carr's seminal critique, *The Twenty Years' Crisis*, the interwar period has been almost universally conceived as the "utopian" or "idealist" phase of IR thinking. A number of important studies published in the last ten years have demonstrated, however, that this simple image distorts a highly complex reality. Though the so-called interwar idealists can be faulted on a number of grounds, they were not as naïve in their assumptions, as simplistic in their analysis, nor as uniform in their outlook as the received wisdom suggests.

Or at least they were not consistently so. One of the problems with analyzing "interwar idealism" is that the writers often bundled under this label were an eclectic and highly prolific bunch. Some were professional students of the nascent subject of IR. Others were gifted amateurs, politicians, publicists, or political campaigners of one kind or another. All had been scarred directly or indirectly by the blow to civilization and humanity that was the Great War. All were engaged in an intellectual struggle to discover how this grotesque event had been allowed to happen. All, including Carr himself, were engaged in an intellectual and political struggle to prevent such a tragedy ever happening again.

Such was the intensity and sense of urgency of the time that the gap between advocacy and analysis was rarely wide. The protagonists in this drama frequently assumed different roles. They wrote for a variety of audiences. The highly specialized IR audience for which most professional students of the subject write today barely existed. Some of the best works of the period were written for what we would now call "opinion formers." But most works were written for "the intelligent general reader." This type of writing has been, for a number of complex reasons, regrettably squeezed out of modern academic life. But those who dedicated themselves to thinking and writing about international issues in the first half of the twentieth century saw it as their duty, as well as an important purpose, to reach a broader audience. For this reason many of the more unsatisfactory works, from a contemporary professional IR viewpoint, were written with a mass audience in mind.

It must also be remembered that many of those associated with "interwar idealism" had careers that spanned well beyond the 1920s and 1930s. Leonard Woolf provides a good case in point. He began his career as a political writer several years before the outbreak of the 1914 war, and was still regularly penning articles, reviews, and letters on the subject well into the 1950s. So although he is known as an interwar thinker, it is important to record that his intellectual and political engagement with international issues spanned at least four decades.

Given the number of different roles the protagonists assumed, the range of their concerns, their lack of professional inhibitions, and the urgency that dictated much of what they had to say, it is not difficult to represent them in a highly partial way, either flattering or unflattering, with a few carefully chosen examples. Carr represented them in a highly unflattering way. Having lost faith in liberalism, he freed himself from the constraints of the Foreign Office, became a professor, and set about writing one of the most successful polemics in the history of political thought.[1] But in his desire to expose the hypocrisy and cant of the latest manifestation of liberal thinking, which he cunningly labeled "utopianism," he misrepresented the current position of several of his targets, failing in particular to take into account the considerable movement in thought that often accompanies periods of great political turbulence.[2] He also by and large adopted a grapeshot approach, which resulted in a number of unintended casualties. It is certainly doubtful whether a number of figures subsequently denigrated as idealist—especially those of the Left such as G. D. H. Cole, J. A. Hobson, Harold Laski, David Mitrany, and Leonard Woolf—were actually the ones that Carr originally had in mind.

This volume was begun as a University of London doctoral thesis. In the knowledge that Ph.D. theses rarely make good books, allied to a demanding teaching schedule at the LSE, the author did not strenuously pursue publication for a number of years. But encouraged by the head of steam that has built up behind revisionist interpretations of early IR thought, and persuaded by several colleagues that a detailed study of the thought of Leonard Woolf would be a valuable addition to this published pool of knowledge, he somehow stole the nerve to throw himself back into the water, and make all the changes necessary to transform a large and in many ways technical thesis into a readable book.

Apart from some minor adjustments, the book follows the plan of the thesis. The most technical part of the thesis was a detailed analysis of the way in which interwar idealism has been represented in ten well-known postwar accounts, and the relation they bear to the "original" account in *The Twenty Years' Crisis*. To save the reader from unnecessary tedium, and to keep the focus on Woolf, I have summarized the findings of this analysis in a much shorter chapter 2. Those wanting the full account will know where to find it. The conclusion to the volume is new. Most of the biographical material with which each chapter opens is new. The section in chapter 3 examining the influence of George Bernard Shaw's *Fabianism and the Empire* on Woolf is also new. Chapter 8, which discusses Woolf's response to *The Twenty Years' Crisis*, has been substantially revised and updated to take into account the recent outpouring of literature on Carr. I have also added a chronology of Woolf's life and career. Apart from these, the changes made consist of the usual refining, streamlining, and polishing.

It would be foolish to pretend that Woolf was a great political thinker. He wrote several highly original and influential books, a brilliant novel, and an autobiography that many rate as one of the best works in that genre of the twentieth century. Although he did embark on what he considered would be a great work of international political theory, his definitive statement on the subject, his three-volume *After the Deluge*, was largely a failure. Woolf was no Weber, Berlin, or Popper. The painstaking reading and rereading of texts and drafting and redrafting of drafts, which is the *sine qua non* of great scholarship, was not Woolf's métier. It is no accident that the third and final volume of his study, which he revealingly and ill-advisedly called *Principia Politica*, became as it unfolded essentially an autobiography—a mode of writing for which Woolf's talents turned out to be exceptionally well suited.

But the fact that he did not ascend the brightest heaven of political theoretical invention does not mean he is not a figure of considerable importance in the history of IR. Woolf's importance for present-day students of IR is fivefold. First, he was a central figure in the early to mid-twentieth-century attempt to put international relations on a more organized, and orderly, footing. He worked tirelessly both through his writings and his committee work to improve the quality of life at the international level. He was passionate about the need for and the practicability of international reform. Second, in his search for a new way of doing and being at the international level he pioneered what later became known as the functional approach to international organization. This approach was to have a major influence on the development of the social and economic functions of the UN and the process of regional integration in Western Europe. Third, he played a major role in undermining the moral and intellectual foundations of empire. He strenuously argued for the progressive granting of self-government to colonial peoples. Yet he perceptively warned that self-government would only work if it took place within a new framework of international obligation. Fourth, at a time of great political and personal crisis he wrote what was until recently one of the few substantial critiques of Carr's work. Although he was an admirer of Carr and had great sympathy for his unconventional left-wing views, Woolf was not prepared to let the "Red Professor" get away with his sweeping condemnation of the League and all those individuals who had for two decades or more selflessly devoted themselves to the cause of peace and international cooperation. One recent student of the subject has described Woolf's critique as "comprehensive and devastating."[3] Martin Wight used to advise his students not to read *The Twenty Years' Crisis* without Woolf's "deadly reply" in *The War for Peace*.[4] Fifth, as well as being in many ways representative of a particular strand of internationalist thought ("Left-Liberal" or "welfare" or "constructive"), one that enjoyed considerable support during the interwar period (including, paradoxically, from Carr), Woolf is also a thinker who in important ways does not fit with the conventional image of the era. If not a test case, Woolf certainly provides a good case by which the validity of this image can be judged.

In sum one might say that Woolf is an interesting specimen of interwar internationalist (and therefore "idealist"?) thought. But he is also a man who deserves serious attention in his own right. This book attempts to make amends for the neglect that his life and work has suffered for too long.

Over the years the book has been, in some shape or form, in production I have incurred many debts of gratitude. It gives me great pleasure to acknowledge them here. Paul Taylor was instrumental in getting the project off the ground as my doctoral supervisor and was a consistent source of encouragement and sound advice. I have benefited from conversations on the subject with Michael Banks, Erica Benner, Mats Berdal, Ken Booth, Elaine Childs, Michael Donelan, David H. Dunn, Hugh Dyer, Victoria Glendinning, Christopher Hill, Mark Hoffman, Hayo Krombach, Cornelia Navari, Hugh McNeal, James Mayall, Brian Porter, Nicholas Rengger, Hidemi Suganami, Nicholas Wheeler, and the late Philip Windsor. The late and great John Vincent played more than a small role in getting me interested in the history of ideas and was from the outset positive about a detailed study of an "idealist" thinker. Denis Healey shared with me his memories of working with Leonard Woolf in the 1940s and 1950s and provided some typically perceptive insights. Many of my thoughts were forged while working with David Long on an edited book, which grew out of our shared interest in early twentieth-century IR thought. He has been an invaluable source of constructive and creative criticism. I have benefited at various points of the project from the research assistance of Dominique Jacquin-Berdal, Jan-Stefan Fritz, and Nisha Shah. Archivists Leila Luedeking, Nancy Turner, and Elizabeth Inglis were extremely helpful and generous with their time during research visits to the Library of Leonard and Virginia Woolf (Washington State University), the Sir Norman Angell Papers (Ball State University), and the Leonard Woolf Papers (University of Sussex). I have also received valuable help from my secretaries at the LSE over the past seven or eight years, Chris Parsons and Barbara King.

An earlier version of what became chapters 3 and 4 was presented to the British International Studies Association's annual conference held at the University of Newcastle in 1990. The detailed analysis on which chapter 2 is based was presented to the *Millennium* 25th Anniversary Conference held at the LSE in 1996. Various bits and pieces of "work in progress" were presented between 1989 and 1995 to seminars and research workshops at the LSE, and the universities of Birmingham, Bristol, Keele, and Oxford. The comments, suggestions, and criticisms received at these meetings have been invaluable as have those of Katerina Dalacoura, Margot Light, and particularly Spyros Economides who have read various chapters at various stages of their being.

Parts of chapters 1, 3, and 4 were published as "Leonard Woolf and International Government," in David Long and Peter Wilson (eds.), *Thinkers of the Twenty Years' Crisis*, Oxford, Oxford University Press, 1995. Parts of chapters 5 and 6 were published as "Fabian Paternalism and Radical Dissent: Leonard Woolf's Theory of Economic Imperialism," in David Long and Brian Schmidt (eds.), *Imperialism and Internationalism in the Discipline of International Relations*, Albany, NY, SUNY Press, 2003. I am grateful to Professors Long and Schmidt and the publishers for allowing this work to be published here.

My biggest debt, however, is to my dear partner, Debra.

November 2002   PW

List of Abbreviations

CWS	Co-operative Wholesale Society
ECOSOC	Economic and Social Council of the United Nations
FAO	Food and Agriculture Organization of the United Nations
IBRD	International Bank for Reconstruction and Development
ILO	International Labour Organization
IMF	International Monetary Fund
IR	The academic discipline of International Relations
ITU	International Telegraphic Union
NFRB	New Fabian Research Bureau
OECD	Organization for Economic Cooperation and Development
PMC	Permanent Mandates Commission of the League of Nations
UN	United Nations
UNCTAD	United Nations Conference on Trade and Development
UPU	Universal Postal Union
WTO	World Trade Organization

Leonard Sidney Woolf: Chronology of his Life and Work, 1880–1969

1880	Born in Kensington, South West London, November 25.
1892	LW's father, Sidney Woolf, Q.C., dies at the age of 48.
1894	Wins scholarship to St. Paul's School, London.
1899	Wins scholarship to Trinity College, Cambridge.
1902	Receives a First (Third Division) in the Classical Tripos, Part I. Elected to the Cambridge Conversazione Society ("The Apostles").
1903	Receives a Second in Classical Tripos, Part II.
1904	Accepts Eastern Cadetship, Colonial Civil Service. Posted to Ceylon.
1905	Moves from Colombo to Jaffna.
1907	Promoted to Office Assistant, Kandy.
1908	Promoted to Assistant Government Agent, Hambantota.
1911	Returns to England on leave.
1912	Resigns from Civil Service. Joins suffrage movement. Begins writing for *Co-operative News*. Marries Virginia Stephen at St. Pancras Register Office. Honeymoons in France, Spain, and Italy.
1913	Publishes first novel, *The Village in the Jungle*, to widespread critical acclaim. Meets the Webbs. Joins the Fabian Society. Begins writing for the *New Statesman*. VW suffers second serious mental breakdown (first occurred after the death of her father, Sir Leslie Stephen, in 1904).
1914	Publishes second novel, *The Wise Virgins*, to widespread critical disapprobation.
1915	VW's first novel, *The Voyage Out*, published.

1916	*International Government* published. Exempted from military service on medical grounds.
1917	LW and VW found the Hogarth Press. LW's younger brother, Cecil (b. 1887), is killed in the Battle of Cambrai. Publishes *Framework of a Lasting Peace* (ed.), and *The Future of Constantinople*.
1918	Appointed Secretary of the Labour Party Advisory Committee on International Questions. Becomes editor of *International Review* (superceded by the *Contemporary Review* in December 1919).
1919	VW publishes her second novel, *Night and Day*. Monk's House, Rodmell, Sussex, purchased.
1920	*Empire and Commerce in Africa* and *Economic Imperialism* published.
1921	*Stories from the East* published. Resigns from *Contemporary Review*.
1922	Stands (unsuccessfully) for Parliament as Seven Universities' Democratic Association candidate for the Combined English University Constituency. Hogarth Press publishes *The Waste Land*. Appointed political editor of the *Nation*. *International Co-operative Trade* published.
1923	Appointed literary editor of the *Nation*.
1924	Appointed Secretary of Labour Party Advisory Committee on Imperial Questions.
1925	VW publishes *Mrs Dalloway*. LW publishes *Fear and Politics: A Debate at the Zoo*.
1927	VW publishes *To the Lighthouse*.
1928	LW publishes *Imperialism and Civilization*.
1929	VW publishes *A Room of One's Own*. LW resigns as literary editor of the *Nation*.
1930	Founds *Political Quarterly*. Becomes coeditor.
1931	Publishes *After the Deluge*, Vol. 1. Appointed Chairman of the New Fabian Research Bureau, Committee for International Affairs.
1933	*The Intelligent Man's Guide to the Prevention of War* (ed.) published.
1935	*Quack, Quack!* published.
1936	*The League and Abyssinia* published.
1939	Publishes *After the Deluge*, Vol. 2; *Barabarians at the Gate*; and his first and only work of drama, *The Hotel*. LW's mother, Marie, dies aged 91.
1940	*The War for Peace* published. Appointed Chairman, Fabian Research Bureau, International Section. Founds Fabian Colonial

	Bureau with Margaret Cole and Rita Hinden. VW suffers third and final mental breakdown.
1941	VW commits suicide.
1942	Becomes Chairman of Fabian International Bureau. Elected director of *The New Statesman*.
1944	Publishes *The International Post-war Settlement*.
1945	Resigns from the two Labour Party advisory committees.
1947	Publishes *Foreign Policy: The Labour Party's Dilemma*.
1953	Publishes *Principia Politica*. Begins work on autobiography.
1959	Retires from *Political Quarterly*.
1960	Visits Sri Lanka. *Sowing* published. Declines offer of membership of the Order of the Companions of Honour.
1961	*Growing* published.
1964	Receives honorary Doctorate from University of Sussex. *Beginning Again* published.
1965	Resigns as a director of *New Statesman*. Receives W. H. Smith Annual Literary Award.
1966	*The Standard Edition of the Complete Psychological Works of Sigmund Freud* completed and published by the Hogarth Press. LW retires as editorial director.
1967	*Downhill All the Way* published.
1969	Dies, aged 89, at Monk's House. *The Journey Not the Arrival Matters* published.

CHAPTER 1

Fabian, Internationalist, and "Interwar Idealist"

This chapter provides a brief overview of Woolf's life and career. It then seeks to ascertain Woolf's position and reputation in postwar International Relations (IR).

Woolf's Career

Leonard Sidney Woolf was born in London in 1880, the son of a prominent Q.C., and the fourth of ten children. His father died suddenly at the age of 48 when Leonard was only 12. From being well off the family was plunged into financial hardship. The Woolf cubs became dependent on scholarships in order to continue their education. An academically gifted and industrious child, Leonard won scholarships to St. Paul's School in 1894, and after a strict diet of Latin and Greek, to Trinity College, Cambridge in 1899.

For a year or two Leonard was a model undergraduate, earnest in the pursuit of his studies, regular in attendance at lectures, and punctual in producing work for his tutor. But his interest in the formal curriculum tailed off, a process that was accelerated when he was invited to join the Cambridge Conversazione Society, otherwise known as the Apostles. It was as a member of this elite, and avowedly elitist, intellectual, and aesthetic circle that he first met J. M. Keynes, E. M. Forster, Lytton Strachey, Thoby Stephen (whose sister, Virginia, later became his wife), and the philosopher G. E. Moore. Moore's philosophy that all essential truths are simple truths had a profound influence on the group. In a way it constituted the intellectual cement that held it together, in one form or another, long after Cambridge.

On graduation Woolf decided to pursue a career in the civil service. His first choice of department, the Home Office, turned him down. Disappointed, he changed tack and applied, this time successfully, for an Eastern Cadetship. In 1904 he set sail for Ceylon. Woolf served as a colonial administrator in Ceylon from 1904 to 1911, gaining a reputation as a tough but efficient administrator. He was promoted rapidly, becoming Assistant Government Agent of the Hambantota district at the age of 27, the youngest colonial servant of that rank in Ceylon. It is likely that he would have attained high office had he remained in the colony, eventually acquiring a governorship and a K.C.M.G., as he later ironically remarked.[1]

But he missed the rarefied atmosphere of Cambridge and the company of his refined friends, and in 1911 he returned to England, resigned his commission, and embarked on a, at first highly precarious, literary career. Within a few years he had married Virginia and published his first book, a novel subtly critical of imperialism, based on his experiences in Ceylon.[2]

Woolf's first foray into politics came with the suffrage movement and, in particular, the Women's Co-operative Guild. During the early War years he wrote a series of pamphlets for the Guild on Co-operative economic organization.[3] It was at this time that Woolf became a Fabian socialist. His first work for the Fabians, commissioned by Sidney and Beatrice Webb, was a study of professional associations. But before the work was finished Sidney Webb, conscious of Woolf's overseas experience, invited him to write a study on "such international agreements as may prevent another war."[4] Up to this point the Fabian Society had shown little interest in the world beyond Britain. Woolf's study, eventually published in book form under the title *International Government* in 1916, was the first major project on international relations to be commissioned by the Society. As well as being Woolf's first work on the subject it is also his most substantial and enduring. Sir Duncan Wilson has described it as "perhaps the most permanently valuable of his political writings."[5]

The combination of overseas experience and critical acclaim for his books secured for him the position of Fabian "expert" on international affairs, a status he retained throughout the interwar period. He took part in lecture tours and became a prominent member of various Fabian committees including the International and Colonial Bureaux of the Fabian Research Department. In 1918, however, his principal political affiliation shifted from the Fabian Society to the Labour Party. In that year the Labour Party commissioned Woolf to write his influential *Empire and Commerce in Africa*. The book established Woolf's reputation as a leading anti-imperialist thinker. His conviction that every nation, as soon as it had acquired a certain basic level of civilization, had the right to govern, or misgovern, itself was one that did not endear him to certain members of the Fabian establishment. Beatrice Webb once described him as "an anti-imperialist fanatic."[6] It was good government that mattered. Self-government was incidental. But Woolf's belief that the seeds of independence had already been firmly sown in India, Ceylon, Burma, Egypt, and Iraq, and that the days of full imperial control of these countries were numbered, was one that was soon shown to be in step with political reality. Although his involvement in the life of the Labour Party was manifold, two roles in particular stand out in importance. From 1918 to 1945 he was Secretary of the Labour Party's Advisory Committee on International Questions, and from 1924 to 1945 he was secretary of the party's sister committee on Imperial Questions. These bodies played a crucial role in bringing a more nuanced understanding of international and colonial issues to policy debates within a largely parochial Labour Party.

Beyond the Labour movement, Woolf was a cofounder of the League of Nations Society, a prominent member the Union of Democratic Control, and a leading figure in the Anglo-Soviet Society—though Woolf's attitude toward the Soviet Union was never uncritical, a fact that got him into trouble with the Left Book Club in the 1930s.

In 1917 he founded the Hogarth Press with Virginia. The Press quickly established itself as a major publisher of modernist literature and poetry, publishing works by Eliot, Forster, Joyce, Keynes, Isherwood, Spender, Woolf, and some of the first English translations of Tolstoy, Dostoevsky, and Freud. The publication of the first English-language edition of the complete works of Sigmund Freud was in many ways its most important project. Work began in 1924. The edition was not complete until the twenty-fourth volume was guided through the Press, still under the watchful, and now octogenarian, eye of Leonard Woolf, in 1966. One of Woolf's biographers has commented: "No one outside the medical profession did as much as he to introduce Freud to the English-language public or to popularize his ideas."[7] The Woolfs were also, it should be noted, great innovators in book design. Cover and title-page designs were often commissioned from Vanessa Bell, Roger Fry, Duncan Grant, and other Bloomsbury artists.

In the field of political journalism Woolf was a frequent contributor, occasional editor, and for many years director of the *New Statesman*. For several years he was political editor of the liberal establishment journal, the *Nation*, and he was its literary editor for much of the 1920s. In the 1930s he founded, with Professor William Robson, the Center-Left journal *Political Quarterly*, and was one of its editors (as well as a frequent contributor) from its inception in 1931 until 1959. During his editorship of the short-lived

International Review (and its successor, the *Contemporary Review*) he pioneered documentary journalism. Each month the journal featured a large section devoted to the publication and review of important international documents. The object was to contribute to the new spirit of openness and optimism generated by the League and the Wilsonian principle of "open covenants, openly arrived at."

Woolf wrote on a wide range of subjects, but his abiding concern was international relations broadly defined. During his long career he wrote more than two dozen books, most notable among them being *International Government*, *Empire and Commerce in Africa*, *Imperialism and Civilization* (1928), and *The War for Peace* (1940). He wrote many pamphlets, most notably *Fear and Politics: A Debate at the Zoo* (1925), a clear forerunner of *Animal Farm*, *The League and Abyssinia* (1936), *The International Post-War Settlement* (1944), and the controversial *Foreign Policy: The Labour Party's Dilemma* (1947). Woolf's articles on politics and international affairs in weeklies, monthlies, quarterlies, and edited volumes are legion. Woolf was also a prolific reviewer of books, reviewing many hundreds on a wide range of topics with a strong preference for biographical and historical works.[8] His crowning achievement, however, and the one for which he will be long remembered, is his five-volume autobiography. Beginning with *Sowing* in 1960 and ending with *The Journey Not the Arrival Matters* in 1969, it was awarded one of the top literary prizes of its day, the W. H. Smith Award. It is regarded by many as a masterpiece. That most erudite senior British politician, Denis Healey, has described it as the "best general introduction to the history of the early twentieth century yet written."[9]

Leonard Woolf died at his beloved Monk's House, Sussex, in 1969 at the age of 89. His brilliant wife, whose genius he had nurtured, and whose literary reputation he fastidiously guarded, predeceased him in 1941.

Woolf's Reputation

There are few references to Woolf's work in the landmark texts of post-1945 IR. This is mainly due to the fact that Woolf is generally regarded, along with many other more or less like-minded thinkers, as an "idealist" or "utopian."[10] Since the publication of E. H. Carr's famous assault on utopianism such thinkers have been generally viewed, in Bull's words, as "not at all profound" and "not worth reading now except for the light they throw on the preoccupations and presuppositions of their time and place."[11] Yet Woolf does not feature in Carr's remarkably short inventory of utopian thinkers.[12] Like so many men of his time his fate seems to have been sealed by his association with (a) the interwar period, (b) progressivist writing, and (c) the League of Nations. Even though it is far from certain that Carr meant the term to be understood in this way, it seems to be the case that all those writing at that time who believed in the desirability and possibility of progressive change, and who saw the League as a useful instrument for bringing it about, have stood condemned of idealist inclinations.

The concept of idealism will be scrutinized in chapter 2. At this point it is interesting to note that those postwar scholars who looked at Woolf's work in any detail have tended to shy away from using such a simple label. Martin Wight, for example, describes Woolf as a rationalist. J. H. Grainger describes him as a "strenuous rationalist world-citizen in politics." George Modelski sees him as a pluralist. Craig Murphy, to cite a further example, characterizes him as a "critical liberal internationalist."[13]

In the postwar study of international relations three authors in particular have discussed Woolf's work. The fact that each of these authors offers a different interpretation as to the kind of thinker Woolf was suggests that his contribution to the subject is considerably more complex than the simple terms idealist or utopian imply. In order to set the scene for the chapters that follow it would be helpful to take a brief look at what they have to say.

Thomson, Meyer, and Briggs on Woolf

In an impressive and regrettably neglected study of the principles and processes of peacemaking, Thomson, Meyer, and Briggs assess contemporary proposals for a "New Order" in terms of the dichotomy between realism and utopianism.[14] The differences between the two, they contend, are (a) psychological and (b) sociological. Concerning (a), the two perspectives differ with respect to "the capacity of human nature to adapt itself to organized society." Utopians tend to be optimistic about the extent to which by deliberate and rational effort human beings can control their own lives and the social environment in which they live. As a consequence "the gist and tone of [their] argument tends to become a sustained effort to persuade all men to accept one set of beliefs: and the assumption is that if only enough people can be converted to these beliefs, the problem will be solved." Realists, by contrast, tend to be pessimistic and skeptical. Their argument takes the form of "a demonstration of the consequences which are likely to follow from actual developments...a warning rather than an exhortation...an analysis of prevailing and probable conditions, and a calculation of the likely trend of events."

But theories and proposals differ not only with regard to the conception of human nature on which they are premised, and their assessment of human capabilities. They also differ on (b) what human beings should try to achieve. At one extreme, utopians "propound a long range vision of what is desirable, with their eyes on the furthest horizon and their minds fixed on ends rather than means." At the other extreme, realists insist that "only the most short-range vision of what is attainable in the given circumstances has any practical importance."

An important set of proposals, however, do not fall neatly into either the utopian or the realist categories. Thomson et al. therefore propose a further category, "semi-utopian." In this category "Utopianism and optimism predominate" but proposals are "considerably qualified in detail and application." Semi-utopian proposals "try to keep in tune" with existing political, social, economic, and psychological conditions, but recognize that the real world of tomorrow may not be the same as the real world of today. Even though the targets set by semi-utopians may not be realistic now, they may become so with changed circumstances in the not-too-distant-future.

For Thomson and his team the writings of Leonard Woolf constitute the "most striking example" of proposals of this kind. They describe *International Government* as

> a brilliant examination of the technique of peacemaking, and of how rational order and the rule of law might replace the disastrous "balance of power" sought by pre-war diplomacy. It was a prophetic book, called utopian at the time, yet making proposals of the very kind that were attempted in 1919.

Moreover,

> after the failure of the League and the breakdown of all international government, Mr Woolf re-stated his thesis in modern terms. He adhered to the basic principles of the League of Nations (or rather of *a* League of Nations), as distinct from the cult of federalism then prevailing, and at the same time he counter-attacked the "Realists" who regarded the conceptions of the League as dead and discredited. Again, with the shift of prevalent opinion away from federalism towards the notion of a "revised League," Mr Woolf has had the sad satisfaction of seeing his "utopian" proposals reaching their target a few years later.

It is also worth noting that the authors of this study placed Woolf's *International Government* and his *The War for Peace* alongside Carr's *The Twenty Years' Crisis* and *Conditions of Peace*, Hayek's *The Road to Serfdom*,

Mannheim's *Ideology and Utopia* and *Man and Society*, and David Mitrany's *A Working Peace System*, as books "which have evolved a more scientific approach to international relations, and which have exerted a special influence on contemporary thought about peacemaking." With respect to one important study at least, therefore, Woolf's idealism was qualified and not of such a kind as to preclude him from serious scholarly attention.

Archer on Woolf[15]

In his wide-ranging historical survey and theoretical analysis of writings on international organization, Clive Archer identifies four broad approaches: traditionalist, revisionist, Marxist, and Third World. The primary distinction between them is the level of analysis. Traditionalists conceive international relations in terms of interstate relations; revisionists in terms of inter-societal or transnational relations; Marxists in terms of class; and Third World writers in terms of class and core–periphery relations. Within each paradigm Archer identifies several main lines of thought. The traditionalist paradigm, for example, contains four lines: international law, world law, international government, and realist.

Woolf is chosen as an exemplar of the international government perspective. Archer does not define what he means by "international government." Nor does he reflect on the various meanings that have been given to the term in the past. He nonetheless proceeds to highlight Woolf's view that international government was not an entirely new phenomenon and that by the twentieth century a good deal of it already existed in regular diplomatic gatherings, public and private international unions, and commodity agreements. He outlines Woolf's plans for a "Supranational Authority to Prevent War." He records Woolf's proposal for a twelve-month "cooling off" period. He further records Woolf's plan for a generalized system of sanctions in which all states would be bound to make "common cause, even to the point of war, against any state violating a fundamental obligation."

Although Archer regards Woolf as an exemplar of, and indeed the main contributor to, the international government perspective, he also recognizes that he was a forerunner of functionalism, and that there is therefore a considerable "revisionist" element in his work. Indeed, Archer draws extensively on *International Government* for his own account of the nineteenth-century development of both international governmental organizations *and* international *non*governmental organizations.

Archer notes that Woolf along with other practical and intellectual supporters of the League are often classified as idealists or neo-Grotians.[16]

He relies in his assessment of the international government approach on Hedley Bull's analysis and critique of neo-Grotianism. Accordingly, Woolf: (a) overestimated the degree of solidarity in international relations; (b) exalted the international interest over the national interest (without explaining how the former could be determined); (c) advocated constitutional reform over revolution as a means of transcending international society (without enquiring into whether "states could become the agents of their own extinction"); (d) gave priority to respect for legality over the need for change; and, (e) failed to recognize the static nature of the international legal system as they construed it.[17]

The extent to which Woolf is guilty of these charges will become apparent as the analysis unfolds. The significant thing to note at this stage is Archer's hesitation to use "idealist" as a descriptive label for Woolf's thought on international government, and his preference instead for "traditionalism," "revisionism," and "neo-Grotianism."

Suganami on Woolf

In his important study of the role of the domestic analogy in world-order proposals, Hidemi Suganami selects Woolf as a representative of those thinkers who have applied the analogy in a straightforward, unsophisticated, way.[18] Suganami arrives at a fivefold typology of the various proposals for world order that have been put forward in the last two centuries: legal, diplomatic, democratic confederal, federal, and welfare institutional. The first two types are accurately seen as poles on a spectrum, with most proposals lying somewhere in-between according to the extent to which they accept (or reject) the idea that the best way to achieve law and order internationally is to replicate at the international level those institutions that most effectively provide law and order domestically. Suganami considers Woolf's views as representative of those on the legalistic end of the spectrum. These thinkers advocate the "peace through law" approach, which urges the creation of an international organization equipped with judicial, legislative, and executive functions, parallel to those found in well-ordered domestic societies. Suganami contrasts the approach of Woolf with the American opponent of the League of Nations, Edwin Borchard. Borchard rejected the domestic analogy and insisted that the pre-1914 system was superior to the League system. Legal prohibitions on the resort to war, the division of belligerents into aggressors and victims, and collective action to assist victims, while central to Woolf's thinking, were considered by Borchard to be not only ineffective, but positively harmful. Woolf argued that a collective security system was essential if war was to be prevented. Borchard argued that such a system was more likely to result in the extension and intensification of conflict rather than its mitigation and resolution.

Suganami points out that Woolf did not consider the problem of war and the maintenance of peace to be *sui generis*. In Woolf's view the resolution of international conflict was qualitatively the same type of problem as the resolution of any other conflict. It was not therefore true that there was no experience to draw on in building a new international order. On the contrary, Woolf asserted, there was 4,000 years of experience on which to draw. Just as cannibalism, duelling, cockfighting, witch burning, and slavery had been largely eradicated, so could war. Woolf accepted that the prevention of war may be a more complex problem, but it was not an essentially different one.

Suganami also points out that Woolf was one of the principal exponents of the "reformed League idea." Soon after the onset of the Second World War the question arose as to whether a new organization should be created to replace the discredited League and, if so, what form it should it take. By this time the League had many critics, ranging from those who wanted a revision of the Covenant, especially the strengthening of its collective security procedures, to those who believed that the whole idea was flawed. Woolf maintained that the League's approach to the problem of world order was essentially correct. He recognized that it had failed to preserve the peace, but contended that one instance of failure did not prove that the whole idea was wrong. He had an answer to those critics, like Carr, who condemned the League as utopian. Carr's view that the interests of nation-states were inherently incompatible and that leagues of nations were therefore impossible was nothing more than a realist dogma. For Woolf there was no *a priori* reason why power had a different nature and reality in the international sphere than it had in domestic society. Both were "equally amenable to elimination and control." The failure of the League did not mean that the League idea was intrinsically utopian any more than the failure of appeasement, Carr's preferred policy, meant that the idea of appeasement was intrinsically utopian. As Suganami explains, the main cause of the League's failure in Woolf's view was "lack of psychological motivation on the part of its members to uphold its principles." Another devastating war, he argued, would serve to induce such motivation in the future. Woolf thus recommended moderate reform of the League, particularly the regionalization of its collective security procedures.

In Suganami's view, Woolf's approach is underpinned by two problematic assumptions: (a) that the punishment of a murderer is the central problem of government (aggressors being analogous to murderers); (b) that the problem of maintaining order between two large, organized groups of individuals is the same as maintaining order between a small number of individuals. He argues with respect to (a) that the main job of government is not to cope with individual murderers, but to manage the demands of large, powerful groups. Following Carr, Claude, and Brierly, he asserts that if experience tells us anything it is not how certain states manage to successfully deal with murderers but how some states manage to avoid civil wars. With respect to (b) he argues that when united a group of individuals possess a strength qualitatively different from that which each possess individually. Following Claude, he describes the tendency to draw simple analogies between individuals and groups when thinking about social order as "schoolboyish."

Conclusion

Estimates of the value and nature of Woolf's contribution to international thought, therefore, vary considerably. According to Thomson et al. Woolf's work was not only influential but prophetic and marked by the adoption of a more scientific approach to international questions. His outlook is best seen as "semi-utopian." While he desired deep change of current reality, his aspirations took account of existing conditions and were based on a realistic appraisal of not-too-distant-future possibilities. Archer sees Woolf's approach to international organization as traditionalist in that it focuses on interstate relations, but he also acknowledges the existence of a significant revisionist, or transnational, component. Implicitly he holds Woolf guilty of the errors that Bull associated with the neo-Grotians. Suganami takes Woolf as an exemplar of the legalist approach to world order, which bases its ideas on a straightforward, and problematic, application of the domestic analogy.

So while the tone and thrust of postwar IR discussion of Woolf's thought is mostly critical, there is, nonetheless, a marked reluctance to dismiss him as utopian.

CHAPTER 2

What is Idealism?

Those postwar writers who have taken a closer look at Woolf have been reluctant to employ the term idealist to characterize his international political thought. Yet it is nonetheless true that such characterization is pervasive in IR. Indeed, virtually everyone who wrote about the international scene during the interwar period, who supported the League, and who held progressivist social and political beliefs, has been labeled in this pejorative way.

But it is not only a pejorative label. It is also an ambiguous one. Indeed, as a realist rhetorical device, which is how some see it, its pejorativeness and its ambiguity go hand in hand. It has enabled swathes of thought and the thinkers who thought it to be dismissed on the most general grounds.

In order to assess the degree to which Woolf can be characterized as an idealist we first need to establish its meaning. We need, that is, to establish its central tenets, its core assumptions or beliefs, those attributes in the absence of which it could not be regarded as a distinct school of thought. We need, in other words, to identify the properties that make "idealism" idealistic.

This is not as simple as it may appear. The first hurdle to overcome is that while some writers have identified idealism almost exclusively with the interwar period, others see it as something much broader. According to the latter view, idealism is an approach to international relations that may ebb and flow in influence, but it is one that can always be found where independent political communities exist in a condition of anarchy. Idealism is a doctrine that advocates various means of controlling or transcending the international anarchy. It may have been strongly manifest in the interwar period but it is not exclusive to it.

Another hurdle to overcome is that while some authors use the term idealist interchangeably with terms such as utopian, liberal, liberal internationalist, or rationalist, others imply that there are subtle and perhaps important differences between them. One frequently encounters statements such as "X was an idealist but not of the utopian kind" or "Y was criticized for holding liberal and even idealist beliefs." But those who imply that these terms signify different things rarely attempt to lay bare the basis of any such distinction.

Idealism in IR Historiography

In order to make progress on the question it may be helpful to have a brief look at some of the standard accounts of the growth of the discipline and idealism's place within it.

In one of the most widely cited short accounts of the growth of IR theory, Hedley Bull states that the "distinctive characteristic" of idealism is belief in progress. Indeed, his preferred term for idealism, which he consistently puts in inverted commas, is "the progressivist doctrines of the 1920s and 1930s." Idealists held that the system that gave rise to the First World War was "capable of being transformed into a fundamentally more peaceful and just world order." Such an order was, indeed, already in the making as a result of "the awakening of democracy," the growth of the "international mind," the creation of the League of Nations, the strengthening of international law, and the good works and teachings of "men of peace [and] enlightenment." The responsibility of IR students was to "assist this march of progress to overcome the ignorance, the prejudices, the ill-will, and the sinister interests that stood in its way." The War and the creation of the League represented a sharp break with the past. The "pre-war system," idealists felt, did not provide a source of guidance but "a series of object lessons" about anarchy and disorder. Present and future possibilities were not limited by the "test of previous experience" but were "deducible from the needs of progress."[1]

In his trenchant analysis of the predictive power of realism, John Vasquez does not so much emphasize progress as its close ally reason. One of the distinctive qualities of the idealist paradigm, he says, is the ability of reason to overcome the problem of war. This is accompanied, indeed fortified, by a belief in a basic harmony of interests between nations and the existence of a nascent world community. However, in contrast to Bull, Vasquez upholds that the "Wilsonian contention" that democracy leads to peace whereas dictatorship leads to war constitutes the "heart of the paradigm."[2]

In one of the more detailed accounts of the "utopian school" to be published in the last few decades, Trevor Taylor emphasizes, like Vasquez, the role of reason in world affairs and the existence of a harmony of interests between nations, actual or potential. But he adds, "in general utopianism is concerned with the formation of an ideal polity and, to a lesser extent, how such a polity might be established." He also interestingly adds that one of the by-products of the utopian faith in reason is belief in a universal code of morality and objective justice discoverable through reason.[3] Like Bull he posits that a common belief of utopians was that the flames of war were often fanned by sinister interests such as weapons manufacturers.[4]

Belief in reason, progress, and the harmony of interests are also stressed in an account by Michael Joseph Smith. This author disputes, however, the often-made claim that these beliefs were facile. The idealists, for sure, did not think that human beings were naturally bellicose. But it did not follow from this that they, the human beings, were naturally pacific and reasonable. On the contrary they had a tendency to follow passion not reason and to be "frustratingly stubborn in their attachment to outmoded ideas." The chief obstacle to peace and internationalism was muddled thinking. The duty of the scholar-publicist therefore was to "educate people of all nationalities to a higher notion of internationalism." This higher notion involved the rejection of the futile pursuit of narrow national interests, and the abandonment of the self-destructive policy of the balance of power.[5]

A variety of accounts emphasize the importance of institutions to the idealist way of thinking, meaning the creation of new or the strengthening of old ones. Both Vasquez and Knutsen assert that one of the core prescriptions of idealism is the creation at the global level of those institutions that have been effective at preventing violence at the domestic level.[6] Kegley and Wittkopf link the question of institutions with the issue of human nature. They assert that for idealism "bad behavior is the product not of evil people but of evil institutions and structural arrangements that motivate people to act selfishly and to harm others." War can therefore be eliminated by eliminating or radically reforming the institutions that encourage it.[7] For Booth, a large part of the idealist faith in progress is derived from the belief that institutions are human constructs which, once created, can extensively influence people's thought and actions. Human nature is therefore not hidebound. The facts of international life are not immutable. Institutions can make an important difference.[8]

Two further commonly cited facets of idealism are worth noting briefly. First is the idea that the *scientific* study of international relations has a large role to play in the prevention of war and the construction of a more peaceful world order.[9] Second is the notion, stretching back to the classical political economists, and a constant refrain of British radical thought in the nineteenth century, that war is incompatible with economic progress and that free trade will lead to peace.[10]

This brief overview provides some idea of the variety of beliefs and assumptions that have been held in recent decades as characteristic of the idealist or utopian school, vision, approach, tradition, or paradigm, as it is variously called. This variety is highlighted if we look at the prescriptions that have been commonly ascribed to idealism. Along with those already mentioned such as the strengthening of international law and education in internationalism, prescriptions for change frequently cited include: the expansion of the number and role of international organizations; the establishment of permanent judicial organs for the settlement of international disputes; the establishment of formal procedures for mediation and arbitration; the creation of an international police force; disarmament; open diplomacy; collective security; peaceful change; self-determination; the encouragement of greater social and economic cooperation; the legal prohibition of war; the abolition of alliances; and a just and impartial settlement of all colonial claims.

This diversity is symptomatic of the fact that there is a good deal of uncertainty in the IR community about the defining characteristics of idealism, its parameters, and its principal exponents. With regard to its exponents, in their popular IR textbooks Dougherty and Pfaltzgraff on the one hand, and Kegley and Wittkopf on the other, cite just one idealist: Woodrow Wilson.[11] Hollis and Smith, in their valuable introduction to the methodology of IR, cite just two: Woodrow Wilson and Alfred Zimmern.[12] Most commentators, however, follow closely, and in one or two instances almost exactly, the fairly extensive group of idealists cited by Bull.[13] This suggests that few commentators have done any substantial research of their own. For reasons we do not need to go into here they have relied on one or two staple accounts. Given the dire need in IR for knowledge of a cumulative kind this is not necessarily a problem. In this instance, however, it is symptomatic of a rather uncritical attitude that many academics have taken toward established interpretations and evaluations of the "idealist phase."

Uncertainty about the nature and scope of idealism is strongly evident, for example, in Olson and Groom's otherwise helpful introduction to the history of the IR discipline. They start their account by stating that idealism dominated the "first period of consensus." But they go on to say that the "mainstream literature" of the 1920s did not "particularly reflect" the "idealist internationalist" paradigm "however much some of those outside the IR professional literature may have done so." The clear implication is that by mainstream literature they have in mind those works produced chiefly by professional IR scholars, and that idealism (used interchangeably with "liberal internationalism," "idealist internationalism," and "the new internationalism") was primarily an outlook shared and promulgated by nonprofessionals. But Sir Alfred Zimmern, the first Wilson Professor of International Politics at Aberystwyth, and the first Montague Burton Professor of IR at Oxford, and a mainstream figure by any standard, is described as "the consummate idealist." Olson and Groom provide no evidence to suggest that he was in any way exceptional, that is a professional scholar but also, uncharacteristically, an idealist. Moreover, despite to a large extent disassociating the "mainstream literature," and therefore IR, from the obloquy of idealism, they nonetheless describe the first period of "disciplinary consensus" as the "innocent phase," an adjective, following Carr, usually applied to idealism. This rather confusing picture is not, regrettably, clarified by Olson and Groom's definition of mainstream literature: "works dealing systematically with the entire world, taking into account insights from several disciplines." A number of books by such consummate nonprofessionals as H. G. Wells, H. N. Brailsford, J. A. Hobson, and indeed Leonard Woolf, fit this definition depending on one's interpretation of "dealing systematically." They certainly sought to deal with the world as a whole and they utilized material from a wide variety of sources both from within the academy and without.[14]

It is not difficult to find similar confusions in the literature on interwar IR thought.

The Legacy of Carr

The foundational text with regard to how idealism is understood in IR is, of course, E. H. Carr's *The Twenty Years' Crisis*.[15] Bull's essay has been highly influential in shaping conventional understandings. But Bull himself was greatly influenced in his understanding and evaluation of idealism by Carr. *The Twenty Years' Crisis*, as well as being generally regarded as one of only two or three classic texts in the field, is still regarded by many as the definitive statement on the subject. To get any kind of grip on the notion of idealism in IR, therefore, it is necessary to go back to Carr.

Carr was the first student of the subject to describe its evolution in terms of certain phases, with the idealist or utopian phase being the first. In Carr's view the science of international relations was created to serve a specific purpose. In this respect it followed the pattern of other sciences. As with Geometry, Medical Science, Engineering, Political Economy, Political Science, and (somewhat incongruently) socialism, the new field of IR did not begin its investigations in the spirit of detached enquiry but in order to achieve certain normative goals. "The initial stage of aspiration towards an end," Carr declared, "is an essential foundation of human thinking. The wish is father to the thought. Teleology precedes analysis."[16]

The field of international politics arose from one of the greatest and most disastrous wars in history, and the "overwhelming purpose which dominated and inspired the pioneers of the new science was to obviate a recurrence of this disease of the international body politic." This passionate desire to prevent war determined the initial course and direction of study.

This course began to change, however, in 1931. From this point onward, events began to clearly reveal the "inadequacy of pure aspiration as the basis for a science of international politics" and it became possible for the first time "to embark on serious analytical thought about international problems." Hard, ruthless analysis of reality was forced on the student of intentional politics as an essential ingredient of his study. This development, the impact of thinking upon wishing, marked the end of the specifically idealist period of study, and the arrival of realism.[17]

What in Carr's view were the core features of utopianism/idealism? Unfortunately, the answer to this question again is not simple. This is because Carr does not set out systematically the key features of idealism but, on the contrary, builds up an impressionistic picture of it sometimes by explicit assertion, but often through inference and insinuation. This problem is compounded by the fact that it is difficult to separate Carr's explication of idealism from his critique of it. The way in which Carr represents a number of idealist propositions and assertions is, to say the least, rather loaded.

A further obstacle in the path of a clear understanding of Carr's position is that he uses the term utopianism/idealism in the two senses outlined at the beginning of this chapter, but without stipulating, in given instances, in which sense he is using it. For example, it is not always easy to determine whether Carr's withering criticisms of free trade or the beneficence of public opinion apply to idealism in the narrow sense or idealism in the broad sense or both. This partly explains why some of the principal victims of Carr's acerbic pen—Angell, Toynbee, and Zimmern in particular—felt they had been misrepresented or unjustifiably tarnished with a very broad brush.[18]

Carr makes so many claims and assertions about the interwar utopian school, and utopianism in general, that it would be impractical, even impossible, to provide a full account. There are, nonetheless, certain features of the doctrine as understood and communicated by Carr that stand out. First, utopianism is an incorrigibly voluntarist doctrine. Utopians believe that reality, no matter how seemingly intractable, can be radically transformed by an act of will. They see political theory, not as a reflection of political practice, but as a norm to which political practice ought to conform.[19] The very purpose of studying IR is to bring an end to the gravest ill of the international body politic, war. Utopians thus see it as their principal task to not only discover the causes of war but to expedite its cure. They sought to do this by impressing on everyone the rationality and justness of their views.[20] Indeed, the elements of faith in reason, the independent validity and importance of morality as a guiding light, and faith in the transformatory potential of individual human agency are inextricably linked facets of utopianism. Its proponents believe in a fixed and absolute standard by which policies and actions can be judged.[21] This standard is not written down in sacred texts or inscribed on tablets of stone but resides in the conscience of every individual human being. Human conscience is thus the final court of appeal in moral questions ("individualism"). But it is also the voice of reason ("rationalism"). What is rational cannot be wrong and vice versa.[22]

This essentially Benthamite faith in reason and the access it gives to universal standards of good, issued in the twentieth century in hitherto unparalleled faith in public opinion. According to Carr, utopians assumed that pursuit of the good was a question of right reasoning. With the spread of knowledge, on international affairs for example, it would soon be possible for everyone to reason rightly. It was further assumed that everyone who reasoned rightly would necessarily act rightly. Carr called this "the utopian doctrine of the efficacy of rational public opinion."[23] Public opinion could not only be relied upon to be right, it was also politically compelling. With the advent of the League of Nations world public opinion had for the first time a universal organ through which its voice could be expressed. The voice of reason could thus for the first time be brought to bear against war. It was now possible to eliminate power from international relations and put reason and discussion in the place of armies and navies.[24]

If voluntarism is the first salient feature of utopianism according to Carr, the second, third, and fourth features, intimately connected, might therefore be regarded as faith in reason, belief in a universal standard of morality, and faith in the efficacy of public opinion. But there is a fifth feature without mention of which any account of Carr's understanding of utopianism would be incomplete. This is belief in the existence of a natural harmony of interests. According to utopians there is no necessary incompatibility between the economic good of individual nations and the economic good of humanity as a whole (the "natural harmony of interest in free trade"). Similarly there is no necessary incompatibility between the security of individual nations and the security of international society as a whole (the "natural harmony of interest in peace"). On an even more general plane there is no essential incompatibility between nationalism and internationalism. Utopians inherited the nineteenth-century Mazzinian belief in a natural division of labor between nations. Each nation had its own special task to perform, as its special attributes befitted it, and its own special contribution to make to the well-being of humanity. If all nations were to act in this spirit, international harmony would prevail. By developing their own nationalism, therefore, nations promoted the cause of internationalism. In serving themselves, nations also served humanity. In the twentieth century this doctrine of the latent harmony between nationalism and internationalism provided the philosophical basis for the Wilsonian conviction that national self-determination was the key to world peace.[25]

Belief in the existence of a harmony of interests is often cited as a characteristic of utopianism. It is important to note at this stage, however, that this was not Carr's view. Carr did not object to the notion of a harmony of interests *per se*, but the nineteenth-century liberal assumption of a *natural* harmony of interests: the assumption of some kind of hidden hand, which, if allowed to function freely, would conjure up not only the greatest wealth and security for this or that nation, but the greatest wealth and security for the world as a whole. Contrary to general supposition, *The Twenty Years' Crisis* could be read as a defense of the doctrine of the harmony of interests: conceived, that is, as a practical process of harmony building; of creating "a new harmony by artificial means."[26]

Carr's Critique

Readers familiar with Carr's famous book will recognize this account as heavily compacted. It does, however, have the merit of conveying briefly and in relatively neutral terms some of the key characteristics of utopianism as Carr conceived it. Yet no account of Carr's book would be adequate unless it also conveyed some of the many criticisms that he leveled at utopianism. Indeed, one of the difficulties with constructing a neutral account of Carr's views is that the language Carr uses is anything but neutral. Disapproval is implicit in the very terms he employed to describe the doctrine. So what did Carr think was wrong with this motley set of beliefs he called utopianism?

The answer is: a lot of things. He decries the utopian tendency to disregard facts and analysis of cause and effect, preferring instead "the elaboration of visionary projects" the "simplicity and perfection" of which gives them an "easy and universal appeal."[27] Utopians, he says, privilege wishing over thinking, generalization over observation, and the discussion of ends over "critical analysis of existing facts or available means."[28] He dismisses the supposed indivisibility of peace and universality of free trade as "items in a political programme disguised as statements of fact." The utopian, he adds, "inhabits a dream-world of such 'facts,' remote from the world of reality where quite contrary facts may be observed."[29] Collective security, general disarmament, world federation, and other such schemes are, he asserts, "the product of pure theory divorced from practical experience."[30] The notion of a common interest in peace, he declares, "masks the fact that some nations desire to maintain the *status quo* without having to fight for it, and others to change the *status quo* without having to fight in order to do so." The statement that it is in the interest of the world as a whole either that the *status quo* should be maintained, or that it should be changed, is contrary to the facts. Further, the idea that it is in the interest of the world as a whole that whatever conclusion is reached, whether for maintenance or change, it should be reached peacefully, "would command general assent, but seems a rather meaningless platitude."[31] He rejects the utopian search for an ethical standard outside of politics as "doomed to frustration." Ethics is rooted in politics and must be interpreted in political terms.[32]

This crescendo of disapproval reaches its pitch with the observation that "the intellectual theories and ethical standards of utopianism, far from being the expression of absolute and *a priori* principles, are historically conditioned, being both products of circumstances and weapons framed for the furtherance of interests."[33] Free trade, peace, international law and order were not universal interests but time-honored slogans of privileged groups designed to uphold their privileged position. In fact, the "supposedly absolute and universal principles [of the utopian] were not principles at all, but the unconscious reflexions of national policy based on a particular interpretation of national interest at a particular time."[34] Consequently, the attempt to base a system of international morality on the supposed harmony of international interests was exposed as "misleading," "bankrupt," and "a hollow and intolerable sham."[35] The problem was not that utopianism had failed to live up to its principles, but that it had failed "to provide any absolute standard for the conduct of international affairs."[36] International morality as expounded by utopian writers became "little more than a convenient weapon for belaboring those who assailed the *status quo*."[37] In truth there was no international harmony of interests. On the contrary there was a clash of interests that was real and inevitable. The whole nature of the problem was distorted by the utopian attempt to disguise it.[38]

Two further important criticisms levelled by Carr at utopianism should be briefly noted. First, he condemns the view that international public opinion was sufficiently potent to render material sanctions obsolete as an "outworn creed." Those who clung unto to it were guilty, in the words of Winston

Churchill in 1932, of "long-suffering and inexhaustible gullibility."[39] Moreover, taking direct aim at the Benthamite doctrine of the efficacy of public opinion, he states that it was undeniable that during the interwar years "public opinion was almost as often wrong-headed as it was impotent."[40] Second, contrary to the utopian wish to eliminate power from politics Carr asserts, "power is a decisive factor in every political situation."[41] "Power, used, threatened, or silently held in reserve is an essential factor in international change." Change would, in general, only be effected in the interests of those by whom, or on whose behalf, power could be invoked.[42]

Conclusion

Idealism in IR: A Framework for Analysis

If we ask ourselves to what extent any given thinker or actor is guilty of utopianism we are faced with the problem of what criteria to apply. In order to make progress the most influential text on our understanding, in IR, of idealism has been examined. But even here there is a problem since its author, E. H. Carr, makes an almost bewildering number of assertions about it, and objections to it are seemingly legion. Yet strip away some of Carr's colorful and engaging rhetoric and it is apparent that for the most part the criticisms Carr makes fall into three broad camps. First, utopians pay little attention to facts and analysis of cause and effect, devoting their energies instead to the "elaboration of visionary projects for the attainment of ends which they have in view." Second, utopians grossly underestimate the role of power in international politics, and overestimate the role, actual and potential, of morality, law, public opinion, and other "non-material" sanctions. Third, utopians fail to recognize that their espousal of universal interests amounts to nothing more than the promotion and defense of a particular *status quo*. Here, as in other areas, utopians fail to appreciate the self-interested character of their thought.

In this chapter we have noted the diversity of characteristics attributed to this amorphous category idealism/utopianism. The fact that there is uncertainty as to its very name suggests that its identity is far from unproblematic. Our review of the IR literature and Carr's influential text in particular has shown that the list of characteristics commonly cited as definitive of idealism is a long one. While reference will be made to a number of these characteristics as this study unfolds, Carr's three broad objections to utopianism will be employed as the principal framework of analysis. Thus, with respect to the various areas of Woolf's international political thought I will ask: to what extent, if any, did he "ignore facts" and "pay little attention to the analysis of cause and effect"? (Charge 1). Is it true to say that he "grossly underestimated the role of power" and correspondingly "overestimated the role, actual and potential, of morality, law, public opinion, and other 'non-material' sanctions"? (Charge 2). Can it be said fairly that his "espousal of universal interests amounted to nothing more than the promotion and defense of a particular *status quo*" and, following from this, that he "failed to appreciate the self-interested character of his thought"? (Charge 3). Answering these questions will enable us to make a fairly reliable judgment on the extent of Woolf's idealism. While debate about the essence of idealism will go on, at least we will know the degree to which Woolf's thought stands up in the face of the three principal criticisms of idealism levelled by its principal expositor and critic.

CHAPTER 3

International Government: An Exposition

London and life with Virginia brought with it a wholly new set of friends and associations. It was through one of these friends, the formidable Margaret Llewelyn Davies,[1] and subsequent involvement in the Women's Co-operative Guild, that Leonard Woolf first met Sidney and Beatrice Webb. Within the space of a year his life had completely changed. From political innocent in the jungles of Ceylon, Woolf metamorphosized into a politically conscious and active member of the Labour Party and the Fabian Society.

The Commissioning of International Government

During the autumn of 1914 Beatrice Webb invited Woolf to become involved in a project on professional organizations then being conducted by the Fabian Research Bureau.[2] Neither Beatrice nor Sidney Webb were particularly interested in international affairs—it was "not their subject"— and they did not give much thought to the possibility of the Bureau getting involved in them.[3] It was George Bernard Shaw who suggested that the Bureau should become active in this area, and with this in mind he managed to secure £100 from Joseph Rowntree for the purpose of producing a study on how future wars might be prevented. Shaw persuaded Beatrice Webb of the need for such a study, and Mrs. Webb, knowing Woolf possessed considerable knowledge of colonial affairs, asked him to shelve his current work and get involved in the Shaw–Rowntree project. The original plan was that the work would be undertaken by a small committee with Woolf as secretary. But early in 1915 a decision was made to allow Woolf to write the report himself, with complete freedom to proceed as he saw fit.[4]

Woolf set to work "like a fanatical or dedicated mole" and within four months had produced the first draft.[5] Part One of the report, "Suggestions for the Prevention of War" was published as a special supplement to the *New Statesman* on July 10, 1915. Part Two, "Articles Suggested for Adoption by an International Conference at the Termination of the War" (the Fabian Draft Treaty), was published in the same form one week later. This was written by Woolf with Sidney Webb and was one of the first detailed plans for a league of nations to be published.

While working on these two projects Woolf became convinced that the prevention of war was part of a wider problem—the development of international government. At the time, as he later recorded,

> It was commonly said or assumed that international government did not exist and could not exist among sovereign independent states; but a very little investigation convinced me that this was not true and that a considerable field of human relations had been subjected to various forms of international government. But practically no books existed on the subject and no attention had been given to it.[6]

Woolf consequently impressed upon Webb that it would be "well worth while doing some serious work" on this subject since it would throw important light not only on the prevention of war but "on the whole field of international relations."[7] Woolf was given a further £100 to write a second report. This report was published, together with the first report and the Fabian Draft Treaty, as *International Government* in 1916.[8]

The Fabian Background

At this point it is worth taking one or two steps back. In the making of *International Government* how much Fabian intellectual material did Leonard Woolf have at his disposal? The short answer is: very little. The Fabian Society's relationship with the outside world had been for decades one of neglect. In the early years of the Society the existence of an international realm was barely acknowledged. During these years the Society, and more specifically its most senior members—the "Old Gang" of Webb, Shaw, Pease, Bland, and Olivier—concentrated their efforts on the "Condition of England" question, in particular how to bring about a root and branch socialist transformation of a country whose wealth and imperial grandeur stood in pitiful contrast to the desperate poverty and baseness of life found in many of her towns and villages.[9] The early work of Fabians covered a wide range of economic, social, and political questions: from the causes of mass poverty and the role of women in society to the improvement of public health, the municipalization of basic utilities, the control of the liquor trade, and the restriction of industrial working hours.

Thought on the important international dimension of many of these questions is entirely absent. During this period Fabians clearly believed that events in the outside world had little relevance. As Bernard Porter has observed, apart from William Pember Reeves's *The State and Its Functions in New Zealand* (Fabian Tract No. 74), the object of which was to provide Fabians with a model of working socialism, "none of the first hundred or so Fabian Tracts was on external affairs; and the First series of *Fabian Essays* scarcely touched them."[10] A recent historian of the Society has reiterated this observation in an account of its involvement in socialist internationalism.[11] Fabians were far from enthusiastic participants in the proceedings of the Second International and paid little more than lip service to its proclamations. The British views expressed at international socialist gatherings immediately prior to the outbreak of war in 1914 were mainly those of Keir Hardy and the Independent Labour Party.[12]

War in South Africa

One crisis did briefly jolt the Fabian Society out of its parochial state of mind. This was the Boer War. The greatest empire since Rome found itself embroiled in a bloody conflict, in which it was to lose over 10,000 men, with a ragged, uncouth, but tenacious band of Dutch farmers. It was a war, moreover, that for many months the Great British Empire looked like losing. Only a policy of military ruthlessness, main force, and the isolation of the civilian population in harsh and insanitary concentration camps, prevented an embarrassing defeat. The outcome was the extension of the empire with the conquest, in effect, of the Dutch South African provinces. This was an outcome that few in Westminster and Whitehall desired.

The dilemmas that the war threw up for Fabians were enormous. Should the war be supported or opposed? If opposed, did not this mean leaving the fate of outlanders, fellow countrymen whose pioneering endeavors on the Rand the Empire had ostensibly gone to war to protect, in the hands of the uncouth Dutchmen? Did not opposing war mean condoning murder and brutality? On the other hand was not the war ultimately driven by capitalist cliques and their allies in the jingo press? Was it not capitalist greed, irresponsibility, and inefficiency that the Fabian Society was founded to eradicate? Were not war and imperialism bad things in themselves? Or was war to promote civilization sometimes justified, perhaps even morally required? Was not the Empire needed precisely to protect vulnerable natives from capitalist imperialism? If so, what was the relationship between the Empire and imperialism? Was not the Empire broadly on the side of progress and civilization? And the Boers on the side of reaction and backwardness?

In attempting to answer these questions the Fabian Society found itself being torn in various directions. The debates the war sparked were acrimonious. Eighteen members, including prominent figures such as the artist Walter Crane and the future prime minister Ramsay MacDonald, resigned in protest against the pro-war line the Society seemed to be taking. The very existence of the Society was called into question.[13]

For our purposes, the significance of the war resides in a small volume, drafted by Shaw, the main purpose of which was to bring down the political temperature by arriving at a position on the subject of South Africa, the Empire, and wider international relationships, which all Fabians could accept.[14] Prior to the publication of *International Government* this volume was the only work of any substance on international relations to be published by the Society. Yet its importance in the Fabian canon is overstated. Bernard Porter has said, for example, that *International Government* built "to a great extent on the foundations that had been laid in 1900." Moreover, although it presented new evidence, the central idea of Woolf's book was not new: "With a slightly different emphasis, and in a very different context, *Fabianism and the Empire* had cropped up again."[15]

This not only exaggerates the significance, certainly in terms of international political theory, of Shaw's typically engaging work, but does a great disservice to Woolf. In order to set the scene for the rest of the chapter it may be helpful to explain why.

Brains and Political Science

On the South African War, *Fabianism and the Empire* treads a careful line. Nowhere does it contain an explicit endorsement of the War in whole or in part. The reader is left, however, with the impression that it does endorse the War, albeit with a string of reservations. From the outset, for example, it is made clear that for Fabians individualism, noninterference, and nationalism are obsolete political doctrines.[16] It is also made clear that the "partition of the greater part of the globe" by the Great Powers is, for good or ill, only a matter of time. The key question for Britain being whether she was to remain the nucleus of one of these powers, or be "cast off by its colonies, ousted from its provinces, and reduced to its old island status."[17]

It is interesting to observe that for Shaw the term Great Power had a moral as well as a power-political connotation. A Great Power should do great deeds. This was what British foreign policy currently lacked. It had no social principle to guide it.[18] It was here, of course, that Fabian socialism could step in. Consciously or unconsciously, Shaw asserted, Great Powers must govern in the interests of civilization as a whole.[19] For this reason gold fields and the "formidable armaments that could be built upon them" could not be left in the hands of "small irresponsible communties of frontiersmen." Theoretically such communties "should be internationalized not British-Imperialized." But, he added, "until the Federation of the World becomes an accomplished fact we must accept the most responsible Imperial Federations available as a substitute for it."[20] That is, the British Empire should be accepted as a temporary guardian of the world interest in the gold fields of the Rand.

In a roundabout way, Shaw was saying that the War was a fact, in some respects an inevitable one, and that the best that could be hoped for, and worked for, was a settlement acceptable to socialists. What would such a settlement involve? Shaw put forward a number of proposals including: (a) the extension of local democracy to white inhabitants of the South African territories, involving the establishment of local parliaments. This was a measure called for repeatedly in the Manifesto with respect to other parts of the Empire, particularly India. (b) The regulation of factories and mines to secure the standard of living of all workers, black or white. (c) A protective regime for the natives, to be administered by "Imperial officials" not subject to local parliamentary control.[21]

Shaw was thus not opposed to war in general nor this particular war. The acid test was whether or not such an act led to a desirable outcome, desirability being measured by the degree to which it advanced or hindered the inevitability of Fabian socialism.

Further flesh was put on these Fabian imperialist bones in a chapter on China. Here the most radical claims of the Manifesto can be found. Shaw conceded that Chinese civilization was not necessarily lower than European. But one of its effects was to prevent Europeans from trading freely. Turning the nineteenth-century liberal paradigm on its head, he asserted that the idea that a nation had the right to do whatever it pleased with its own territory, without reference to the interests of the outside world, was as absurd from a socialist point of view as the notion that a landlord had the right to do whatever he liked with his property, regardless of the interests of his neighbor.[22]

In the wake of the Boxer Rebellion (in reality, Shaw insisted, no more a rebellion than the destruction of the Armada), European intervention in China is justified in terms of the assertion and enforcement of "international rights of travel and trade." But the right to trade is a very comprehensive one. It involves, among other things, the right to insist upon a settled government to keep the peace and enforce agreements. If the native government is incapable of doing this, a foreign trading power has the right to set one up. This, Shaw asserts, is the "common historical origin of colonies," and may be regarded as "an irresistible natural force, which will lead sooner or later to the imposition by the Powers of commercial civilization on all countries which are still refractory to it."[23]

The important matter is not size or power, it is claimed, but quality of civilization. Thus if Russia were to annexe Switzerland it would be a "calamity which the rest of Europe would be justified in peremptorily preventing." But if Switzerland were to annexe Russia, and liberalize her institutions, "the rest of Europe would breathe more freely." In the boldest though not unambiguous assertion of the Manifesto, Shaw then says:

> There is therefore no question of the steam-rollering of little States because they are little, any more than of their maintenance in deference to romantic nationalism. The State which obstructs international civilization will have to go, be it big or little.[24]

Britain should thus proceed on the principle, opposed to that of noninterference, that she has "international rights of travelling, trading, and efficient police protection, and communication by road, rail and telegraph in every part of the globe."[25]

There are other features of the Manifesto of interest to students of international political theory. Two in particular are worth mentioning due to their distinctive Fabian qualities and probable influence on future Fabian thinking. First, the Manifesto calls for a radical reorganization of the consular service. It was not enough to have a single imperial institute in Kensington. Imperial institutes should be set up in every significant port and trading center in the world. The job of the institutes would be to supply British traders with local knowledge and to promote their wares. They would also act as "organs of disinterested industrial intelligence"[26] and therefore as a barrier against manipulation by capitalist cliques of the press, politicians, and the public. The role of the institutes would be especially important as free trade and the "utopia of the Manchester School" became further discredited, and regulated and managed trade took its place.[27]

Second, Shaw was at pains to point out that the failings of British foreign policy were not so much due to capitalist conspiracy, or corruption, as incompetence and ignorance. On local conditions, in particular the effect of modern industrial civilization on local conditions, the politicians and the press were woefully ignorant. This made them easy meat for unscrupulous financial and commercial interests. Large scale, impartial, social and economic investigation was required. This was summed up in the Shavian flourish: "what the British Empire wants most urgently in its government is not Conservatism, not Liberalism, not Imperialism, but brains and political science."[28]

According to Porter, *Fabianism and the Empire* was the most original and enduring of Fabian statements on international relations, and it pervaded the Society's thinking on the subject for over half a century. As far as Leonard Woolf's writings go, however, this assessment is well wide of the mark. The evidence suggests that *Fabianism and the Empire* was not especially influential on Woolf's thinking (and it should be borne in mind that Woolf was the leading Fabian expert in the area for much of the 1910s, 1920s, and 1930s). Indeed, compared with *International Government*, the Manifesto is a thin, superficial document. Barely half of its 101 pages are taken up with international issues, and of these the bulk are concerned with the the internal governance of the Empire. As with all manifestos it contains a good deal of political rhetoric but little by way of detailed empirical or sociological analysis. In this respect Woolf's book is far superior.

Porter claims that one of the main things that followed from the argument of *Fabianism and the Empire* was that ultimately a system of world government was needed to replace the obsolete nationalism of the nineteenth century. It was interest in this idea that culminated in *International Government*. But as we shall see, Woolf was nowhere near as ready as Shaw to write-off nationalism as a major force in international politics. Nor was he as convinced as Shaw that world government would be the inevitable conclusion of social evolution. While certainly not antipathetic to the idea of world government, *International Government*, as we shall also see, was predicated on the idea that such an eventuality was unlikely to occur in the forseeable future, and maybe not at all. There are certain parallels between the two works (e.g. the emphasis on "scientific" social investigation, the faith in "machinery" to solve political problems, and the belief that the British Empire provided an instructive example of working internationalism—though whether it constituted for Woolf the "closest approximation to an ideal international authority yet achieved"[29] can be doubted[30]). But a close reading of the two texts suggest that the influence was neither direct nor great.

One further point merits emphasis. *Fabianism and the Empire* is a work of second-image analysis *par excellence*.[31] The explanations it gives, if not always explicitly, for the causes of war are located almost exclusively at the level of the state. Accordingly, war is a product of inefficient, ignorant, lazy, and incompetent governments. It is fermented by capitalist "rings" and "cliques" who fiendishly exploit the natural pugnacity of the press and the public. It is assisted by the cozy relationship between the armed forces, the War Office, and the institutions of the aristocracy.[32] The point here is not to examine the coherence of such a position, but to note that the domestic organization and constitution of the state is consistently identified as the source of international strife.

This stands in sharp contrast to Woolf's analysis. While Woolf paid his dues to these factors, and while his thought contains in many places the heavy imprint of the English dissenting tradition, he consistently locates the fundamental causes of war at the level of the international system. He predominantly adopts, in Waltz's terms, a third-image analysis. It is the lack of international organization, or the right type of organization, and perhaps the right type of psychology to make it work, that is identified as the chief, underlying, cause of war. This fact makes *International Government* a much more modern work than *Fabianism and the Empire*, and links it much more closely with the systematic, professional study of international relations, to which it was an important spur.[33]

The Fabian Legacy

The influence of the main Fabian contribution to international thought in Woolf's *International Government* appears to be slight. As well as the parallels mentioned above one could point to the idea that individualism (if not nationalism or noninterference) was outmoded; that the Great Power politics was a fact of life and that the Great Powers also should behave like "great responsibles"; and that what was needed in international life was more and better government. But these are rather broad notions that Woolf could well have acquired from Fabian thinking in general. He did not necessarily inherit them directly from *Fabianism and the Empire*.

It is certainly true that by the time he came to write *International Government* Woolf had imbibed a good quantity of Fabian doctrine. The Fabian raw material used in the construction of this important and in some ways pathbreaking work was of a general rather than any particular kind. One may point to: (a) the importance attached to "facts" and detailed empirical investigation; (b) the strong attachment to a sociological as opposed to a philosophical mode of enquiry; (c) belief in gradualism and a permeative approach to political change as opposed to militant and revolutionary methods; (d) a commitment to rational and scientific as opposed to ethical or romantic socialism; (e) concern with social efficiency as well as social injustice; (f) faith in "scientific administration" and the importance of the highly trained expert; and (g) dedication to public service and the pursuit of collective well-being. Fabianism is a notoriously difficult political doctrine to define. These facets are undoubtedly, however, ones to which many practising Fabians subscribed.[34] As we shall see, they find ample expression in Woolf's work.

A Practicable Proposal

The outbreak of war in August 1914 had a profound effect on the Fabian Society. Not only did it bring into sharp focus the extent of the Society's neglect of the international realm, it also served to impress on it that domestic reform could not be achieved in the absence of international reform. Fabians could no longer be little Englanders. An understanding of international relations would now have to be a much greater part of their work. *International Government* was the first product of this new attitude.

Given the absence of a serious body of Fabian thought on international affairs it is not surprising that in Part One of his study Woolf drew not on the Fabian writers, or for that matter on the work of other radicals, but on the work of diplomatic historians and international lawyers. For Part Two there was very little work of any description to draw on. As Woolf later recalled:

> You could not become an authority on international government in 1915 by reading books, because the books did not exist[35] ... I had therefore to read Blue Books and White Books and annual reports dealing with such vast organizations as the Universal Postal Union or the International Institute of Agriculture, and I had many interviews with civil servants and others who attended the conferences or congresses of these unions or associations as national representatives.[36]

A large part of Woolf's study, then, was original research.

It is important to note that Woolf conceived his work in the most practical terms. The brief given to Woolf by Sidney Webb for the investigation, which later became Part One of *International Government*, was as follows:

> What is needed is to arrive at a strictly practical suggestion, or rather alternative suggestions, explained and supported by accounts of *what has been tried with useful results*; and of past experiments and analyses suggestive of any new expedients we can devise ...[37]

More specifically Woolf's job was to enquire into the evolution of international law, institutions, and agreements and to suggest ways in which these could be developed in order to make war less likely.

Woolf was well aware that plans for radical international reform were often regarded as utopian. Long before Carr's critique he denounced "this terrifying adjective" as a conservative device for discrediting any new idea or proposal. He also claimed with characteristic irony that "everything is utopian until it is tried." It is important to note that in a sense the dichotomy between realism and utopianism was part of the vocabulary of international relations long before the publication of *The Twenty Years' Crisis*. Woolf contrasted the so-called idealists, utopians, "amiable cranks," and "idealistic dreamers," with "the 'plain and practical men' school of writers," and those who upheld "the dogma of anti-internationalism."[38] His denunciation of the term notwithstanding, Woolf shared the general Fabian fear of being labeled utopian and consequently steered clear of suggestions he felt states would not accept. This is clearly evident in the Fabian Draft Treaty for "A Supernational Authority that will Prevent War."[39] Despite the bold title, the plan does not advocate the merging of independent national units in a "world state" or the creation of a "world government" or a "world parliament." Woolf maintained that such ideas were impracticable since they did not have the slightest chance of being accepted by the world's statesmen. The carnage of the war had made change a matter of great urgency. The system could not be left as it currently stood. But new schemes for world political organization would have to take into account the structure and processes of the old. Reform, perhaps radical, was needed, but revolution in its fullest sense, or a "sudden, large mutation"[40] was not realistic. Nor did he seek to outlaw war. Rather, he recommended the establishment of machinery and procedures whereby states could settle their differences short of war. Similarly, he did not, at this stage at any rate, advocate disarmament arguing instead that this would come about by itself, "just as the individual carrying of arms falls silently into desuetude as and when fears of aggression die down before the rule of law."[41]

Woolf's Conception of International Government

For Woolf government was essentially a regulatory activity. Whether local, national, or international, government involved

> the regulation of relations according to general rules, which to a greater or less extent are understood vaguely to embody the idea in the community of what the *right* relations ought to be.[42]

Or alternatively it was a question of

> making rules which will regulate the relations between the individuals or the groups, of establishing organization which will make it easy for them to co-operate for common purposes, and of devising models of settling disputes and differences when they arise.[43]

These rules included customs, morality, the rules and regulations of voluntary associations, and law.

Woolf defined international government broadly: it meant "the regulation of relations between states, nations or peoples by international agreement."[44] International government was not necessarily, therefore, a centralized activity involving a set of central institutions. Nor was it the exclusive domain of states. Nor was it something completely new. On the contrary it was something that already existed and was evolving. In this respect the nineteenth century had been highly significant:

> ... a profound change in international relations has taken place since the beginning of the Nineteenth Century, and ... the people who repeat and repeat again that International Government is Utopian, and international agreement must betray national interests, simply shut their eyes to the fact that in every department of life the beginnings, and more than the beginnings of International Government already exist ... [45]

Throughout the nineteenth century, Woolf contended, international interests had been gathering strength at the expense of traditionally conceived national interests. By this he meant that the interests of individuals and groups within the state increasingly corresponded to the interests of similar individuals and groups in other states. The corollary of this was that *real* national interests, the interests of the mass of people, had become international interests. Indeed, he claimed that, "[t]he recognition of international interests, and that national interests are international interests, and *vice versâ*, was the great social discovery of the last 100 years."[46]

Given such a broad definition of international government the possibility arises that it takes a number of different forms. Two can be inferred from the way Woolf organized his material in *International Government*. Part One of the book examines the ways in which, from 1815 to 1914, the Great Powers acted in concert. In contrast, Part Two is concerned with what Woolf called cosmopolitan (meaning primarily nonstate) organization. But a third kind of international government, which might be called "international government through adjudication," can also be discerned sandwiched between them. One of the weaknesses of Woolf's analysis, to be discussed in chapter 4, is a failure to adequately distinguish between these different forms. Arguably there is a tension between them. Rather than in harness, as Woolf assumed, it might be the case that they pull in different directions.

Great Power International Government

Woolf observed that during the nineteenth century the Great Powers had gathered together in concerts, conventions, and congresses in order to discuss and settle matters that threatened to disrupt the peace. A new, if rudimentary, international system had come into being, the most significant attribute of which was the tendency of the various congresses and conferences to behave as if they were "rudimentary international legislative organs." The central principle of this new system was the negation of the right of any one Power and the assertion of the right of the Powers collectively to make decisions on matters affecting the peace of Europe.[47]

Woolf felt that his interpretation of nineteenth-century international relations could be verified by reference to a number of international events. He gave special weight to four in particular. The first was the Greek revolt of 1821. The Great Powers agreed that the revolt posed a serious threat to the peace of Europe. Russia proposed collective intervention and an international conference to resolve the conflict. Turkey protested, not without good reason, that the matter fell within her domestic affairs. Russia, France, and Britain, however, "under cover of the specious term 'mediation'...formed themselves into a kind of legislative committee."[48] Over the next ten years, through a series of conferences, they proceeded to settle the conflict between Turkey and Greece, and they were prepared to enforce their decisions when necessary. The most dramatic example of this was the "pacific blockade" and the destruction of the Turkish fleet at Navarino in 1827. This kind of activity on the part of the Great Powers continued throughout the century. Woolf cites a number of examples in support of the claim that the Great Powers had arrogated to themselves the right to collectively "arrange" the affairs of Greece.[49] According to Woolf, "The relations of Greece and Turkey were... continually regulated by quasi-legislative conferences."[50]

The second example concerns the Balkans. In 1876 the insurrection of Bosnia-Herzegovina was supported by Montenegro and Serbia against Turkey. The six Great Powers came forward as "mediators" and two conferences were held at Constantinople. Various proposals were made with respect to the nature of the administrative system to be applied to Bosnia-Herzegovina, and a commitment was made to establish an international force, to be composed of between 3,000 and 6,000 Belgian troops, to police the agreement. But these proposals were rejected by Turkey. Woolf points out that this would have been the end of the matter if the Great Powers were genuinely acting as mediators. But Russia sent a circular to the other Powers asking what measures they were prepared to take "to enforce the decisions of Europe." When the other Powers proved reluctant to take action, Russia went to war and attempted to make her own terms with Turkey by the Treaty of San Stefano. This, however, proved unacceptable to the other Great Powers and they subsequently "insisted upon a European settlement at the international Congress of Berlin." In Woolf's view the conference at Constantinople "clearly... regarded itself as an international legislative organ" though the Powers lacked the courage of their convictions when it came to enforcing their agreement. Yet, by repudiating the Treaty of San Stefano they once again affirmed the principle that the Eastern question could only be settled by the collective decision of the Powers.[51]

The final two examples are dealt with by Woolf much more briefly. In 1867 Holland proposed to sell the strategically important Duchy of Luxembourg to France. There were fears that this may result in war between France and Germany. Even though the transaction would have been perfectly legitimate under international law, the Great Powers intervened and an international conference in London sealed an agreement whereby the eight Powers represented "collectively guaranteed" Luxembourg's neutrality. Finally, in 1905 the Moroccan Crisis threatened to disturb the peace of Europe. France was determined to settle the matter unilaterally, but under pressure from the other Powers she acceded to Germany's wish that an international conference be charged with resolving the dispute. A conference was subsequently held at Algeciras, and its Final Act once again confirmed the principle of "international regulation."[52]

Woolf believed that this new "quasi-legislative" role the Great Powers had assumed for themselves could be extended and refined. Such a development, he felt, was essential if the dragon of war was to be slain. Two obstacles, however, lay in the path of any such development. The first was the tendency for the concert to conceive itself in various, not necessarily consistent, ways. This was especially the case during the years of the Congress system, 1815–1822. At times it saw itself as a "Parliament of Nations," or a kind of European confederation. At other times it saw itself as merely a "hegemony of four great powers, bound by alliance to preserve the *status quo*."[53] Constant uncertainty as to the nature of the new system in the minds of its participants contributed to the Congress system's premature demise.

The second obstacle was that the Great Powers consistently failed to specify the area of competence of the quasi-legislature. Czar Alexander and his continental allies were of the opinion that it should be allowed to deal not only with questions pertaining to the relations between states but also their internal affairs. British Foreign Secretary Castlereagh, and later Canning, disagreed. They were of the view that "our engagements have reference wholly to the state of the territorial possessions settled at the peace; to the state of affairs between nation and nation, not...to the affairs of any nation within itself."[54] Woolf believed that this "common-sense" method of delineating the competence of the quasi-legislature had merit in a large number of cases. But it was lacking when it came to "problems of nationality." It was extremely difficult to say whether cases such as the Greek rebellion and the Bosnian insurrection were national or international. Consequently there was bound to be disagreement over whether such disputes should be resolved nationally or through an international conference. One of the problems this gave rise to was as follows: if the Greek and Bosnian cases were considered to be international, then logically so should the question of Irish Home Rule, the "position of India within the British Empire," and "the position of Finns within the Russian Empire." There was little prospect, however, of the British or Russian governments accepting a right of collective intervention in these matters. Therefore, the permissive principle advocated by Alexander was not practicable, at least not in a consistent way. If the noninterventionist position of Castlereagh and Canning had been adopted, however, the Powers would have been prohibited from settling Turkey's conflicts with Greek, Bosnian, and other minorities. Yet the Powers had in fact done this, and they had successfully avoided war between themselves by doing so.

Woolf was undecided on what position to take on this question. On the one hand, the chances of obtaining agreement between the powers along the lines of the permissive principle were remote. There was no prospect, for example, of Britain giving Russia any say in what she regarded as her domestic affairs, especially given the enormous differences in their administrative, economic, and political systems. On the other hand, if a strictly noninterventionist position were adopted the Great Powers would be prohibited from dealing collectively with one of the most potent sources of contemporary international tension—nationalism. Woolf eventually settled for a pragmatic compromise. During the nineteenth century the practice evolved of treating a question as an international question if there was a consensus among the Powers that it posed a threat to the peace of Europe. Anticipating the underlying logic of Chapter VII of the UN Charter, Woolf accepted this as the only satisfactory way of resolving the matter until the domestic constitutions of states had become more uniform in character.[55]

International Government through Adjudication

Woolf attached great importance to rules of international law. Although sometimes vague and uncertain and noncomprehensive in scope, there was no denying that "a vast body of well-established international law" had been developed "covering a great extent of international relations, and certainly the fundamental relations upon which international society rests to-day." The foreign offices of the world were continually engaged in applying such rules. Hundreds of thousands of Britons had laid down their lives in defense of them. Nine-tenths of international intercourse and nine-tenths of international commerce depended on their daily recognition and application.[56]

One of the products of the emerging quasi-legislative role of the Great Powers was the quantative and qualitative development of international law. International conferences had become involved in making new rules of law; they also become involved in the codification of existing customary rules. As a result, international law was becoming less vague and uncertain, and rights and duties were being created that were "clearly *capable* of being the subjects of judicial decisions."[57] This was significant for Woolf since, in true Webbian fashion, he believed that progress in social affairs depended on transforming "vague" political relations into "definite" legal relations. In the past international society provided only two methods of settling disputes: negotiation and war. A third method was now in the making: international adjudication.

In his wide-ranging discussion of adjudication Woolf essentially makes three points. The first concerns arbitration. During the first two decades of the twentieth century, arbitration was widely seen as the solution to the problem of war. The success of arbitration in the *Alabama* case and the Dogger Bank incident convinced many observers of the need for a general system of arbitration. Woolf, however, felt that the arguments in favor of arbitration were incoherent. In his view, generic use of the term arbitration concealed two kinds of judicial process that needed to be distinguished. With the first kind, the judge or arbiter makes a decision on the basis of law. With the second, a decision is made on the basis of what is considered "fair and reasonable." Supporters of arbitration assumed that the cases they enthusiastically cited were examples of the latter form of judicial decision. In fact, Woolf maintained, they were examples of the former. States had only been willing to accept arbitration when the dispute clearly hinged on a question of law. This was true not only of the vast majority of cases but also of the most famous arbitration case of all. The tribunal in the *Alabama* case made its judgment on the basis of previously agreed rules of international law—*not*, as many believed, on the basis of what was fair and reasonable. The main difference between Britain and the United States concerned the rights of neutrals during war. It was this question that had brought the two countries to the brink of war. It was resolved, however, contrary to popular belief, not by arbitration but by diplomatic negotiation. Arbitration only occurred with respect to the level of damages due. In fact what had happened was that the disputing parties had sought a judicial settlement not on the primary bone of contention, but on a series of subsidiary bones all of which fell within the remit of existing rules of international law.

Woolf's examination of this and other cases led him to the conclusion that a general system of obligatory arbitration was no panacea for war since states were willing to submit only certain kinds of disputes to a judicial body. This was as true of relations between states as it was of relations between individuals. Not all disputes within states were settled by judicial decisions. The range of disputes settled by such means was, in fact, "strictly limited." Political, and what Woolf ambiguously called "administrative" differences, were "never within States referred to judicial tribunals." It was hopeless, for example, to expect the "Home Rule question" to be resolved by such means. It was similarly hopeless to expect the judicial method to settle all disputes at the international level. The type of disputes that could be resolved by judicial methods were, in Woolf's words, "legal disputes": that is, those involving the interpretation of a legal document, the existence of a legal right or obligation, or a question of fact.[58]

In an attempt to define this type of dispute more precisely Woolf challenged the view that judicial settlement is impossible in questions that affect "national honour and vital interests." This is the second point he makes in his discussion of adjudication. According to Woolf the attempts made to devise a system of obligatory adjudication at the Hague conferences had foundered because diplomatists had insisted on ruling out adjudication in disputes involving honor and vital interests. An attempt to draw up a list of disputes that did not impinge on such matters resulted, unremarkably, in a brief list of disputes of no importance. The central problem was that honor and vital interests could not be objectively defined. In principle any question might affect the honor and vital interest of a nation. It followed that giving individual states the right to decide whether or not such matters were involved was not a step forward since adjudication would in effect be optional not obligatory. If they wished to avoid adjudication on a particular question they merely had to deem that it involved a question of honor.[59]

Woolf contended that such an approach, as well as being flawed, was also unnecessary. The historical record showed that in fact states had been prepared to submit their differences to a judicial tribunal when honor and vital interests were involved provided that: (a) a "rational and suitable" judicial procedure exists; and (b) the question could be put to the tribunal in a legal form.[60] The Dogger Bank incident, for instance, had been successfully resolved by an International Commission of Inquiry even though one of the issues at stake was the honor of the Russian Fleet. Other cases resolved by judicial settlement, for instance the Alaskan and Venezuelan Boundary questions, had also involved either national honor or vital interests. These cases demonstrated, in Woolf's view, that there were five categories of disputes that could be put to a tribunal in legal form: (a) disputes that could be reduced to questions of fact; (b) questions of title to territory and boundaries; (c) questions as to the interpretation of law; (d) questions concerning the responsibility of national agents for the results of their actions; and (e) questions concerning certain kinds of pecuniary claims.[61]

In Woolf's view it was "both practicable and reasonable" for states to bind themselves to submit these five categories of questions to judicial decision. He also maintained, however, that "in the present state of affairs" the prospect of states actually doing so would be increased "if an additional safeguard to national interests could be introduced."[62] This is Woolf's third point. In effect he proposed two safeguards. First, he proposed that states should not be bound *absolutely* to submit such disputes to a judicial tribunal. Rather they should be given the option to bring them before an International Conference, which would make a decision not only on the basis of law, but also on the basis of equity. This provision was necessary because of the conservative nature of law. Strongly anticipating Carr's analysis of law and peaceful change, Woolf argued that states whose interests were not invested in the *status quo* would not accept compulsory adjudication. This was the case even with respect to the limited range of questions he had identified since a judicial tribunal, by its nature, inevitably upholds the existing order.[63] What was required was a method by which the *status quo* could, in certain circumstances, be upset in an orderly manner. Woolf vested this function in his International Conference.

The second safeguard proposed by Woolf involved giving states some say on the *type* of tribunal before which their unresolved disputes would ultimately have to be brought. "The art of administering and interpreting International Law," according to Woolf, "has only just been born, and we know so little about it that, by trying to confine it to rigid lines, we may easily kill it in infancy."[64] Thus although referring "legal disputes" to a tribunal should be obligatory (notwithstanding the first safeguard), the type of tribunal should be optional. Woolf saw no reason why a number of tribunals, variously constituted, could not exist side by side. The Permanent Court of Arbitration established at the first Hague Conference could thus exist alongside the Judicial Arbitration Court proposed at the second conference, and alongside other courts, commissions, and tribunals established by specific treaties. In the event of a disagreement between the disputing parties over which tribunal was most suitable, states would be bound to submit the dispute to a conference or to the Permanent Court of Arbitration.

In summary, Woolf's proposals for compulsory adjudication, firmly based on his interpretation of the recent past, were as follows. It was possible to identify a class of disputes—legal disputes—which could always be settled by the decision of a judicial tribunal. However, because of the uncertainty and incompleteness of certain points of international law, and because deciding matters within the existing framework of law was an inherently conservative method, states would be reluctant to fully subscribe to it. Woolf proposed, therefore, that they be permitted, in certain circumstances, to submit the dispute for decision by an international legislative conference. There was no reason why a plurality of judicial bodies could not coexist with each other. The need for a single, central, judicial organ had been much exaggerated. Reference to a tribunal should be obligatory but the choice of tribunal should be voluntary.

Cosmopolitan International Government

Woolf's principal analytical contention on this type of international government was that during the nineteenth century the economic, social, and to a much lesser extent, political structure of the world had become more cosmopolitan than it had ever been before. His main prescription was that organization along cosmopolitan lines should be extended, especially in the political sphere. Indeed, an extension of such organization was necessary to fill the gap—which had become a breeding ground for international tension—between the organization of social and economic life of the world and the organization of its political life.

The growth of cosmopolitan organization was a product of the revolution in communications. This led to a massive increase in international intercourse between economic, social, cultural, educational, scientific, and political actors. Increased intercourse led to increased interdependence and to the "discovery," referred to above, that true national interests were in fact international interests. The practical manifestation of this discovery was the "spontaneous creation and evolution" of a new and multifarious range of international and cosmopolitan bodies and groups.[65]

In Woolf's view this range of new actors consisted of four basic types. First, there were those bodies and associations composed exclusively of states. Primary among these were the public international unions such as the UPU ITU. Unlike the conferences and congresses of Woolf's first conception of international government, these were intended to be permanent bodies, which operated on a day to day basis through a bureau or secretariat. They came into being, starting with the Riverian Commissions established at Vienna, as a result of a growing awareness among states that certain important common interests could not be protected in an extemporary fashion.

Woolf's second category of international bodies had grown side by side with the public international unions. These were the "unofficial" congresses and associations consisting of individuals and groups other than states. Starting with the World Anti-Slavery Convention held in London in 1840, a plethora of such bodies had come into being. As with the first category, the impetus for the creation of such bodies was the realization that there was "an interest to serve or an object to attain which was international rather than national."[66] Woolf calculated that by 1914 over 500 international associations of this kind had been created, and over 400 of these had a permanent existence. This meant that

> ... there is hardly a sphere of life in which a consciousness of international interests has not penetrated, and led to men of every tongue or race joining together in order to promote those interests. Practically every profession, from engineers and architects to nurses and commercial travellers, is represented. Industry and commerce, from Chambers of Commerce to bird-fanciers and cinematographic film makers; labour in some forty separate International Federations; Science, from the powerful Electro-technical Commission to the International Society of Psychical Research; Medicine, with as many as thirty-nine distinct associations; Art, Literature, Learning, and Religion have all entered the field of international organization.[67]

Along with these were "innumerable" associations dedicated to the achievement of particular social or political ends such as women's suffrage, temperance, or the eradication of prostitution.[68]

A third, less common, kind of international association were those comprising a heterogeneous membership. The Association Internationale pour la Lutte contra le Chômage, for example, had among its membership, states, provinces, municipalities, employers, trade unions, professional associations, and individual economists. Such bodies came into existence when a number of individuals and groups, often representing different constituencies, realized that they had a common interest in solving a particular problem. In Woolf's opinion they represented a "new type and experiment in human co-operation." These bodies paved the way for the most striking example of this type of cooperation: the International Labour Organization.[69]

The fourth and final kind of international association was concerned exclusively with commerce. Producers and suppliers had increasingly gathered together in order to regulate international trade. In its simplest form such regulation consisted of the agreements on price and market share. More sophisticated forms of regulation included the formation of rings, cartels, and international companies.

Woolf not only identified these new international bodies, he also had a lot to say about their broader significance. Their birth was part cause and part effect of four highly important developments. First, administration was being internationalized. During the nineteenth century the functions of the state had gradually expanded to satisfy the needs of a changing society. But with increasing internationalization of society there came a point when national administration was no longer adequate. One of two things had to occur: either the emerging fabric of that society had to break down; or the independence of states had to be compromised. Woolf contended that, in fact, the latter had begun to occur, and administration on international lines had firmly taken root. The UPU, for example, established a single postal territory for the exchange of correspondence. The day to day running of the UPU was entrusted to a permanent International Bureau, which undertook research, supplied information, provided machinery for the resolution of disputes, and acted as a clearing house for the settlement of accounts. Similar administrative functions had been invested in the Bureau of the ITU, the Danube Commission, an International Administration for the suppression of slavery in Africa, and the various international sanitary councils.[70]

Second, lawmaking was becoming increasingly cosmopolitan. Social progress not only necessitated the internationalization of administration but also the harmonization of national laws. Woolf called the process whereby national laws are harmonized "cosmopolitan law-making," and the most striking example of it could be found in the field of maritime law. An international voluntary association, the International Maritime Committee, had been founded in 1898 for the purpose of putting pressure on states to progressively unify their divergent maritime codes. As a result a convention was signed unifying laws relating to salvage and collisions at sea. A draft convention had also been drawn up covering safety at sea and the carriage of freight. A similar, though less successful, process had also begun to take root in the area of labor law. The International Association for Labour Legislation, had been set up in 1900. As a result of its efforts a large number of industrial countries agreed to adopt laws proscribing night work for women and prohibiting the manufacture, import, and sale of matches made from white phosphorus. The Association also had some success in impressing on states the need for wage boards and minimum rates of pay in certain industries.[71]

Third, standardization was occurring on an increasingly international scale. International scientific associations had taken the lead in the standardization of scientific nomenclature. Before 1880 there existed a plethora of standards with respect to the measurement of heat, color, time, electrical current, and so on. In the decades that followed, however, agreement was reached on single international standards for all these phenomena. This pattern of standardization was repeated with respect to, among other things, medical nomenclature, actuarial methods, chemical analysis, food analysis, and the testing of materials. Woolf believed that this process of standardization was immensely important. It signalled not only the "internationalisation of society," but the growth of an "international social tissue." Peculiar national habits and customs were being broken down. And this was highly significant since, in Woolf's words, "it is where nations represent different levels of 'culture' and are yet in intimate and continual relationship, that the difficulties of applying government to their relations are most formidable."[72]

Finally, commerce and industry were increasingly becoming international in organization and scope. Indeed, Woolf claimed, "In no department of life has International Government been more firmly or widely established."[73] He also claimed, "[t]he business man in every country is a confirmed internationalist." This was demonstrated by resolutions of the International Congress of the Chambers of Commerce. These resolutions were "almost entirely occupied with pressing the governments to take steps to internationalize administration, legislation, etc."[74] Furthermore, capitalists increasingly sought to regulate competition and substitute for it some form of cooperation. An array of trusts, cartels, combinations, and other arrangements had come into being to maximize economies of scale, divide up markets, and regulate output and prices.[75] The apparatus of international government had also been erected in the world of labor—although it was true that the international trade union movement was stronger on paper than in practise. Trade unionists had organized themselves into various international federations in order to more effectively combat the forces of international capital. These federations performed a variety of functions ranging from dramatic attempts to organize international strikes, to less sensational activities such as research into labor conditions.[76]

International Government in the 1920s and 1930s

The preceding account is based largely on Woolf's wartime writings, *International Government* in particular. He had little to say about international government as such in the 1920s. He wrote widely on such matters as mandates and international cooperative trade—matters that unquestionably fall within his initial definition of international government. But he did not discuss these matters from what might be called an international government perspective: he did not consider them explicitly in terms of his network of intergovernmental rules and regulations.

The same could be generally said about the 1930s. During this period Woolf had many interesting and prescient things to say about the rise of Fascism and Hitlerism,[77] about Soviet Russia and communism,[78] about the World Disarmament Conference,[79] the Abyssinian crisis,[80] the League,[81] Labour,[82] the foreign policy of the national government,[83] pacifism,[84] and so on. But he did not add anything substantial to his *theory* of international government.

It would be unfair, however, to say that he did not add anything at all. Woolf made a number of interesting points and observations about international government during this period, three of which are particularly worthy of mention.

First, he put forward a novel theory about how it was possible, despite the "quiet growth" of a "vast system" of international government in the nineteenth century, for war to break out so suddenly and ferociously in 1914. He contended that there were essentially two, for the most part, conflicting methods of political organization—nationalism and internationalism—which, in turn, were always to some extent the effect or expression of two, for the most part, conflicting currents of communal political psychology—communal nationalist psychology and communal internationalist psychology. The former was rooted in patriotism:

> The nationalist thinks of a world of completely independent States or nations, and regards himself as an individual belonging to and owing loyalty to only one unit in that world. He identifies his own interests passionately with those of his own nation, and he is rarely, if ever, conscious of any common bond of interests between nations.[85]

Nationalist psychology reached its peak in Europe during the first decade of the twentieth century. During that time

> [e]verything calculated to influence a man's political beliefs or emotions combined to make him think and feel nationally and imperially, the schools, the press, the churches, literature and painting, sculpture in our streets, and the military bands in our parks.[86]

Such was the potency of nationalist psychology that most people believed that government and society was organized entirely on national lines. Few realized that this was no longer the case and that, in fact, international government had either modified or taken the place of national government "in almost every department of life."

But unlike organization on national lines international organization "was not so much the result or reflection of conscious political psychology as the inevitable result of changes in the structure of human society." The industrial revolution of the eighteenth century and the scientific revolution of the nineteenth had knit the world so closely together that the national frontier had rapidly become a social, economic, and political anachronism. Modern commerce, industry, and finance had been internationalized. So too had the post, the telegraph, the railway, and the prevention of disease. In these areas and many others frontiers were being increasingly ignored and "international government...silently substituted for national."[87]

But although the scope of international government had by 1914 become very extensive it "had behind it little or no international psychology." Few people "thought or felt internationally." In consequence internationalism had made few inroads into the "strictly political" relations between states. These relations were still determined by "a fantastic system of diplomacy and war based on the anachronistic myth that every State was a sovereign, independent unit."

By the turn of the century the world was thus faced with two competing systems and two competing types of communal psychology. A choice had to be made between one and the other. In the Triple Alliance and the Entente and at Sarajevo it chose nationalism and war.

Second, he put forward an interesting interpretation of the Versailles settlement. The horror of the war provoked widespread revulsion against nationalism, the glamor of which had for many people "evaporated...in the mud of Flanders or during a London air raid." A patriot declared that "patriotism was not enough" and the speeches of President Wilson began to diffuse a "thin film of international psychology over hundreds of thousands of people who had also found that patriotism was not enough."[88]

Yet in some places the temperature of nationalist psychology had been heated as much as it had been cooled in other places, and international psychology, though real, was for the most part "vague" and "uneducated." As a result the framework for the new Europe was arrived at largely as if the international civilization of the nineteenth century "had never been heard of and we were living in the time of Frederick the Great." Territorially the Balkanization of Europe was carried to lengths that "in the milder days before the war, the most optimistic statesman in Sofia or Belgrade or in the mountains of Montenegro and Albania could never have dreamed of."

But the architects of the settlement were not of one mind. The desire for vengeance jostled with the desire for peace. The nationalists at the conference were forced to listen to the president and "the masses crying for peace at the door." Compromise was the result. A building that had begun as an Arc de Triumphe was hastily finished off with "the stucco cupola of a Temple of Peace": "The Wilsonian League was superimposed upon the territorial, military, naval, and economic settlement, and Geneva was created as an antidote to Serajevo and Versailles."[89]

Third, he provided a suggestive account of the state of the League and international government "ten years on." "The outstanding fact," Woolf asserted, "is the unexpected strength and position developed by the League in the short time of its existence." In the everyday international government of commerce, industry, culture, and science, the League had assumed a particularly important role. Geneva had become the nucleus of a new system of international government dealing with a vast array of questions and problems: from the arms trade to the ray treatment of cancer, from the administration of the Saar to the standardization of economic statistics, from the treatment of minorities to the relief of refugees.[90] The architects of the peace had not altogether intended this. But in unloading an array of practical problems from their own shoulders onto those of the League they had enabled it "at once to become a real entity in the society of nations."

Yet the importance of the League was both overestimated and underestimated. The nationalist underestimated the importance of the League in not appreciating the immense development of international government that was taking place under its auspices. He viewed the League as a "foreign body," which on no account should be allowed to meddle with matters of high politics. The League, on the contrary, should stick to the performance of tasks the unimportance of which was in keeping with its inferior status. But in taking this view the nationalist had unwittingly strengthened not weakened the League. It was through the performance of these "unimportant," "every-day" tasks that the League had been able to attain "a position of importance and stability, which it could not possibly have won in ten years if it had merely remained an instrument to be used in emergencies for preventing war and for the pacific settlement of international disputes."

But the importance of the League was also overestimated. The internationalist, for his part, failed to appreciate that nationalist passions still persisted and that nationalist psychology was still dominant. It was true that if the world were allowed to enjoy a century of unbroken peace, the bonds of common interests might become "so closely and intricately bound" by the growth of international government that both national psychology and the structure of the society of nations would be "completely altered" and a second Serajavo made "impossible." It was also true that the League had succeeded in training its secretariat in international psychology and had even had some success in encouraging its wider growth. But the danger of nationalist war remained. It was a cold fact that international psychology was still for the most part weak, vacillating, uninstructed; and where vital interests were thought to be involved the dominant psychology was nationalist not internationalist. This was demonstrated *inter alia* by: the "persistent refusal of the Conservative Government to sign the Optional Clause"; by the outcry in *The Times* when it eventually was signed; by the prejudice against and contempt for the Permanent Court of International Justice (whose judges were considered either not learned in law or learned in an inferior, Latin, school of law); and by the attitude of *The Times*, Lord Salisbury, and Sir Austin Chamberlain and others, who saw the League as merely an "ideal" or something "good enough for France and Germany and other foreigners, but...unnecessary for the British Empire." This *mental* condition, Woolf concluded, was a perpetual obstruction to the development of a "sane and stable system of international politics."[91]

Apart from these three points Woolf had little to say of significance about international government in the 1930s. Why?

Stephen Spender once said that "Leonard and Virginia were among the very few people in England who had a profound understanding of the state of the world in the 1930's."[92] There is something in this. Leonard Woolf began to warn his readers about the growth of "barbarism"—the growth of hatred, unreason, violence, and intimidation and acceptance of them as normal methods of conducting political affairs—even before the rise of Hitler. In a prescient article written in 1932 he argued that unless this savage phenomenon was vigorously resisted it would inevitably land Europe in another world war.[93]

But although often insightful, Woolf's work during this period was far from systematic. One finds observations of genuine insight and prescience buried beneath mountains of turgid political rhetoric. As the tragic years of the 1930s unfolded, and the international political scene progressively darkened, the balance in Woolf's work between careful argument and angry polemic shifted markedly in the direction of the latter. The Woolf we encounter is mostly Woolf the radical pamphleteer not Woolf the Fabian social investigator. This combination of events, temperament, and overriding purpose accounts for his failure to develop the concept he had devoted so much time and energy to, a decade or so earlier.

International Government in the 1940s

The same could be said about his quite extensive writings on postwar reconstruction in the 1940s. In these writings the term international government appears more frequently than it did in the 1930s but there is no attempt to further refine the *concept* or develop the *theory*. In a pamphlet written for the Labour Party containing the term in its title, for example, Woolf covers much the same ground as before. He talks, among other things, of the growth of interdependence, the obsolescence of (and the need to "drastically limit") sovereignty, the need for rules and "organs of government" to make, amend, and interpret these rules, the growth of international administration, and the need for "organisation and procedure for controlling and preventing the use of force or violence." But all this is done in a highly simplistic manner. He says, for example,

> There is nothing essentially different in the government of a football club, a village, a town, a country, of Europe, or of the world, except that the scale is bigger and the organisation more complicated.
>
> In every case it is a question of making rules which will regulate the relations between the individuals or the groups, of establishing organisation which will make it easy for them to co-operate for common purposes, and of devising methods of settling disputes and differences when they arise.[94]

The problems with this passage are legion. First, even if one accepts the initial premise—which makes no allowance, of course, for ethnic, cultural, religious, ideological, and socioeconomic diversity—the qualification is potentially so large as to cast serious doubt on the whole proposition. Questions of scale and complexity are nowhere near as trivial as Woolf rather complacently implies. Second, the issue is put in the form of an axiom or a conclusion when in fact it is at best no more than a broad hypothesis.

Third, the general tone of the passage is acutely at odds with the difficulty of the problem.

But one should perhaps not make too much of this since the point of the pamphlet is not to advance scientific knowledge but to "educate, agitate, organise." It is nonetheless important to note that in the process Woolf irons out the complexity and much of the subtlety of his previous work and presents us in effect with a set of assertions based on a simple analogy between individuals and states. The problems with this kind of analogy will be examined in chapter 3.

Other works of the period though less obviously didactic in purpose offer substantially the same fare of repetition,[95] oversimplification,[96] platitude,[97] invective,[98] and the occasional dazzling insight.[99] Woolf's ideas for postwar international economic reconstruction will be discussed in chapters 7 and 8. Here it is important to note that during this period his ideas turned decidedly—though not in name—in the direction of world government. He called for "drastic national disarmament," the "abolition of national airforces," and "real international control of national armament" as requisites for a new system of collective security.[100] In response to both federalists and functionalists he asserted the need for a "central world authority" to "coordinate the activities of regional or functional international organs and to deal promptly and authoritatively with any action or situation which may threaten the world's peace or prosperity." Such an authority would need to have "effective control of international force adequate to meet the threat of national force" and/or "control of sufficient armed forces to maintain international law and order under all circumstances."[101] Though broadly welcoming the foundation of the UN (he particularly welcomed Chapter VII of the Charter and the creation of the ECOSOC) he condemned (as emasculatory) the power of veto granted to the permanent members of the Security Council and called for compulsory settlement of all disputes through adjudication, arbitration, or conciliation.[102]

Most radically of all, he advocated, with the advent of the atomic bomb, centralization of the production of atomic energy under a "world authority" and the concentration of all armaments other than those required for purely internal police purposes in the hands of the UN. The invention of the atomic bomb, he argued, had turned the balance of international power upside down, and rendered collective security, and especially the system of collective security as devised at Dumbarton Oaks and San Francisco, obsolete. Great Powers were no longer invulnerable to small Powers. Armed with atomic bombs a small Power could "completely paralyse" a Great Power or at least "inflict appalling and irreparable damage before being wiped off the map itself." The UN placed no restrictions on the acquisition of atomic weapons. It was therefore highly likely that within a comparatively short time a large number of states would own them. The collective security system of the UN was thereby undermined. Would-be aggressors were now in a position to threaten their victims *and* the Security Council as much as the Security Council could threaten them. Collective resistance to aggression was now as much of a threat to civilization as aggression itself. It followed that nothing could save civilization as long as the sovereign state was free to manufacture, arm, and use the atomic bomb.

But by what means could this freedom be denied? President Truman and Mr. Attlee proposed "international control of atomic energy to the extent necessary to ensure its use only for peaceful purposes" and "elimination from national armaments of atomic weapons." This answer, however, did not, in Woolf's view, amount to much. Military exploitation of atomic energy depended on almost exactly the same methods and processes as those required for industrial uses. This meant that international control as previously envisaged was no longer adequate: international *inspection* could not ensure that the uses to which atomic energy was being put were always and everywhere purely industrial. Some state somewhere was bound, sooner or later, to give in to temptation and "the mere fact that there was good ground for fearing this would cause the whole system to break down and lead to general atomic armament 'for defensive purposes.'"

It followed that if atomic disaster was to be avoided, and the "elimination from national armaments of atomic weapons" achieved, production of atomic energy had to be concentrated in the hands of a world authority. It was difficult to say whether this would be permanently, even temporarily, feasible. But more than a ray of hope existed in the fact that the production of atomic energy on any considerable scale was currently a gigantic operation requiring enormous plant, labor force, and expenditure. If the United States, USSR, and Britain could reach agreement it would be possible to restrict such production exclusively to "plants directly controlled by an international authority under the United Nations." The authority would then distribute the energy for industrial uses to other countries. This, at least, would provide some breathing space until a more effective system could be devised.

But things could not stop there. It was not possible, in Woolf's view, to prevent by international control the use of atomic weapons unless the same kind of control was applied to other weapons. The alternative was a world in which the production of atomic energy was controlled but states remained perfectly free to arm themselves with every other kind of armament that modern science provided. In such a world the threat of war and the competition to produce more and more destructive weapons would clearly remain and the UN would have no alternative but to manufacture atomic bombs in order "to prevent aggression." But the use of atomic weapons by the UN to prevent aggression and thereby "keep the peace" was neither feasible nor logical.[103] This meant that the only solution was to put *all* armaments except for those needed for domestic purposes under the control of "the world authority of the United Nations." The implications for national sovereignty were necessarily profound. Such a solution required states not only to surrender control over their armaments but also to partially surrender control over their industrial production. Realists, of course, would condemn this as utopian. But if this were true, Woolf bleakly concluded, the strange pass had been reached at which humanity had to choose between utopia and annihilation.[104]

CHAPTER 4

International Government: Analysis and Assessment

Woolf's analysis of the growth of international government established his position as the leading Fabian authority on international matters. His books on the subject firmly put *Fabianism and the Empire* into the shade. But how great was Woolf's stature further afield? What impact, if any, did his work have on practice? What significance does it have in the history of thought? What accounts for the fact that Woolf's ideas failed to be taken seriously much beyond 1945? This chapter seeks to answer these questions. Its main task, however, is to determine the extent to which Woolf's work in this area can be deemed idealist. In doing so it addresses the related question of the extent to which it is based on the "domestic analogy." It concludes with some reflections on Hedley Bull's damning judgment that, among other works, *International Government* is "not at all profound" and not worth reading now "except for the light it throws on the preoccupations and presuppositions of its time and place."

The Stature of Woolf's Thought During the Interwar Period

International Government was one of the most important IR texts of its time. The prominent Independent Labour Party intellectual, Henry Noel Brailsford, considered it "a brilliant book."[1] An American reviewer described it as "a remarkable contribution to the literature of constructive internationalism."[2] Woolf's research was extensively utilized in one of the first textbooks on international organization.[3] Another American writer, C. Howard-Ellis, described *International Government* as a piece of "striking analysis" and a "remarkable study."[4]

Woolf's work continued to be highly regarded in the 1930s and 1940s. Edmund Mower described *International Government* as "valuable," and "prophetic."[5] According to A. C. F. Beales, *International Government* and *The Framework of a Lasting Peace* were the most important contributions to thinking on peace during the 1914–1918 period, and he acknowledged the former book as "an invaluable source of guidance" for his own work on peace and cooperation.[6] Similarly, Sir Alfred Zimmern described Woolf's analysis as "masterly" and drew extensively from it in his account of international administration in the "pre-War system."[7] The distinguished international lawyer J. L. Brierly recommended Woolf's account of the evolution of "quasi-legislation by conference" for its "admirable combination of scholarship and humour."[8] As late as 1945, as recorded in chapter 1, a team of Oxbridge historians commended Woolf's study as not only "prophetic" and "pioneering" but also "a brilliant examination of the technique of peacemaking."[9]

Even critics of the book acknowledged it as an important contribution to the war and peace debate. A reviewer in the New York *Nation* decried it as "aggressively Fabian" but conceded that it was "suggestive in general framework" and contained "evidence of careful study."[10] J. A. Hobson criticized Woolf's scheme for putting too much power in the hands of the Great Powers, but nonetheless regarded it as "very able."[11]

Practical Impact

It is impossible to precisely determine the influence of Woolf's ideas on the creation of the League. The Woolf–Webb draft was one among many plans debated both officially and unofficially at the time. No single plan or blueprint proved decisive. Several of them, however, provided the intellectual raw material from which the Covenant was constructed. One of these was Woolf's book and the Woolf–Webb plan based on it.

It is certainly the case that the Woolf–Webb plan bears a close resemblance to the League Covenant. The similarities are striking, especially with respect to: the outlawing of aggression; the notion of making "common cause" against any state in breach of its fundamental obligations; the emphasis placed on economic sanctions; the distinction between justiciable and non-justiciable disputes; the obligation to submit all justiciable disputes to an international tribunal; the obligation to refer all other unresolved disputes to an International Council; the idea of a "cooling-off period" (twelve months in the Woolf–Webb plan, three months in the Covenant); the obligation to submit all treaties to a League Secretariat for registration and publication; and the obligation to promote cooperation in the economic and social spheres. There were some important differences between the two documents—most notably with regard to the composition of the Council and on disarmament—but the similarities are sufficient to suggest that a substantial filtering through of ideas took place.

There is evidence, however, that at least in respect of the technical, social, and economic functions of the League, Woolf's influence was more direct. Late in 1918, Sydney Waterlow, a member of the newly formed League of Nations Section of the Foreign Office, was asked to write a paper on "International Government under the League of Nations." Waterlow had recently read Woolf's book on the subject and was greatly impressed. He drew extensively from it when writing his paper, and "lifted almost verbatim"[12] the sections dealing with international cooperation on labor conditions, public health, transport, and economic and social policy. The paper was well received by Lord Cecil, the head of the section, and the bulk of it was subsequently incorporated into the British Draft Covenant. This later formed the basis of discussions between the British and U.S. delegations at Versailles.[13] A copy of *International Government* was also sent by the U.S. Naval HQ in London to Colonel House, U.S. delegate to the Peace Conference and a chief architect of the Covenant, with the comment: "Mr L. S. Woolf...has collated in a most scholarly way, a mass of data carefully sifted of experiences and precedents for international government which may prove of use to you, as a scaffolding."[14]

Significance in the History of International Thought

The significance of Woolf's work on international government in the history of international thought is fourfold. First, and most basically, Woolf helped to establish the belief that international organization was both a feasible and an efficacious way of promoting common interests and reducing international friction. This belief is nowadays so firmly entrenched that it is easy to forget that there was a time when such thoughts were considered eccentric and regarded by many with deep suspicion. In the decades immediately prior to the First World War, thinking on war and peace, to the extent that it existed, was dominated by two views. Conservatives saw international relations as a realm of competition, struggle, and conflict. War was seen as an almost natural phenomenon, which inevitably broke out from time to time as nations struggled against each other for power, influence, and prestige. Progressives, on the other hand, whilst not dismissing the conflictual side of things, tended to see the world in terms of growing economic, social, and cultural intercourse between individuals and nations. These relations were seen as inherently pacific and the principal method for transmitting civilization and its benefits around the globe. War was far from an intractable problem. Benthamites, for instance, maintained that the achievement of international harmony depended on just three things: arms limitation, arbitration, and a free press.[15] By the late nineteenth century, faith in the healing powers of arbitration had become one of the hallmarks of progressive opinion.[16]

Woolf was one of a number of writers who showed that war was not a natural, inevitable, phenomenon, but a human artefact and therefore potentially controllable.[17] He demonstrated that a system of arbitration, though desirable, was not in itself sufficient to prevent war. Perhaps most importantly, he demonstrated that international organization was not only viable, but that a good deal of it already existed.[18]

Second, and allied to this, Woolf was one of the first political analysts to recognize the importance of the nineteenth-century concert system from a theoretical point of view. From the standpoint of historical scholarship, Woolf's analysis is in a number of respects unsatisfactory. He underestimated, for example, the extent to which the "new, rudimentary, system" or "quasi-legislature" did not replace the old balance of power system, but was grafted on to it. As K. J. Holsti has demonstrated, the nineteenth-century "system of governance" was a mixed system where "[b]alance and concert went hand in hand."[19] The territorial balance of power established at Vienna and intended to be permanent, was a necessary precondition for the creation of the concert. When, due to the growth of nationalism and the increasing infirmity of two of the powers, the permanence of the compact could no longer be guaranteed, the existence of the concert facilitated adjustment of the *balance* short of all-out war.

To give a further example, Woolf failed to identify the different phases in the operation of the concert system: he speaks of it as if it constituted an undifferentiated whole. To do this is misleading. Robert Jervis has argued, for instance, that the concert system operated from 1815 to 1854, and in its strongest form only from 1815 to 1822. In his view the system cannot be said to have operated in the late nineteenth century because Great Power pursuit of self-interest was not sufficiently constrained.[20] Holsti, by contrast, has identified four relatively distinct periods 1815–1822, 1823–1856, 1857–1875, and 1876–1914. In terms of agreement on common objectives, use of common institutions, and the degree to which decisions had authority, the efficacy of the concert varied considerably from one period to the next, with the concert operating highly effectively on all three counts in the first period, and highly ineffectively on all three counts in the third.[21]

But from the standpoint of theory, Woolf's analysis of the concert system is highly significant. His main concern was not the system itself but what could be learned from its experience. He attached great importance to the fact that the peacemakers of 1814–1815 had attempted to build a new international system that went beyond eighteenth-century "*laissez-faire*" balance of power politics. They wanted to put international relations on a more organized footing. Writing during the next great European conflagration, Woolf felt that this was still the most urgent task facing mankind. A large part of his inquiry was an attempt to discern "where we are now," to discover the strengths and weaknesses, the limits and the potential, of the nineteenth-century order, for the explicit purpose of determining "how we should go forward." Woolf's importance in this regard resides in his identification of, and the weight he attached to, the profusion of rules, regulations, procedures, and institutions that had emerged in a world which fell well short of possessing a single, centralized government. This interest in the nature of and potential for cooperation or "governance" within an essentially "anarchical" setting has come to occupy a central place in IR. Indeed, the kind of inquiry Woolf initiated into the lessons of the concert system is one that recently has been the subject of considerable attention.[22]

Third, Woolf was an early and far from insignificant contributor to modern interdependence theory—"modern" because not only did he show, as Cobden and others had done in the nineteenth century, that interdependence between nations was growing, but also that it had profound implications for state sovereignty and therefore for the future organization of international relations. Woolf's view, as we have seen, was that the communications revolution had set in motion a train of events the culmination of which was to make the interests of individuals, firms, and other groups, increasingly international in scope. In many areas of life the state has ceased to be independent in any meaningful sense. Sovereignty had been eroded. This process, however, was not an inevitable one. People had a choice before them. Either they could continue to develop their present "modern" patterns of life, the logic of which was greater international government, or they could revert back to a simpler, more localized mode of life the logic of which was a greater degree of autarky, independence, and sovereignty.[23]

Woolf was by no means the first person to propound this thesis on interdependence. Others, notably Angell and Hobson, had done so before him. In his account of the growth of official and unofficial international organizations, however, Woolf provided new evidence of the phenomenon, which proved invaluable to later, more sophisticated, analysts of interdependence like David Mitrany.[24]

Fourth, Woolf was a pioneer of international functionalism. All of the standard accounts of functionalist doctrine acknowledge the important role Woolf played in laying the foundations for functional theory.[25] Arguably, however, his importance has been only partly recognized. In building his theory of functionalism Mitrany drew on Woolf's ideas on international government perhaps more than he himself realized.[26] As a consequence of their close working relationship in such bodies as the League of Nations Society and the Labour Party Advisory Committee on International Questions, Mitrany had an in-depth knowledge of Woolf's ideas. Many of these ideas were strongly functionalist in flavor. It is perhaps no accident that Mitrany's first attempt to develop a functional theory of international relations was entitled *The Progress of International Government*. It should also be noted that whereas other writers who influenced Mitrany took the domestic scene as their field of study, Woolf took the international scene. Woolf was the first thinker to show how a functionalist-type analysis could be applied to international relations. This is not to say that he put together the coherent and systematic functionalist theory as Mitrany did later. And it is true that Mitrany became a severe critic of the statism and the legalism that underlie Woolf's first two conceptions of international government. But Woolf did provide the skeleton of a functional theory and some of the flesh in the form of numerous examples of practical cooperation.[27]

The following examples illustrate the functionalist aspect of Woolf's work. First, the pluralism that underpins Mitrany's work[28] is strongly present in Woolf's. He contended,

> ...State government is everywhere...insufficient for the manifold relations of the manifold groups into which our society divides and subdivides itself. This is well recognised in individual states, where the development and working of voluntary associations, such as churches, trade unions, associations of employers, joint stock companies, clubs, etc., have been studied and traced. All these bodies are organs of government, and therefore combine with the State organs to regulate the relations of citizens. The whole problem of international government, and therefore of the prevention of war, consists in the elaboration of a similar organised regulation of international relations.[29]

A large part of *International Government* is devoted to identifying such "manifold groups" and "organs of government" as exist internationally, and analyzing them in terms of structure and function. He felt there was no reason why such groups could not be "combined" with states in a complex governmental framework. Only by such means could "the organisation of government and the organs of government follow strictly the complication of group interests in the world of facts."[30]

Second, like Mitrany, Woolf was convinced that the ability of the sovereign state to fulfil the needs of its citizens had been called into question by the developments of the modern world. Complete independence of legislation and administration, for instance, had become "incompatible" with the "complex material world" and contemporary "aims and desires and modes of life." It was the recognition of this incompatibility that had led to the first tentative advances toward cosmopolitan lawmaking and international legislation.[31] More generally, the conception of the state as "an isolated entity" and "absolutely independent" did not "mirror the realities of life and the world." Much misery resulted from trying to apply "these obsolete conceptions and beliefs to a world which they no longer fit."[32]

Third, Woolf described the growth of international associations and organs of government in terms that presage the functionalist principle of technical self-determination. These bodies, Woolf insisted, had not been the invention of political idealists but had grown "spontaneously" in order to "meet international needs." Woolf also spoke of there being "a natural tendency of the world towards International Government."[33]

Fourth, Woolf argued, as did Mitrany, that social change had brought about "the breakdown of representative political government."[34] The organs of government had failed to keep up with the increased complexity of social life. As a result a "serious gap" had opened up "between the organisation of our life and the organisation of our government."[35] In particular, the geographical basis of representation had been called into question. The primary interests of individuals and groups within society no longer coincided with geography:

> A man's chief interests are no longer determined by the place he lives in, and group interests, instead of following geographical lines, follow those of capital, labour, professions, etc. But government and organisation of government have not kept pace with this change of social organisation....[36]

Both domestically and internationally new institutions were needed to provide for "due representation" of "vital group interests." The international association had emerged precisely to meet this need.

Finally, Woolf emphasized, as did Mitrany, the effect that international associations could have on the attitudes of individual officials. As well as helping to forge an international public opinion on any given matter, participation in such associations also led to the "internationalisation of the mind." The degree to which states had been successful in harmonizing their labor laws, for example, was a product not so much of formal international agreements, but the informal influence of the "internationalised official."[37]

Analytical Weaknesses

Yet there are certain weaknesses in Woolf's analysis and it is this fact rather than the putative utopianism of his work that accounts for its failure to be taken seriously, especially by an increasingly professionalized discipline, much beyond 1945. It is important to register, first of all, the sloppiness of which Woolf was sometimes guilty. Etherington has noted this with respect to Woolf's writing on imperialism.[38] Evidence of it is plentiful in his writing on international government. Shortly after taking great pains, for example, to distinguish arbitration from other kinds of judicial settlement he inexplicably abandons the distinction and proceeds to use the term "arbitration" in a generic way. The confusion of the reader is not spared by a footnote stating, not unambiguously: "By arbitration in this and the following paragraphs I mean the decision of international disputes by a judicial body."[39] Similarly, Woolf asserts that (cosmopolitan) international government began in 1838 with the creation of Conseil Supérieur de Santé in Constantinople. On realizing, however, that he had previously stated that it began several decades before with the formation of the Riverian Commissions, he adds a footnote: "The new Internationalism *really* began with the Congress of Vienna in 1815."[40] Much of this sloppiness is accounted for by the fact that Woolf wrote very quickly and he rarely revised the first drafts in any substantial way.

But there is another element of clumsiness in Woolf's writing. Woolf the serious social investigator was always the servant of Woolf the political publicist. There is a propagandist element in all Woolf's writings on international government. As well as contributing to our understanding of international cooperation Woolf was also seeking to promote a political program. Not surprisingly, therefore, he tried to discredit the groups, practices, and political programs he was opposed to. Along with Conservatives and conservatism these included, in true dissenting fashion, the Foreign Office, the aristocracy, diplomatists and secret diplomacy, generals, and the balance of power.[41] But in doing so Woolf unwittingly makes a number of clumsy analytical errors.

Woolf's interpretation of the nineteenth century provides an interesting example. As social investigator, and also as Fabian socialist, Woolf argues that the nineteenth century is a century of steady progress toward international government. But Woolf the Labour propagandist and dissenter argues that the nineteenth century is a century of war, reaction, repressiveness, and stupidity. The reason for this is that Woolf the propagandist does not want to give any credit for the progress that was made in that century to his conservative enemies who were, of course, by and large running the show. He also wanted to lay the blame for the First World War squarely on their shoulders without at the same time incriminating the attempt, in part *their* attempt, to put international society on a more organized footing. This schizophrenic tendency resulted in some astonishing contradictions. For instance, Woolf castigates the world for giving plenty of opportunity to militarists, imperialists, and nationalists whilst "refusing to give even a trial" to international government. But the bulk of his work up to this point had been dedicated to showing that international government had already become an important part of the fabric of international society.[42]

Some striking analytical shortcomings of a similar kind can be found in his writings of the 1940s. In response to Clarence Streit's argument for a federation of democracies, for instance, Woolf contended that although world federation should be the "ultimate aim of international organisation," and that there was little doubt that a federation of "France, the British Empire, the U.S.A., a democratised Germany, a democratised Italy, and the smaller democracies would go a long way to rid the world of the threat and fear of war," it was none the less extremely doubtful whether "national and international psychology" made such a "revolution" immediately possible. This was because federation required "a very high degree of political co-operation and a common attitude towards the bases of government and perhaps of society."[43] Few would doubt the validity of this proposition. It does not, however, sit easily with Woolf's assertions about "real international control of national armament," nor his call for a "central world authority" to "deal promptly and authoritatively with any action or situation which may threaten the world's peace or prosperity," nor his argument for the centralization of the production of atomic energy under a "world authority," and the concentration of all armaments other than those required for purely internal police purposes in the hands of the UN. If the current state of "national and international psychology," "political co-operation," and "common attitudes towards government and society," made a worldwide federation of democracies infeasible, then surely it made international control of atomic energy and national armaments infeasible too? While rejecting, on the grounds of feasibility, the limited idea of a limited federation, he for all intents and purposes advocated (without discussing its feasibility) something much more far-reaching—world government.

It is also worth adding that these assertions, along with his strictures about the need to "drastically limit" national sovereignty, also do not sit easily with such statements as:

> Sooner or later, the German state must take its permanent place in the world of states and the German people re-enter *the comity of nations*, if the world is to have peace and prosperity... The problem which faces Allied statesmen is to discover what concrete steps can be taken to encourage the rise of a democratic and pacific Germany which can be trusted to cooperate *as a free nation with free nations*.[44]

Again, the wisdom of extending the hand of friendship and peace to a defeated Germany cannot be doubted. But Woolf's terminology throws his vision of a postwar world order in which national sovereignty is, at a minimum, severely limited, into much confusion.

Before moving on to the conceptual weaknesses in Woolf's work, another kind of analytical shortcoming should be briefly mentioned: assertions and arguments made by Woolf have been shown as flawed by subsequent, more rigorous analysis. The following four examples are illustrative. First, in trying to identify the causes of war, Woolf puts far too much emphasis on "disputes and differences." Specifically, he puts far too much emphasis on war being due to lack of machinery for the resolution of disputes. There are various problems with this approach. One is reminded of Carr's distinction between "underlying and significant" causes and "immediate and personal" causes.[45] Woolf often seems concerned only with the latter. He failed to analyze the *sources* of international tension in any depth, and consequently tended to neglect the role of power, ideology, and domestic factors. He also failed to recognize that disputes and differences are sometimes used by statesman merely as pretexts. In such cases disputes and differences are not the *real* causes of war but simply circumstances that statesmen find convenient to exploit.[46]

Second, Woolf had far too much faith in the possibility of selecting "ten men good and true" to hear and settle disputes "fairly and reasonably." He underestimated the reluctance of states to grant authority to such bodies in advance of any particular dispute breaking out, not only for reasons of sovereignty and national interest, but also for ideological and cultural reasons. With respect to the latter Woolf did not take into account the problems that cultural relativism presents for such notions as "fairness" and "reasonableness." In his defense, of course, it might be said that he was writing at a time when the world was dominated by seven or eight for the most part European powers. For men like Woolf the world seemed much more culturally uniform than it actually was. The uncritical way in which he presents his case is, nonetheless, a considerable analytical weakness.[47]

Third, Woolf had a tendency to brush aside certain awkward questions. For example, after delineating the kinds of disputes that would be suitable for compulsory adjudication he asks the question: how is it to be decided whether a particular dispute falls into one of the categories of "suitable disputes"? Given the generality of each of the categories (e.g., "questions of fact"), and especially given that all disputes have aspects that fall into one or more of them, this question is obviously a crucial one. However, Woolf casually dismisses it thus:

> This, of course, is an example of a question as to the competency or jurisdiction of a court which continually arises wherever there is a judiciary. Municipal courts frequently have to decide questions as to their own competency, and there seems no reason why an International Court should not be given the power to do the same.[48]

End of story. The answer is woefully inadequate. Not only does it ignore any difficulties there may be in transplanting a domestic procedure onto the international stage, it also underestimates the complexities involved—with respect to precedent, the right of appeal, and the role of public prosecuting authorities—in making such decisions in domestic legal systems.

Woolf similarly brushes aside the vital question of how the various obligations to submit justiciable disputes to an international court are to be enforced. While he shrewdly rejects the idea of a permanent international police force, he does not offer much by way of an alternative. He asserts, "[t]he whole question of sanctions is of theoretical rather than practical interest"; and blandly adds, "If the International Authority, the Society of Nations, has the power to compel a member to comply with its obligations, and if it has the will to do so, a way in which to exercise the power will be found."[49] There is no discussion of the problems and prospects of collective enforcement in any of its forms. Subsequent practice and theory has, of course, shown that questions as to the collective power and collective will of the society of states are nowhere near as straightforward as Woolf supposed.[50]

Finally, Woolf's thought on the nature of international law has been wholly superseded by later scholarship. As described in chapter 3, Woolf took international law very seriously. In writing *International Government* he made use of a number of books on international law, especially Oppenheim's well-known treatise.[51] Not surprisingly therefore Woolf's discussion of international law is often astute. Woolf never quite managed, however, to liberate himself from the view that international law was a primitive form of domestic law; that is, he never quite managed to see international law as a distinct body of law, with its own unique characteristics. For instance, he notes that much international law is "vague and uncertain," and implies that a more advanced body of law could only be successful in a "highly organised society of nations." Woolf tantalizingly suggests, therefore, that the quality of international law is related to the degree of solidarity that pertains in international society. But in the final analysis Woolf abandons this sociological approach to law and insists, limply, that international law is vague and uncertain "largely due to two facts: there is no recognised international organ for making International Law, and no judicial organ for interpreting it."[52] The work of Kelsen and Manning, among others, has subsequently shown this to be a highly superficial answer.[53]

Conceptual Weaknesses

Woolf's theory of international government also contains a number of conceptual weaknesses. Conceptual clarity was not one of Woolf's strong suits. It is difficult to pin down, for example, what he means by an "international authority." The term suggests the creation of a single actor over and above states, which has the right and perhaps the power to determine the shape of at least some of their relations. The fact that the term "supernational authority" is used in the Webb–Woolf plan, further suggests that Woolf's international authority should be conceived in this way. But sometimes Woolf uses international authority as simply a collective noun for his proposed international conference and judicial tribunals: he speaks, for instance, of an international authority "consisting of" these bodies.[54] The picture, however, is far from clear: he occasionally suggests that an international authority is something much more specific and separate from other bodies.[55]

Given this, and given his pluralist rejection of the more far-reaching kinds of central control that the term implies, one has to conclude that Woolf's international authority is largely devoid of content. Why then did he use the term? One answer is that it enabled him to hedge his bets. He could answer critics who accused him of advocating a world government by saying that, on the contrary, he advocated something much more modest: international government defined as process (Woolf hardly ever speaks of *an* international government *vis à vis an* international authority).[56] Similarly, he could answer critics who accused him of being too conservative by saying that, on the contrary, he was proposing something very radical: an international authority.

The blame lies as much with Woolf's conception of international government as it does other concepts. The first point to note here is that Woolf's usage of the concept is far from consistent. Although he initially defines it in very broad terms he sometimes unwittingly adopts a more restricted definition. He withheld the title of international government from the Automobile Conference and Convention of 1909, for example, on the grounds that it did not create permanent organs of international government.[57] The problem with this, of course, is that according to his initial definition—to recapitulate, "the regulation of relations between States, Nations, or Peoples by international agreement"—conventions and other agreements are acts of international government regardless of whether they provide for the creation of "permanent organs."

Woolf's use of the concept in the 1930s provides a further example. Although he characterizes the nineteenth century, in line with his original thesis, as a struggle between nationalism and internationalism, he effectively abandons his first two conceptions of international government by restricting the meaning of internationalism to "cosmopolitan international government" or, as he called it in the 1930s, "every-day international government."[58] When he speaks of the growth of internationalism in the nineteenth century he thus has in mind only "cosmopolitan"/"every-day" international government. This is a departure from his original thesis according to which *all three* types of international government are types or aspects of internationalism.

He puts in the place of this thesis a rather crude dichotomy between the "pre-War system"—of competitive nationalism, patriotism, diplomacy, security through national armaments, hostile alliances, and the balance of power—and the "system of internationalism"—meaning "an association of disarmed states, pledged by treaty under no circumstances to resort to war, to settle their differences and disputes by a process of law or international conciliation, and to promote and regulate their common interests by common action."[59] Little intimation is given of the fact that in his major work on the subject he rejected such a crude dichotomy—in *International Government* the "pre-War system" *is* a "system of internationalism"—at least in embryo.[60] It is worth briefly adding that these rather muddy conceptual waters are not clarified by Woolf's habit of using a number of other terms as synonyms for his system of internationalism. Examples include "pacific international system," "system of international cooperation and pacific settlement," and "system of pacific internationalism."[61] One can only conclude that the descriptive and analytical value of the concept he deemed so important is significantly diminished by his inconsistent, indeed quite reckless, use of it.

Doubts about the term's descriptive and analytical value are paralleled by doubts about its prescriptive value. International government in the broad sense is an amalgam of not necessarily compatible things—from arbitration treaties to the growth of organized international crime,[62] from economic combination to gatherings of scientists. It may be questioned whether the emergence and growth of these phenomena were part of the same sociological process, though Woolf was correct to highlight the precipitative role of the communications' revolution. To describe these things, however, as acts of international government is to conflate several international developments, different not only in character, but also in their respective ramifications. To be an advocate of international government may not at the end of the day amount to much. The capitalist can be an advocate as much as the socialist, the conservative as much as the radical, the feminist as much as the white slave trafficker. An undifferentiated concept of international government becomes as useful as, say, an undifferentiated concept of "justice." Virtually everyone can safely become a true believer. What we need to know is the *kind* of international government being advocated. There is, after all, a major difference between an "international capitalist system of government"[63] and a system of international government run along socialist lines.

Woolf appears to have been unaware of the pitfalls of defining his key concept in such a broad way. Confusion and contradiction inevitably follow. Indeed, one such contradiction can be found at the very heart of Woolf's thesis. It might be argued that two of his strands of international government— great power concert and cosmopolitan organization—pull in opposite directions. Lawmaking in international conferences and collective enforcement of law pulls the world in a statist direction, whereas unofficial, cosmopolitan, organization pulls the world in a non-statist direction. The implication of the former is that states tighten their grip on the world, whereas the implication of the latter is that their grip is weakened. It follows that while it makes sense to prescribe one or the other, it does not make sense to prescribe both.

When one moves from the prescriptive level, however, to the analytical level, Woolf's ground may be firmer. After all, this contradiction may be one that exists in the real world. There is much evidence to suggest that the power and authority of the state, *vis à vis* other actors, may be increasing in some respects though diminishing in others. One manifestation of this is that although sovereignty is as popular as ever, the ability to maximize the benefits of possessing it is constantly diminishing.[64]

It also might be said in Woolf's defense that the reason why he advanced such a broad conception of international government is understandable. Woolf's introduction to politics came not only from the Fabian Society but also from the Co-operative Movement. He inherited Robert Owen's vision of a new society "in which all would work together in a rational manner for the common good, without need of violent revolution."[65] He also inherited, from Graham Wallas, the belief that the way to achieve this end was to substitute cooperation for competition as the fundamental principle of social organization.[66] Nineteenth-century *laissez-faire* liberalism was moribund: the task for the future was to replace it with regulation, coordination, and organization. Woolf's *International Government* was an attempt to apply this belief to the field of international relations. Its flaws can be attributed not only to the way in which he went about his task, but also to the belief itself. It is, however, not unreasonable that Woolf sought to build his theory out of materials that were familiar and, as far as he knew, reliable.

Utopianism

Having set the scene historiographically and conceptually, it is now possible to tackle head-on the central concern of this chapter.

Although Woolf was not a specific target of *The Twenty Years' Crisis*, it is important to note that he viewed Carr's book as an attack on his own position. He took particular objection to what he felt was Carr's arbitrary and irresponsible use of the word utopian, and he attempted, with mixed results, to refute some of his assertions in an article, "Utopian and Reality," published in *Political Quarterly* and in a book, *The War for Peace*, published shortly afterwards. Woolf's response to Carr is examined in detail in chapter 8.

The question whether Woolf, or indeed any of the other "thinkers of the twenty years' crisis," deserves to be labeled utopian is an extremely complex one. This is because the term, as demonstrated in chapter 2, has no settled meaning. If by utopian is meant the belief that radical reform of the international system is both desirable and possible, then Woolf's ideas about international government are without doubt utopian. The problem here, however, is that if this definition is adopted Carr himself becomes a utopian given his endorsement of functionalism and certain forms of international collectivism.[67] If, on the other hand, it is taken to mean a complete rejection of the existing system in favor of some blueprint for an entirely new world order, Woolf is not utopian. He did not completely reject the existing order, and although he was never reticent in putting forward quite radical proposals for change, he rarely engaged in the drawing up of blueprints—not, that is, if we mean by blueprint a comprehensive and detailed plan of what a new world would look like and how it would work. The only example of such a scheme is the Woolf–Webb plan.[68] Similarly, if by utopian we mean the refusal to acknowledge the existence of, or tendency to understate, the unseemly aspects of international politics, then Woolf is not a utopian since his estimation of the quality of international life was just as grim as later realists. That is precisely why he wanted so much to change it.

With respect to the three broad charges against utopianism identified as key in chapter 2, the following points can be made.

Charge 1: Facts and Cause and Effect

Much of Woolf's work is polemical in purpose, rhetorical in style, and lacking in detailed empirical analysis. He had a tendency to see the world in sweeping, Manichean terms such as "civilization" and "barbarism." This tendency is particularly pronounced in his articles and books of the 1930s. His controversial tract published by the Left Book Club in 1939, *Barbarians at the Gate*, provides a good example.[69] In this book Woolf analyzed the intensifying European crisis in terms of the forces on the side of civilization and the forces of barbarism. A keen supporter of the Popular Front, Woolf managed to squeeze Stalin's Russia into the former camp, but not without difficulty. The result is a contorted and procrustean account, which fails to convey the complexities that characterized the diplomatic scene of the 1930s. Woolf condemned the ruthless suppression of personal and intellectual freedom in Soviet Russia but nonetheless argued that she would sooner or later align herself with Britain against the fascists *not* for power political reasons but because their "ultimate social aims" were those of "freedom and civilization." The book came out shortly after the signing of the Nazi–Soviet Pact.[70]

Woolf's writings of the 1930s are especially propagandist and exhibit few traces of the kind of factual analysis called for by Carr. It will be recalled from chapter 2 that Carr denounced collective security, general disarmament, and other such schemes as "product[s] of pure theory divorced from practical experience." It will also be recalled that he denounced many of the writers of the time for their ignorance of strategy. The solutions they proposed were "neat and accurate on the abstract plane" but were obtained only "by leaving out of account the vital strategic factor." He concluded with the damning words: "If every prospective writer on international affairs in the last twenty years had taken a compulsory course in elementary strategy, reams of nonsense would have remained unwritten."

There can be no doubting Woolf's ignorance of strategy. He was a staunch believer in a system of collective or "pooled" security. This required states to renounce their right to use force as an instrument of national policy and to entrust their security instead to "the machinery of pacific settlement and a common obligation to resist an aggressor." But such a system of "pacific internationalism" could not possibly work in a world of heavily armed Great Powers. A precondition of collective security or pacific internationalism was, therefore, national disarmament.[71] But although he castigated pacifists for refusing to accept the full implications of the "common obligation to resist an aggressor,"[72] he never himself explained how such an obligation would be met in a disarmed world.[73] If by disarmament he did not have in mind what has since become known as "general and complete disarmament," it is similarly unclear what he considered to be the *optimum level* of disarmament: that is, the lowest level of national armament consistent with the effective performance of common obligations.

This is a matter Woolf never got to grips with. In his outline for an "independent" and "impartial" foreign policy for Britain of 1947, for example, he boldly asserts, "[w]e should reduce our military commitments to a minimum consistent with any obligations which might become necessary for real collective security if UNO should become an effective instrument of peace." But he makes no attempt to spell out what these obligations might be nor specify the nature and level of the armaments that would be needed to fulfil them. The drastic reductions in armaments he recommends as an interim measure suggests that he did not expect the requisite level to be high. This expectation is so dubious that one wonders whether Woolf ever gave the matter serious attention. One also wonders whether he ever considered the possibility that a high level of armaments might be needed to transform the UN into an "effective instrument of peace" in the first place.[74]

In this connection it is a curious fact that by 1937 Woolf was suggesting that "collective" as opposed to "national" defense necessitated "a very high measure of rearmament." It would not be unfair to say that in Woolf's outlook "things collective" seem to possess certain magical qualities. It does not seem to have occurred to him that collective rearmament might upset the balance of power and trigger a preemptive war, or a lethal arms race, in exactly the same way as national rearmament tended, so he believed, to do.[75]

Again this feature is also apparent in Woolf's 1940s writings. Although he repeatedly dismissed the possibility of deterring aggression through "power political" methods he maintained complete confidence in the efficacy of collective methods. Not once does he question whether the shortcomings attributed to the former (the generation of a climate of fear and hostility leading to an arms race and a "preventive" war) might also apply to the latter. Indeed there is a sense in which Woolf's argument is tautological: "real" collective security through a "real" international authority would, it seems, present a front so united, so powerful, and so imbued with moral authority, that it could not possibly fail. Anything falling short of such a front could not be considered a "real" system of collective security.[76]

It is also a curious but important fact that the allegations of muddleheadedness and pusillanimity that Woolf levelled at the pacifists might equally be leveled at Woolf himself. Woolf was adamant in the early 1930s that the central object of British foreign policy should be to "prevent the outbreak of a European war."[77] But he also wanted the British government to pursue a "more militant policy" of using the League as an "instrument against Fascist militarism." The League, he argued, should be used to "force" Fascist states like Italy and Germany to "show their hand." If they were not prepared to comply with their obligations under the covenant they should be made "openly to repudiate them" and, in light of this, "forced out of the League." "A League," he continued, "purged of militarist and Fascist states, composed of democratic and socialist governments, determined by every means in their power to prevent war, would be a much stronger instrument for peace and civilisation than the half-sham League which we have today."[78]

Yet Woolf stopped short of calling this new League an alliance, a notion that, in typical dissenting fashion, he continued to denounce.[79] He also stopped short of admitting that such a "militant policy" could bring nearer the very thing it was designed to avoid—war. The anodyne, some would say evasive, phraseology of the following sentence is illustrative:

> What exactly that common action [against aggression] should be may be a subject of argument, but that an alternative to armed nationalism requires that every state should assume some obligations to stand by the side of the victim of aggression and to resist the aggressor is indisputable.[80]

The employment of euphemisms such as "stand by the side of" (or "support" or "come to the assistance of" or "fulfil its obligations to"[81]) is almost exactly the kind of weakmindedness for which he arraigned the pacifists. Woolf rarely admits that "sanctions" might involve "military sanctions" and that "military sanctions" meant war. Indeed, in characterizing the "pre-War" or "Balance of Power" system as a "system of war" and the "League system" as a "system of peace" he occasionally implies that collective security, though involving sanctions, did *not* involve war.[82]

There are in fact two dimensions to this problem in Woolf's thought. The first is the one stated in the previous paragraph: Woolf is at least partly guilty of the weakmindedness of which he accused the pacifists, because, like them, he shies away from a full and frank disclosure of the implications of collective security. The second is more complicated. On the few occasions he does come close to a full and frank disclosure, he purposefully stops short of using the word "war." He talks stoically of the "risks" of collective security.[83] He strongly implies on one occasion that "the application of sanctions" necessarily entails "the use of force."[84] He even suggests that collective security could, in principle, produce more violence than it prevents.[85] Nonetheless he refuses to call this violence "war."

The reason for this is at root psychological. Woolf was so badly scarred by the horrors of the Great War—a war in which one of his younger brothers, Cecil, was killed and another, Philip, was seriously wounded by the same shell—that he could not see war in anything but the blackest terms. One of the ramifications of this was that he could not accept that the new system of international relations built around the League might ultimately depend on such an "evil," "vile," "bestial," "barbarous," "stupid," and "senseless" thing as war for its survival.[86] He consequently called it something else. He maintained, "[t]he use of force to resist aggression by states organized in a League to eliminate war is not war unless the use of force to resist violence by a state organized to eliminate crime is crime."[87] Some of the pitfalls of this form of analogical reasoning will be discussed in the next section. At this stage the point to note is that such reasoning simply obscures even further the price that may ultimately have to be paid by law-abiding states to "maintain" peace and "preserve" collective security. War is a grave word. But collective security may require grave action. In choosing words the gravity of which did not correspond to the gravity of the action, Woolf is, I think, guilty of being less than sincere and *ipso facto* of undermining, albeit unwittingly, the very foundations—resolve and preparedness—upon which the success of such action almost by definition depends. Woolf sometimes speaks as if resolve alone would be enough to deter aggression, thereby rendering graver action unnecessary. He is silent, however, on how such resolve can be continually demonstrated in the absence of such action.[88]

A further puzzling and ultimately deficient feature of Woolf's position on collective security concerns his conception of the League. He insisted that the League was not a "foreign body in the comity of nations and endowed...with a personality transcending or even outside the States of which it was...composed." It could not "act by itself or...be a force for good or evil in international affairs apart from the Governments which are represented upon its organs." On the contrary it was simply a "political organisation" or "pacific machinery" the efficacy of which is contingent on the sincerity and determination of its members.[89] When discussing this matter in the abstract, therefore, Woolf's position could hardly be clearer.

But the logic of his rather sketchy thoughts on the *practical* dimensions of "pooled security through the League" suggest a quite different conclusion. Woolf was against "armed nationalism" and in favor of "disarmed internationalism." Collective security meant "collective, not national defence, by collective instead of national armament." Security would be provided not by national armies and navies but "collectively" by "the League."[90] Is the implication of such statements that the League could or should have armed forces of "its own"? Or is it the case that Woolf had in mind the *secondment* of national forces, as part of the process of national disarmament, to the League? In either case, who is in control of these "no longer national" forces? And if they are no longer national, does not this mean that the League *has*, inevitably, acquired a personality of its own?

While worrying in themselves, such disregard of key practical and conceptual strategic considerations also gave rise to some highly superficial judgments on contemporary events. The Japanese invasion of Manchuria, to give one example, occurred, quite simply, because Japan rightly calculated that France and Britain would not comply with their obligations under the Covenant. This was a product partly of "muddled ignorance" on the part of the French and British governments, and partly of their manifest lack of the "will to peace." Woolf does not stop and ask *why* Japan felt that the League Powers would not comply with their obligations, nor *why*, except for these two sweeping assertions, the League Powers steered clear of any action that might get them involved in the conflict. The complex strategic equation in Asia and its potential impact on the strategic equation in Europe is not even considered.[91]

Strategy, armaments, and collective security is undoubtedly an issue-area within which Woolf's "attention to facts and analysis of cause and effect" is far from adequate. I have spent some time dealing with it precisely because it is one area in which Carr's pronouncements are, I believe, accurate and fair.[92]

It would be wrong to conclude, however, that Woolf's inattentiveness to the "facts" and "cause and effect" with regard to collective security is representative of the normal pattern. A good deal of Woolf's work was written for the heavily empiricist Fabian Research Department. His statement of purpose in *International Government* is typically Fabian empiricist: "The object of this inquiry is to give data which may, if possible, enable people to transform the vague 'some sort of [international organization]' into a more definite object of their hopes."[93] Throughout his career he was deeply wedded to the Webbian belief that the truth of socialism, and by extension internationalism, could be rationally demonstrated by "the facts." The task of the investigator was to gather enough facts to prove these Fabian truths both in their positive and normative aspect. It is not surprising therefore that several of Woolf's works contain a wealth of empirical data—though not necessarily the kind of data considered important by later realists. Indeed, as mentioned, the importance of Woolf's work to a large degree resides in the mass of information he collected on official and unofficial international associations.

Charge 2: Power in International Politics

Woolf generally viewed power, or at least its unilateral exercise, as a defect of the international system. He was consequently more inclined to censure it than to analyze it. He frequently asserted that the opposite of power was law and did not investigate in any detail the degree to which law is underpinned by a particular distribution of power.

But although Woolf failed to give the role of power the attention it deserves, he did not entirely ignore it. This is evident, for example, in his acknowledgment that nationalism, patriotism, and the sovereign state could not be wished away and that any proposal for a new international order had to take account of them.[94] It is evident in his rejection of "any such revolution as world-parliaments and world federation."[95] It is evident in his rejection of the idea of a world state:

> For however attractive a world-State may be to our imaginations, a little reflection, aided by the sobering study of protocols, blue-books, and white papers, will show that in the world of actual facts there if no ground prepared for the reception of so strange a plant.[96]

It is evident in the special position he granted to the Great Powers in his proposal for an International Council, and in his recognition of the probable permanence of international inequality:

> If... the world is ever to organise itself for the peaceful regulation of international affairs, that organisation must provide for the essential inequality of States. If such inequality is not reflected in the pacific machinery, it will make itself felt in war, while the machinery will be left to rust unused.[97]

To the extent that Woolf saw the growth of international government as an inexorable process, there is an implicit endorsement of the positive role of power—social power—at the heart of his thesis. And in common with other supporters of the League, Woolf believed that power also had a positive role to play in providing collective security and upholding the international rule of law.

Finally, it would be incorrect to assume that Woolf was entirely dismissive of the "power of power politics." He often utilized the conceptual and explanatory tools of power politics in analyzing particular episodes and events. His analysis of the early Cold War international context, for example, focuses on such impeccably power political factors as: the relative power position—economic, political, and military—of the three former allies; the dangers of widespread misperception ("erroneous beliefs") of this power position for Russian and American policy; the fear and suspicion among the Russian leadership of Anglo-American collusion; the fear and suspicion in America and Britain of the spread of Communism and Russian territorial ambitions; the self-fulfilling nature of policies based on fears and suspicions; the growing tendency in the policies of the United States and the USSR to treat issues not on their merits but in terms of their effect upon their relative economic and military power; the dangers inherent in exclusive U.S. possession of the atomic bomb; and the impact of Britain's disengagement from empire on her power and status.[98]

The point to be emphasized, however, is that although Woolf sometimes analyzed particular events in terms of power politics he did not believe that such an undesirable state of affairs was endemic or immutable. He never abandoned faith in the possibility that power politics could be transcended through international government and a "real" system of collective security. To continue with the same example, although Woolf's estimation of the Cold War international situation was bleak (due to *inter alia* the "hostility and power politics of the USA and USSR," the "consistent hostility" of Russia toward Britain, the abuse by Russia of its power and status within the UN, the opportunistic nature of Soviet foreign policy and the unscrupulous methods employed in its efforts to spread communism and totalitarianism abroad, the dangers of domination by "the powerful and militant capitalism of the USA," and the "terrible vulnerability" of Britain's geographic and economic position in a war fought with atomic weapons), he did not concede any ground to the realist view on how to deal with it. He continued to condemn national deterrence, armed alliances, and the balance of power. He continued to argue for collective security through the UN. And he continued to call for an end to and immediate dissociation from power politics.[99]

Charge 3: Universal Interests and the *Status Quo*

Woolf uncritically assumed that peace was a universal interest, justice a universal value, and that both of them could be determined, if needs be, by a majority vote in a conference of Powers. Following Cobden and Angell, he felt that war benefitted no one except a small and exploitative clique. War was a barbaric act parallel to cannibalism and slavery. It was also an act that, because of the increasing destructiveness of modern weaponry, threatened not only this or that nation, but also civilization itself.

But Woolf's convictions about war and his singleminded pursuit of peace did not blind him to the fact that the preservation of peace might have as its corollary the solidification of a particular, and perhaps unjust, *status quo*. His radical liberal belief in the need to uphold the rule of international law, for instance, was tempered by his socialist understanding of law as an instrument for maintaining the existing order of things. The following passage on the question of compulsory adjudication succinctly sums up Woolf's view on what he called "the problem of the *status quo*." It is worth quoting at length not only because it reveals the extent to which Woolf was aware of the hypocrisy and the "inner falsehood and cant"[100] that often accompany earnest declarations on the sanctity of international law, but also because it anticipates in important respects the argument that Carr was to make more than two decades later. According to Woolf, it was not advisable for any state to bind itself absolutely to refer disputes to a judicial tribunal because such a tribunal

> ... would be compelled to decide every issue strictly in accordance with the existing law.... It would be essentially that conservative element... necessary in every society and which maintains the existing order of things. Nor must we forget that it so happens that it is always our particular interest as a nation to preserve the existing order of things. In the international system Great Britain is naturally in the position which the rich capitalist employer holds in the industrial system. She has usually nothing to gain by a change.... She is always conservative and therefore in favour of arbitration and a rigid adherence to existing treaties. But... it may be in the interests of other nations and of the world generally that changes should take place, and that, if an arrangement which maintains the existing order of things is essential, an arrangement which makes it possible to upset it in an orderly manner is no less essential.

At the present moment there are only two methods by which the existing order of things can be upset—negotiation and war. It is only obtuseness and lack of imagination on our part if we do not see that no nation, whose interests are not in preserving the *status quo*, will give up the power of going to war...unless some other possible method of varying the *status quo* is assured to it. The fact that Germany opposed and Britain supported obligatory arbitration at the Hague Conference does not prove the wickedness of Germany and the pureness of Britain, any more than the refusal of wage-earners to accept the employers' proposals—namely, to give up their weapon, the strike, and bind themselves to arbitrate—proves a moral superiority of the employing over the employed class.[101]

There are of course considerable differences between Woolf and Carr on the question of compulsory adjudication. Carr rejected as illusory the distinction between justiciable and non-justiciable disputes.[102] He poured scorn on the notion that political relations could be converted into legal relations.[103] He also had grave doubts about the thrust of Woolf's argument, namely, that what was required was a "rational" noncoercive method of peaceful change.[104] The quotation is significant, however, because it shows that Woolf was not utopian in the sense of being an unthinking defender of the *status quo*. It also shows that Woolf's thought is considerably more complex and sophisticated than certain critics have contended.

The Domestic Analogy

It might be contended that one of the main weaknesses of Woolf's thought on international government is his reliance on the "domestic analogy." In his incisive study of the role that the domestic analogy has played in proposals about world order, Hidemi Suganami defines it as a form of

> presumptive reasoning which holds there are certain similarities between domestic and international phenomena; that, in particular, the conditions of order within states are similar to those of order between them; and that therefore those institutions which sustain order domestically should be reproduced at the international level.[105]

Suganami proceeds to show that the domestic analogy manifests itself in a range of ways and takes a number of different forms. These forms differ according to the similarities that are held by users of the domestic analogy to be significant (e.g., between treaties and contracts, or between conferences and legislatures); the domestic institutions that are held to be relevant (e.g., police forces or the welfare state); and the prescriptions for change that logically follow (e.g., reform of the society of states or the creation of a single world state). Not surprisingly given this variety, some forms of the domestic analogy are more cogent than others. Suganami, to some extent justifiably, cites Woolf as an example of someone who uses the analogy in a straightforward, highly problematical, way.[106] Straightforward in the sense that the state is personified and it is presumed that the bases of order between states in international society are essentially the same (and not merely "similar") as the bases of order between individuals within the state. Problematical because, *inter alia*, this approach assumes that enforcement of law against miscreant individuals is the central task of government when in fact it is the management and conciliation of conflict between large and powerful groups.[107]

Reliance on this type of domestic analogy is particularly evident in Woolf's later writings. He contended, as may be recalled from chapter 3,

> There is nothing essentially different in the government of a football club, a village, a town, a country, of Europe, or of the world, except that the scale is bigger and the organisation more complicated.[108]

Similarly,

> To prevent war is a problem of politics and government, not essentially different from the problem of preventing duelling or cock-fighting or of regulating the relations between the inhabitants of Middlesex and those of Surrey. It may be easier to prevent cock-fighting than war or to regulate the relations between Middlesex and Surrey or England and Scotland than those between France and Germany. But there is nothing in the last problem which suggests it is essentially different from the others.[109]

Thus Woolf did not see the problem of war and the maintenance of peace as *sui generis*. The experiences of domestic societies in dealing with ills such as robbery and murder were directly relevant for thinking about how to deal with international ills such as war. The common answer to such ills was government. All civilized life, Woolf claimed, depended on the effective functioning of six "essentials of government": the existence of recognized and accepted rules; a legislative body for making and modifying these rules; judicial bodies for interpreting them; organs and procedures through which changes could be made to the constitution or principles of society; administrative bodies to promote common interests; and some means of controlling or preventing the unilateral use of force. These essentials of government applied no less to international society than they did to domestic society.[110]

Evidence of this straightforward reliance on the domestic analogy can also be found in Woolf's more sophisticated earlier work. He criticized what he felt was an imbalance in the laws of war in favor of *ius en bello* by asking: "What should we think of a State in which there were no laws to prevent riot and murder and violence, and no police to enforce the law, but yet there were very detailed and complicated laws governing the conduct of persons engaged in riots, murder, and violence?" And he maintained that the difference between "a nation enforcing its own will by violence" and "a nation enforcing the will of an international authority by violence" was "the difference between a hooligan and a policeman."[111]

Although illuminating there is, however, no need to reproduce further specific examples. This is because the very form and structure of much of what Woolf has to say is based on an uncomplicated domestic analogy. By advocating *judicial* settlement, the further development of an international *legislature*, the founding of a stable international *constitution*, and, of course, the importance of international *government*, Woolf was clearly suggesting that hopes for a more orderly international society resided in making it more like domestic society.

There are, however, several aspects of Woolf's work suggesting that the overall picture is not as clearcut as it at first seems. This can be illustrated by following three examples.

First, Woolf explicitly rejected the straightforward analogy between individuals and states in his analysis of arbitration and judicial settlement. As we have seen, Woolf rejected general obligatory arbitration as neither practicable nor reasonable. Those who advocated this assumed that just as judicial decisions had been substituted for private war between individuals, international judicial decisions could be substituted for war between states. Woolf pointed out, however, that only a limited range of disputes within states were in fact settled by judicial decisions. Many disputes concerned not the interpretation of the law but what the law ought to be. To suggest that such disputes could be settled judicially was to confuse two different processes: the judicial and the legislative. Significantly, Woolf added that disputes such as the Irish Question were the kind of disputes that most closely resembled international disputes. This was because they involved groups of individuals and not individuals *per se*.[112]

Thus Woolf was aware of some of the problems inherent in a direct analogy between states and individuals. This awareness led him to incorporate the aforementioned measure of flexibility in his proposals for judicial settlement. Although still reliant on the domestic analogy in the sense that his proposals for international order are informed by a reading of domestic experience, the type of analogy he employs is, in this instance, more subtle than the one prevalent in later writings.

Second, Woolf sometimes employed a more subtle version of the analogy by virtue of his pluralistic understanding of domestic society. Accordingly, government not only consisted of the "Houses of Parliament, the Courts of Justice, the policeman, and the Borough Council," but also the church, the guild, professional associations, joint stock companies, clubs, associations of workers, consumers, employers, scientists, sportsmen, and the like. Woolf argued that the prevalence of the "narrow vision of government and the functions of government as limited to State or Municipal organisation" led to "much misunderstanding of the history and the future of International Government."[113] As has been seen, Woolf advocated not only the reproduction of "State or Municipal organisations" at the international level, but also the elaboration and development internationally of nonstate organizations. Thus, his pluralistic conception of international government was at least in part informed by his pluralistic conception of domestic government.[114]

Finally, there is a sense in which Woolf's theory of international government rests only to a small degree, if at all, on the domestic analogy. He claimed, not without reason, that his proposals for international reform were based on international processes and institutions that were already firmly rooted in the international system. His recommendations for the development of "cosmopolitanist" international government in particular were based on a reading of recent *international* experience as much as they were on a reading of *domestic* experience. Following on from this, to the extent that lawmaking had been cosmopolitanized, administration internationalized, sovereignty eroded, and an international social tissue created, the distinction between the domestic and the international had been blurred. A single society was emerging out of the collectivity of societies. To the extent that this had occurred there was, strictly speaking, no distinct domestic or international realms upon which analogies could be drawn.

These examples indicate that although Woolf often employed the domestic analogy in a straightforward and highly simplistic way, he also used it in a more subtle way, and in some areas he hardly used it at all. Again, the picture of Woolf's thought that emerges is a complex one. The crude publicist was also in some respects a subtle and prescient analyst. Once again this suggests that the prevalent image of interwar "idealists" as simplistic, one-dimensional, wishful thinkers is in need of substantial revision.

Conclusion

I would like to conclude by offering a few thoughts on Bull's contention that Woolf's work on international government is "not at all profound" and not worth reading now "except for the light it throws on the preoccupations and presuppositions of its time and place." It should first be noted that this contention rests on a conservative premise. Bull held the view that the international system was characterized by certain enduring features: anarchy (meaning "absence of government"); society (meaning at least some agreement on common norms, rules, and institutions); war; alliances; the balance of power; and the primacy of the sovereign state.[115] Profundity for Bull meant recognition of the central role these enduring features played in international life. This is the conservative premise: continuity is assumed to be more fundamental than change. Writers like Woolf, in Bull's view, had little to say of significance about the elements of continuity in international politics, and this meant that their relevance to their *own* age was limited let alone their relevance to ours. Hence his damning judgment.

In some respects it is a fair one. Many of Woolf's presuppositions and preoccupations are outmoded in that they have subsequently been shown to be either naïve, inaccurate, or inconsequential. Some of the most striking examples have been commented on: his belief that conflict was largely due to "lack of machinery"; his belief in the possibility of identifying an objective category of "legal disputes"; his assumption of extensive cultural homogeneity— an assumption symptomatic of the imperial mind-set shared at the time by even some of the most anti-imperialist thinkers; his habit of thinking in terms of a simplistic domestic analogy; and his tendency to underestimate the problems involved in the collective enforcement of international law. To these may be added Woolf's unswerving belief in the efficacy of reason. Reason, one critic once suggested, was Woolf's panacea. "A little more reason would have saved us all" was his leitmotif.[116] More than anything else it is his undiluted rationalism that separates Woolf from modern analysts of the subject. It never occurred to him that there is a tragic element in international politics, which reason alone is powerless to resolve.

However, although Woolf may not have been a profound thinker according to Bull's criteria, it would be wrong to conclude that his thought is entirely bound by time and place. Many of Woolf's ideas and observations, especially those concerning the processes of and prospects for change, continue to have relevance in the contemporary world. His view that technological change not only has major implications for the economic and social structure of the world, but also for its political structure, is one that is now widely accepted. His analysis of the "internationalisation of administration" and the growth of an "international social tissue" is one that continues to find expression in modernization theory and analyses of globalization. His observation that when the "national question" is involved it is often extremely difficult to determine whether the scope of a dispute is "national" or "international," is one that has acquired new relevance with the end of the Cold War and the reemergence of ethnic conflict. The same can be said of his misgivings about relaxing the rules on nonintervention in the absence of a much wider consensus on domestic political values and organization. Finally, Woolf's starting point for thinking about world affairs is one that continues to offer a provocative alternative to the one advanced by realists. Woolf did not see the world as an unmitigated anarchy. On the contrary, he believed the world was characterized not by the *absence* of government but by its gradual *evolution*. There is room for debate about the usefulness of Woolf's broad conception of "government." It is, however, interesting to observe the recent resuscitation of the notion, under the slightly different designation, "governance." The revival of interest by scholars and statesmen alike in the complex network of international rules, organizations, and regimes, which lie at the heart of the process of governance, suggest that Leonard Woolf's vision of international order is one that is still very much alive.

CHAPTER 5

Imperialism: An Exposition

Great Power war was not the only threat to mankind in the first half of the twentieth century. A further and potentially equally disastrous threat was imperialism. In his autobiography Woolf wrote:

> There were in fact two vast, œcumenical problems which threatened and still threaten, mankind and are interrelated: first, the prevention of war and the development of international government; secondly, the dissolution of the empires of European states in Asia and Africa which seemed to me inevitable and which would cause as much misery to the world as war unless the Governments of the great imperial powers recognised the inevitability, and deliberately worked for an orderly transference of power to their native populations, educated for self-government by their rulers.[1]

The nature, cause, and cure of imperialism were Leonard Woolf's abiding political concerns. In the growing chorus of opinion against imperialism in the 1920s and 1930s Woolf's voice was one of the clearest and most persistent. He wrote about the subject, like Hobson before him, in broad theoretical terms combining the detailed empirical analysis of the Fabian social investigator with the causticity and moral passion of the radical pamphleteer. Woolf's importance lies largely in his continuation of the Hobsonian tradition. In many ways he assumed Hobson's mantle as Britain's foremost anti-imperialist theorist.[2]

Many of his ideas developed *pari passu* with his work as secretary of the Labour Party's Advisory Committee on Imperial Questions and his work, in various capacities, for the New Fabian Research Bureau (founded in 1931), and the influential Fabian Colonial Bureau (founded in 1940). In the 1920s Woolf was the Labour Movement's leading anti-imperialist thinker, and the authority of his opinions continued well into the 1930s.[3] His work influenced many prominent anti-imperialist thinkers of the time including Sydney (later Lord) Olivier, Norman Leys, Leonard Barnes, George Padmore, and Rita Hinden.[4] In 1920 he drafted, with Charles Buxton, the first policy document committing the Labour Party to the "ultimate aim" of a "political system of self-government" in Africa.[5]

Woolf was one of several prominent men—Olivier and George Orwell among them—whose anti-imperial ideas were informed by direct experience of empire. This gave them added weight not only among the practical utopians of the Fabian Society, but also with a wider British public notoriously skeptical of theory and abstract ideas. His experiences as a young and ambitious colonial administrator in Ceylon from 1904 to 1911 were, indeed, tremendously important for the future development of his social and political ideas. Above all else it was Ceylon, he later claimed, that had turned him into a "political animal." His first published work was a novel based on these experiences, *The Village in the Jungle*.[6] In this work Woolf explores the complex relationship between traditional village society (charming but brutal), its natural jungle environment (beautiful but cruel), and British colonial rule (necessary but perverse). One imperial historian has described it as

> ...one of the finest pieces of social analysis which British Ceylon produced. Its understanding of traditional peasant society is astonishing, its delineation of the process whereby that society succumbs to economic pressure, masterly. All subsequent historical research on the problem in Ceylon has merely endorsed what Woolf asserts.[7]

Though its praises go largely unsung, *The Village in the Jungle* ranks alongside *Heart of Darkness*, *Passage to India*, and *Burmese Days* as one of the great fictional explorations of the impact of the West upon the non-Western world. Unlike these works, however, *The Village of the Jungle* looks at its subject from the inside-out rather than the outside-in. Loathing the ex-patriot life, Woolf "went native," immersing himself in traditional life and culture, and acquiring fluency in Sinhalese in the process. As vividly recounted in the second volume of his autobiography, Woolf gained an understanding of traditional Sinhalese life and village society that was unique.[8]

The publication of *The Village in the Jungle* was followed a decade later by the publication of a collection of shorter fictional works in which the same themes are further explored.[9] During the intervening period Woolf wrote his major work on imperialism, *Empire and Commerce in Africa*, the more popular-oriented *Economic Imperialism*, and a number of articles along similar lines.[10]

Above all it was Woolf's voluminous *Empire and Commerce in Africa*, written for the newly formed Labour Research Department, that established his reputation as a leading anti-imperialist thinker. The book, which stretches, according to his own calculation, to 166,604 words,[11] started out its life, in the autumn of 1916, as a study of international commerce parallel to *International Government*. Over the next twelve months, however, Woolf narrowed it down, on the advice of Sidney Webb, to a study of "imperial trade and exploitation" in Africa.

The incorporation of a vast amount of statistical data—gathered largely from the library of the London School of Economics and Political Science—made the book an invaluable work of reference for anticolonial publicists and campaigners. It soon joined Hobson's groundbreaking but empirically thinner study as a standard work on the subject.[12]

Shortly after the publication of *Empire and Commerce in Africa*, Woolf turned his attention away from economic imperialism toward the question of mandates under the League of Nations. This change in focus was married to certain modifications in outlook. The predominantly mono-causal thesis of *Empire and Commerce in Africa* gave way to the more pluralistic perspective of *Economic Imperialism* and *Imperialism and Civilization*. The latter book is Woolf's most considered and mature work on the subject. Its central theme, in contrast to earlier works, is that imperialism is best viewed as a "clash of civilizations": as a tremendous conflict between disparate and contending values, ideas, and beliefs. In the kind of questions it asks it can be seen as a forerunner, albeit in a more populist and radical vein, of Bull and Watson's *Expansion of International Society*.[13]

Later in the 1920s Woolf also began to view the white settler rather than the European state as the chief villain of economic imperialism. Far from being too imperialistic, Woolf now began to attack the state for not being imperialistic enough. He strongly urged European governments to resist the selfish and duplicitous demands of the white settlers for self-government. The real reason behind these demands was not "freedom" or "democracy" but the desire of a small self-selecting racially exclusive clique to further extend their autocratic power. The logic of such demands was not only the further enslavement of native peoples, but bloodshed and war as the white minority applied evermore desperate measures to curb the black majority's growing political awareness and appetite for self-rule. The answer lay in enlightened colonial administration from the center, involving a genuine commitment to prepare "backward peoples" for self-government.

Woolf wrote little on imperialism in the 1930s despite being in close contact, through his Labour and Fabian activities, with many leading African and Asian nationalists. As one might expect, the darkening international scene in Europe dominated his thoughts during this period. But he returned to imperial and colonial questions in the 1940s, writing a number of articles on colonial responsibilities and the preparation of African peoples for self-government. Woolf's interest in these more practical aspects of imperialism is a product of the fact that by the mid-1940s the anti-imperialists had by and large won the day. The key political agendum now was not the ends of colonial rule but the most appropriate means of bringing about its dissolution.

Woolf continued to write on imperialism and colonialism well into old age. The detailed diaries he kept as Assistant Government Agent in the Hambantota district of Ceylon, 1909–1911, were published in 1962; he continued to review books on the subject (which, he unblushingly claimed, confirmed all his views of the 1920s); and he gave in his autobiography a fascinating account of the development of the anti-imperialism in Britain.

For the student of imperialism Woolf is, therefore, a fascinating and important figure. His involvement with the subject spanned over half a century; he wrote extensively; he was concerned with both theory and practice; he had a considerable impact on progressive opinion; and he was one of the few critics of Empire who was at one stage involved in running one. He was, moreover, the only major critic of Western imperialism of the early twentieth century—among whom I include Hobson, Brailsford, Luxemburg, Morel, Olivier, and Lenin—who lived to taste the fruits of victory with the dissolution of the British and French colonial empires in the 1950s and 1960s.

Woolf's thought on imperialism can be conveniently divided into four areas of concern: the theory of economic imperialism; mandates; the problem of white settlers; and the education and political advancement of "backward peoples." I will now summarize Woolf's thought in these four areas before moving on to an analysis and assessment in chapter 6.

Theory of Economic Imperialism

Woolf's theory of economic imperialism is divided into two parts: the first concerning the nature and causes of late nineteenth-century imperialism; the second concerning its effects.

Nature and Causes

Woolf's thesis was that the imperialism of the late nineteenth century, unlike previous imperialisms, was motivated purely by economic factors. The cause of this was the profound change that had occurred in the "structure and sphere of the State," the most immediate symptom of which was the "immense and almost overwhelming importance" that the state had assumed in economic affairs. This development was of relatively recent origin: "The state, as we know it today, is a growth of very recent years: in its present form and with its present attributes it did not exist even in 1820."[14] But the pace of change had been rapid: by the first decade of the twentieth century there was hardly a single department of "individual life and activity" that had not been "subjected to State control or interference."[15]

Woolf attributed this change in the structure and sphere of the state to three phenomena that had begun to emerge in the late eighteenth century: democracy, nationalism, and industrialism. Democracy and nationalism ensured that the autocratic state conceived as the personal property and preserve of kings, was replaced by the democratic nation-state organized for the pursuit of national interests conceived as "the greatest good of the greatest number," "the realization of the best life," or "the materialization of the mysterious and sacred general will." Interacting with democracy and nationalism, the growth of industrialism ensured that the state became increasingly preoccupied with economic efficiency and commercial well-being. "Nobody in the eighteenth century thought of asking whether the state was efficient, for the main functions of the state were not economic: to-day, despite the enormous increase of patriotic nationalism, we instinctively regard the state as a kind of super-joint-stock-company."[16]

The changing role of the state was part and parcel of a general shift in ideas and beliefs. Industrialism and commercialism had begun to permeate every walk of life. In this respect the capitalists of Manchester were no different from the Mercantilists of an earlier era or the imperialists of a later era: all assumed that material profit was the main standard of value, and that the chief duty of the state was to promote, or at least not impede, its maximization. During the mid-Victorian era the policies of free trade, noninterference, and anti-imperialism were held to be the best means of attaining this end. But with the "intensive growth of industrial and commercial organization" in the late nineteenth century things began to change. "Vast and complicated organizations"—the big factory, the trust, the cartel, the syndicate, the multiple shop—came into being. They were increasingly seen as essential for industrial and commercial efficiency. The possibility of using the power and organization of the state for economic ends was not overlooked for long:

> If trade and industry were the ultimate goals of national policy, the golden goal might surely be attained more effectively by an active and aggressive

use of national power and organization than by a policy of passivism and pacificism.[17]

This chain of cause and effect—from the emergence of nationalism, democracy, and industrialism, through the change in the state, to the "active and aggressive" use of the "power and organization of the state" for the economic purposes of its citizens—culminated, around the year 1880, in economic imperialism.

Woolf's definition of economic imperialism was clear:

> Under this term I include the international economic policy of the European States, of the U.S.A., and latterly of Japan, in the unexploited and non-Europeanized territories of the world. The policy of Economic Imperialism includes colonial policy and the acquisition by the Europeanized State of exploitable territory, the policy of spheres of influence, and the policy of obtaining economic control through other political means. These various kinds of policy are all distinguished by one important characteristic; they all aim at using the power and organisation of the European form of State in the economic interests of its inhabitants in lands where the European form of state has not developed. I call it imperialism because the policy always implies either the extension of the state's territory by conquest or occupation, or the application of its dominion or some form of political control to people who are not its citizens. I qualify it with the word economic because the motives of this imperialism are not defence or prestige nor conquest nor the "spread of civilization," but the profit of the citizens, or of some citizens, of the European state.[18]

The method adopted by Woolf was essentially *verstehen*: Max Weber's term for what he claimed was the characteristic method of the social sciences: interpretive understanding of actor behavior. Woolf drew the bulk of his evidence from the writings and speeches of those statesmen, soldiers, and businessmen to whom the formulation of state policy had been entrusted.

The following quotations and passages are indicative of the kind of evidence Woolf brought to bear.

Lord Rosebery, British prime minister 1894–1895, stated in the 1890s that imperialism meant "pegging out claims for posterity."[19] M. Etienne, the French colonial under-secretary, 1887–1892, declared in 1898,

> We have built up and we intend to preserve and develop a colonial empire in order to assure the future of our country in the new continents, in

order to reserve there an outlet for our products and to find there raw material for our industries.[20]

Earlier, in the formative years of economic imperialism, Georges Clemenceau defended in the Chamber of Deputies (in 1881) the use of troops in Tunis on the grounds that Tunis was necessary as "an outlet for our manufactures" and "a lucrative means of investing capital."[21] The German chancellor, Otto von Bismarck, emphasized the economic factor when he told the Reichstag in 1884, at the point of his "conversion" to the imperialist cause, that beyond Europe Germany wanted "not provinces, but commercial enterprises."[22]

Woolf places most store by the statements of two British spokesmen: Joseph Chamberlain[23] and Captain, later Sir Frederick, later Lord, Lugard.[24] In the theoretical part of his study he repeatedly refers to the claims of these prominent statesmen. Chamberlain, Gladstone's trade minister, 1880–1885, and Colonial Secretary in the Conservative Unionist governments of Salisbury and Balfour, 1895–1903, claimed in 1894 that it was the government's job to ensure that "new markets shall be created and old markets... effectively developed." There consequently existed "a necessity as well as a duty for us to uphold the dominion and empire which we now possess" and "a necessity for using every legitimate opportunity to extend our influence and control in that African continent which is now being opened up to civilization and commerce."[25]

Chamberlain explicated this view in more detail in a speech to the Birmingham Chamber of Commerce in 1896:

> Our most important duty... [is] not the party legislation which occupies probably the largest part of our public discussions, but the development and maintenance of that vast agricultural, manufacturing, and commercial enterprise upon which the welfare and even the existence of our great population depends.... All the great offices of state are occupied with commercial affairs. The Foreign Office and the Colonial Office are chiefly engaged in finding new markets and defending old ones. The War Office and the Admiralty are mostly occupied in preparation for the defence of those markets and for the protection of our commerce... Commerce is the greatest of all political interests.[26]

Speaking about his recent expedition to Uganda for the British East Africa Company, Woolf's second key witness, Sir Frederick Lugard, claimed,

> The scramble for Africa... was due to the growing commercial rivalry, which brought home to civilized nations the vital necessity of securing the

only remaining fields for industrial enterprise and expansion. It is well to realise that it is for our advantage—and not alone at the dictates of duty—that we have undertaken responsibilities in East Africa. It is in order to foster the growth of the trade of this country, and to find an outlet for our manufactures and our surplus energy, that our far-seeing statesmen and our commercial men advocate colonial expansion... I do not believe that in these days our national policy is based on motives of philanthropy only.[27]

Through such statements Woolf was able to show that economic considerations were of considerable importance in motivating the nineteenth-century imperialism. He was also able to show that these considerations assumed greater and greater importance as the century unfolded. The era of Ferry, Rhodes, and Chamberlain differed markedly from the era of Metternich, Wellington, and Talleyrand. For the latter group, imperialism was primarily about the balance of power, alliances, the Eastern Question, and maintaining or disturbing the *status quo*. Even Disraeli's conception of empire was in the main "sentimental"—"pomp and circumstance and titles, dominion and war, ships and men and money too"—"a policy conceived in terms of Power and Prestige rather than of money-making and markets." But "in the ninth decade of the nineteenth century" economic imperialism "fully and finally established itself."

In the great States of Europe, now completely industrialized, political power passed from the hands of birth into the hands of wealth, and the political ideals of rule and power and prestige gave way to those of commerce, industry, and finance.

European policy became "dominated by rival imperialisms, colonial policies, spheres of influence, commercial treaties, markets, and tariffs."[28]

Woolf's evidence, however, is not entirely consistent. He is unable to sustain his initial contention that imperialism was motivated *purely* by economic factors. Bismarck may have become more interested in economics in the 1880s, and he may have been much influenced, as Woolf claimed, by "traders, shippers and financiers"—men like Godeffroy, Woermann, Luderitz, and Hansing. But, as his own account shows, questions of strategy and great power competition were never absent from his mind, and although Bismarck eventually complied with the wishes of German trading and financial interests, and thus initiated Germany's imperial policy, Woolf does not prove that he did so for *their* reasons. The German chancellor was clearly perturbed by the expansion of British power in Africa and was eager to check it. This is confirmed by his involvement in the Congo controversy of the early 1880s culminating in his convening of the 1884 Congo Conference at Berlin, and by his successful bid to prevent an Anglo-Portuguese alliance.[29] But why exactly did he abandon his earlier indifference to colonialism? The arguments of those representing economic interests may have been an important factor, but they were not the only, nor necessarily the most important one. The quotations Woolf selects from Bismarck's speeches do not clinch the matter in quite the decisive way he assumed. The following statement taken from Bismarck's public announcement of his new policy could be interpreted as testimony to his concern for "Power and Prestige" as much as his desire for "money-making and markets":

> It is not possible to conquer oversea territories by men of war or to take possession of them without further ceremony. Nevertheless the German trader wherever he has settled will be protected, and wherever he has assumed possession of territory there the Administration will follow him, as England has continually done.[30]

This statement contains a tacit acknowledgment of both Britain's naval mastery and, arguably, the importance Bismarck attached to great power rivalry.

Similarly, although the statements of Etienne and Clemenceau suggest the dominance of economics, a lengthy statement by Jules Ferry, also quoted by Woolf, injects a degree of uncertainty. Jules Ferry, it should be noted, was one of the principal architects of French colonial policy during the crucial first decade of the "era of economic imperialism" in the 1880s. Ferry claimed that empire was necessary in order to secure outlets for French exports and capital. But he also gave other reasons: the need for an outlet for emigration; the need for strategic ports; and the need to maintain the power and prestige of France.[31]

It is also significant that Woolf makes a distinction between North and Tropical Africa. After 1880 European statesmen began to "deal" with the latter in terms of the new policy of economic imperialism. But with respect to the former, the "older policy of Wellington and de Polignac" never entirely lost its hold:

> The statesmen who played for and won and lost Egypt, Tunis, Tripoli, and Morocco all believed that commerce was the greatest of all political interests, and on the Niger, the Congo, and the Zambezi they put their beliefs into practice: but in Egypt, Tunis, Tripoli, and Morocco their economic

imperialism was never pure; it was always mixed with considerations of European strategy and alliances and the balance of power.[32]

Even more evocatively

> ...although economic forces played strongly upon the chief actors at Algeciras and in the Agadir incident, the spirit of the dead statesmanship of Metternich, Wellington, and de Polignac seemed to haunt and "possess" Prince Bülow and Declassé, Herr Kiderlen-Wächter and Sir Edward Grey.[33]

If not the spirit of Metternich et al., the spirit of the church missionary societies of Victorian Britain might be said to have haunted the statesmanship of Chamberlain and Lugard. Lugard's references to the "dictates of duty" and to "motives of philanthropy" indicate that the idea of the "civilizing mission" was not entirely absent in his explanation of Empire. The same could be said of Chamberlain's references to "duty" and "civilization." In addition, although it may have been correct to say that "all the great offices of state are occupied with commercial affairs" this does not mean that the promotion of commerce was their *sole* function.

Along with these specific problems with Woolf's analysis, there are problems of a more general nature. The determination of social causation through analysis of public declarations of social actors is not a hazard-free enterprise. Social purpose and setting invariably condition social pronouncements. The speeches and statements of politicians and major political actors are particularly conditioned by the political context in which they are made. The social investigator, therefore, must always be on her guard. She may be witnessing not social truth but the employment of an age-old political tool. Chamberlain in his speech to the Birmingham Chamber of Commerce was probably exaggerating for his own political purposes rather than giving an "objective" account of what he felt to be the *raison d'être* of empire. Such statements, of course, often contain as much "ought" as "is." Similarly, the fact that Lugard was writing in defense of a much criticized campaign cannot be ignored. He was at pains to point out to reluctant British ministers the considerable material rewards that could be reaped in East Africa. He wanted to convince them that official British involvement would not become the financial albatross that many feared. In a sense Lugard was not only seeking to explain and justify past acts of imperialism but to make a case for its extension and reinvigoration.

Without wishing to encroach too much on the territory of chapter 6, it is worth noting another problem. It concerns the selection of evidence.

Woolf does supply a large number of quotations, but only ones that corroborate his thesis. This raises a general question with the interpretive method. How far should the analyst go in searching for counter-interpretations? As we shall see, a number of critics at the time felt that Woolf did not go far enough. It might be added that relative to all the speeches, declarations, and statements made at the time, those cited by Woolf are, at the end of the day, rather few in number.

There is no evidence to suggest that Woolf was aware of these shortcomings except for the fact that as *Empire and Commerce in Africa* unfolds, Woolf's determination to uphold his mono-causal thesis becomes progressively weaker. Claims to the effect that late nineteenth-century imperialism was notable for "the singleness and purity of [economic] motive" become less frequent, and claims to the effect that economic factors were the "main" motive or "impulse" or the "ultimate" end of policy, more so.[34]

A distinct trend away from mono-causalism is clearly evident in later writings. In *Economic Imperialism* Woolf explicitly says that there was no single and simple cause of the "complex" phenomenon of imperialism, and he proceeds to examine some of the explanations commonly advanced. The "moral" explanation that colonial expansion was motivated by the "white man's burden"—the duty to spread Christianity, law and order, and other "blessings of civilization" (an ironic reference to the Final Act of the Congress of Berlin, 1884–1885)[35]—is dismissed by Woolf as a secondary cause. This view was frequently used as an argument against withdrawing from a conquest once it had been made, or against abandoning control once it had been acquired. Thus in Woolf's view:

> ...the connection between imperialism and moral ideas appears to be this: Europeans have acquired their Empires for selfish motives; they, or many of them, believe that they retain and maintain their Empires for altruistic motives. The white man's burden becomes a duty only after... he has placed it upon his own shoulders.[36]

The same could be said of "sentimental" reasons, that is, the belief that "the acquisition and retention of imperial possessions and dependencies outside Europe reflects great glory on the European State." This explanation, according to Woolf, may have been valid as far as the retention of empire went, but belief in the glory of empire had done little to set the policy in motion.[37]

Military and strategic reasons had more weight, especially with regard to French and Italian imperialism in North Africa. There was also a sense in which imperialism had a strategic logic of its own. Britain sought to control

Egypt not because such control afforded any strategic value for Britain itself, but in order to protect India. Accordingly, "Military reasons are... not to any great extent a cause of imperialism, but they are a reason for making an empire large, and a large empire larger."[38]

In a pamphlet published in the same year as *Economic Imperialism* Woolf dropped the "economic" from "imperialism" altogether:

> By imperialism is meant that world movement which led in 20 years to the partition of practically the whole of Africa and large areas of Asia and all the islands of the Pacific among the four Great Powers, Britain, France, Russia, and Germany, and the smaller Powers, Italy and Belgium. This partition did not mean simply that the territory was conquered and the government of the territories subjected to the direct or indirect control of the imperial Powers; it meant, too, that Europe imposed upon the Asiatic and African peoples the ideal and institutions of Western civilization, her military, legal, administrative, and economic system.[39]

A reader unacquainted with Woolf's writings could be forgiven for not realizing that the author of this definition was one of the principal architects of the radical theory of the "new" imperialism. It contains few traces of his earlier radicalism. Indeed, but for the slightly pejorative verb "impose" and the structural connotations of "world movement," the definition is a conservative one.

Woolf's radicalism returned with *Imperialism and Civilization*. He began the book by pointing out that the relations between civilizations prior to the nineteenth century were largely tolerant and indifferent. "But the new European civilization of the nineteenth century changed all that. It was a belligerent, crusading, conquering, exploiting, proselytizing civilization." Vastly superior technology made this aggressive expansion of Western civilization possible. The need for new markets and new sources of raw materials made it necessary. The picture was as follows:

> Behind the capitalist, the trader, the manufacturer, and the financier, who had emerged from the industrial revolution and were now led by blind economic forces to stretch out their hands to the markets and produce of Asia and Africa, stood the highly organised, efficient, powerfully armed, acutely nationalist modern State which had emerged from the French Revolution and the Napoleonic Wars. Sometimes deliberately and sometimes haphazardly and unconsciously, the power of this terrific engine of force and government was invoked by the capitalist to aid him in developing or exploiting the other continents. The effect was stupendous.[40]

This return after a brief absence of Woolf's radicalism was not matched, however, by a restoration of his earlier mono-causalism. Thus the "inevitability" of the "stretching out" and "imposition" of European civilization on the rest of the world was "especially" due to economic impulses. Though these impulses were a primary cause of imperialism, strategic impulses were a "secondary" cause.[41] The conquests of Greece, Rome, and the Renaissance were about glory and domination. In contrast nineteenth-century imperialism was "primarily" about economic exploitation.[42] The forceful control of the economic life of China by the imperial powers of Europe, the United States, and later Japan was "exercised *primarily* in the interests of the commercial, industrial, and financial classes of the controlling Power."[43] Similarly, the evils caused by imperialism were "*mainly* due to the habit of European civilization of subordinating everything to economic ends."[44]

The phrasing of these arguments amounts to a significant modification of Woolf's initial thesis. It is important to stress, however, that although he abandoned the notion that late nineteenth-century imperialism was motivated *purely* by economic factors, he continued to insist on their *primacy*. His label "economic imperialism" remains therefore a valid one.

Effects

Woolf contended that the effects of late nineteenth-century imperialism were "almost wholly evil."[45] Economic imperialism was bad for the colonized, but it was also bad for the colonizers—except for a small band of traders, financiers, mine owners, and planters who in many cases accumulated vast wealth.

The intellectual and political proponents of economic imperialism genuinely believed that great riches were to be won in the "opening up" of Asia and Africa. For Woolf this was pure delusion. The colonial parties in France and Germany, for example, held "vague and erroneous ideas" about the nature of the empire they wished to conquer:

> This was particularly true of Africa, the mystery of whose forests and lakes and rivers was only just been revealed to Europeans. Undoubtedly a vision of "many goodly states and kingdoms" swam before the eyes of the patriots, who dreamed dreams of German or French Australias and Canadas rising by the side of great rivers, or in the tropical forests of Asia and Africa.[46]

The Congo, to give one example, was seen as an "Eldorado" of rubber, precious metals, and—oddly given Woolf's initial thesis—"savage souls."[47]

Such views were delusory because the historical record showed that the general benefits of economic imperialism were meager. Woolf provided a wealth of data to prove this claim. In 1913, for instance, all of Britain's tropical possessions in Africa accounted for only 1.04 percent of U.K. imports and 1.4 percent of U.K. exports. This meant that tropical Africa was of no more importance economically to the United Kingdom than Chile. In terms of U.K. exports Argentina was three times more important and six times more important in terms of imports. The average value of food and raw materials imported from British East Africa between 1909 and 1913 amounted to 0.15 percent of the United Kingdom's total imports of these commodities, and British East Africa imported only 0.19 percent of total U.K. exports. It had been claimed in the early 1890s, by Chamberlain, Lugard, MacKinnon, *The Times*, and others that Britain should colonize Uganda because it would provide a vital market for British exports and vital jobs for British workers. In classic dissenting fashion Woolf responded as follows:

> Uganda, that country which was to secure the British workman from unemployment, actually takes no more than 0.006% of the total exports of British industries. It is clear that the incorporation of Uganda in the British Empire has had no more and no less effect upon British trade, industry, and employment, than if it had been sunk in the Indian Ocean and blotted off the map of the world.[48]

Woolf also pointed out that imperialists assumed that colonial markets would be closed to foreign competition. But this was not the case. For the period 1898–1913, for example, the increase in value of raw materials imported by British industries from German East Africa was far greater than the increase of value of those imported from British East Africa. Similarly, the rate of increase of British exports to German East Africa was far greater than the rate of increase of British exports to British East Africa. Woolf continued:

> The significance of this fact is obvious when it is remembered that Mr. Chamberlain and the economic imperialists of the British East Africa Company argued that the main reason why Britain should seize and retain Uganda and British East Africa was in order to keep the Germans out and prevent them from closing these territories to the products of British industry.[49]

Woolf concluded that even at the height of the Empire the importance of Britain's tropical possessions in Africa to the British economy was at best marginal. The belief that they provided an important market for British manufactures was a delusion. "The few score inhabitants of Park Lane," he exclaimed, "have a far higher purchasing power and are a far better market for British industries than the millions of Africans in these British possessions."[50]

The importance of British Africa as a source of raw materials was similarly delusory. British imports from East Africa were negligible. Her imports from West Africa were greater but still relatively modest: palm oil, the major export of the region, was a commodity of minor importance when set against cotton, wool, copper, and iron ore. So too was Nigerian tin when set against the much greater amounts of tin imported from Bolivia.

Although not identical, what was true of British possessions was also generally true of French and German. The trade between France and her Algerian and Tunisian colonies was not insignificant, these colonies accounting for 5.5 percent of French exports in 1912. However, this figure was only marginally greater after France established a system of colonial preference, in 1885, than before. Colonization had thus resulted in only a marginal increase in trade. Moreover, the value of French exports to Algeria and Tunisia was two and a half times greater than the value of the exports to all other French colonial possessions. In 1910 the French Empire accounted for 8 percent of French exports and 7 percent of imports. This meant that, as trading partners, Germany and Britain were far more important to France than her colonies: British imports of French goods were twice the value of French goods bought by the entire French colonial empire, and Germany imported 15 percent more. Together Britain and Germany exported to France three times the total exports of the whole French Empire. "Nothing could show more clearly," Woolf concluded, "that the economic beliefs behind economic imperialism are dreams and delusions."[51]

The German experience stood even more roundly condemned. In 1909 Germany's entire colonial empire took just 0.5 percent of German exports and accounted for just 0.4 percent of German imports. In terms of German imports, British West Africa was nine times more important to Germany than German East Africa (figures from 1912), and as a market for German exports German East Africa was only marginally more important (figures from 1910). These figures led Woolf to conclude:

> It is a curious commentary upon the doctrines and policy which we have been examining in these pages, and in which the Germans were the most fervent believers, that in 1909 the trade of Germany with her colonies was just equal to her trade with the British possession of the Malay States: it was one twelfth of her trade with British India![52]

If the European side of the colonial balance-sheet was a bleak picture the African side was even more so. The so-called blessings of European colonialism amounted to very little. "Law and order" had to some extent been established but only in the wake of "persistent and ruthless slaughter of the inhabitants in wars and through 'punitive expeditions.' "[53] Brutal systems of administration existed in many colonies and especially in the Belgian Congo, the French Congo, and German South West Africa. Christianity had spread to some extent but its adoption was more apparent than real. Many of the nine million Africans (out of a total population of 170 million) who had been converted by 1920 were Christian only nominally. The spread of education had fared little better. Even in British colonies, which tended to have a better record on education than the colonies of others, the provision of education in any of its forms was dismal. Local taxation far outstripped expenditure. In 1917, for example, the expenditure on schools in Nigeria amounted to only 1.7 percent of taxation raised. In British East Africa the total expenditure on education for the year 1909–1910 was a meager £1,835 while the expenditure on the post office, which served only the interests of white settlers, was £26,700, that is 1,400 percent more. The colonial authorities, indeed, spent little of the revenue they raised on schemes designed to benefit "the native":

> Though the native is heavily taxed, the revenue derived from such taxation is devoted by Government not to native requirements, but mainly to European interests, e.g., the Chief Native Commissioner of Kenya stated that the Kitui Akamba tribe paid £207,749 in taxes in ten years, and that the only Government expenditure in the Kitui Reserve during this time had been on collecting the taxes.[54]

Similarly, the attempt to establish the "Europeans' economic system" and the "principle of economic efficiency" had produced few benefits for Africans. The colonial record in East Africa was particularly appalling. Local economic systems had been ruthlessly destroyed rather than adapted. No attempt had been made to improve traditional agricultural techniques. The best land had been expropriated to white settlers, and local populations forced into inadequate "native reserves." By various means, some direct others indirect, the native had been compelled to work for poor wages. In many cases the exploitation of African labor by white capitalists was indistinguishable from slavery.[55]

In Asia, although the pattern of economic imperialism had been different the results were equally appalling. Economic imperialism brought corruption, civil war, indebtedness, and foreign intervention in its wake. China, for example, had been reduced to "anarchy and economic chaos."

The phenomenon of economic imperialism thus stood condemned from all sides: neither the Africans and Asians, nor the Europeans benefited from it except for a tiny band of exploitative European financiers, traders, and planters.

Mandates

Woolf believed that the mandates system "honestly applied" held out the best hope for resolving the immense problems wrought by economic imperialism. From the outset he maintained that complete independence must be the ultimate goal, though movement toward it, especially in "tropical Africa," would have to be gradual.

Early Doubts

In his first work on the subject Woolf's faith in the efficacy of mandates was far from absolute. It is worth spending some time spelling out the reasons for this.

Those committed to the "honest" application of the mandates principle, especially in Africa, were confronted with a serious dilemma. The modern European state was an instrument of exploitation, and would remain so as long as the "ideas and beliefs of economic imperialism" prevailed. More specifically, as long as it was considered the "first duty" of the European state to promote the economic development of Africa in the interests of its own citizens, colonial offices and governments, regardless of their nobler professions, would be subject to the "irresistible pressure of the handful of white men who have economic interests in Africa."[56] If these interests dictated that the native should not be educated, he would not be. If they dictated that he work for the white man for a penny a day, "taxation or starvation" would "furnish the necessary inducement." If they dictated that his land should be sold to Europeans, then it would be, and the native forced into reserves. And so on. Any attempt by government to strengthen the position of the native through education was bound to fail since "any real education" would "unfit the native to take his place as a docile labourer on a penny a day in the scheme of economic imperialism."[57]

It was in this semi-structural sense that the European state was "necessarily an instrument of exploitation." Woolf seemed to be suggesting that the ideas and beliefs of economic imperialism were so compelling that the state had no choice but to comply with the dictates of its white standard-bearers in Africa. Yet the immediate withdrawal of the European state from Africa would not necessarily make things better. Withdrawal, in effect, would mean handing over of the fate of the native from the exploitative European state to "the more cruel exploitation of irresponsible white men."[58] Moreover, economic imperialism was itself responsible, paradoxically, for creating conditions that made some form of continued control by Europeans inevitable. "Primitive peoples" had suddenly been confronted with a "highly complex, alien civilisation" and there had been little attempt to equip the native with the knowledge and skills necessary to "control" this civilization. They were unable, as a consequence, of managing their own affairs and, in the language of the League Covenant, "standing by themselves in the strenuous conditions of the modern world."[59]

This was the dilemma. Economic imperialism had created the conditions that made an immediate transfer of power in Africa impossible. A period of transition was needed during which the European state would have to honestly carry out its professions. But how could an instrument of exploitation be transformed into "an instrument of good government and progress, not for a few hundred white men, but for the millions of Africans"?[60] That was the question.

Those who provided answers to it, Woolf suggested, fell into two camps. On the one hand there were those whose diagnosis of the problem was political. Imperialism was a disease of the interstate system. The competition of state against state caused "international hostility in Europe" and "the expropriation, exploitation, and extermination of the natives in Africa." The answer lay in substituting cooperation for hostility through a League of Nations. States would renounce the right to use Africa as a means to their selfish ends and accept President Wilson's principle of "the removal... of all economic barriers and the establishment of an equality of trade conditions among all nations." The "ultimate vision" in this line of thought was the substitution of "some form of international control and administration" for "national possession, ownership, or exploitation."[61]

On the other hand there were those whose diagnosis of the problem was social and economic. "The imperialist policies of Germany, France, and Britain, the hostility and competition of these States, the seizure of territory, the ruthless conquest and massacres of natives" were for these thinkers "merely symptoms." The relations between Europe and Africa were not political or moral but social and economic. Africa was viewed "only in the light of a potentially profitable estate." There was therefore little value in a political remedy such as international administration. This was because social behavior, from this more "scientific" perspective, was not a product of conscious reason, but an automatic and instinctual by-product of "that system...which we call for short the capitalist system." The answer to the problem thus took the form not of "a change from imperialism to internationalism, but of a change of the social and economic relations between the African and the European." The doctrine that all men, regardless of race or color, possessed equal human dignity and were entitled to rights to life, land, and education, would have to replace the doctrine that the "native" was merely "live-stock" on "Europe's African estate," a source of "cheap labour," and "the market for the shoddy of our factories and our cheap gin."[62]

Laying himself "open to attack, on both flanks, from the rear, by friend and foe alike," Woolf confessed to belonging to both camps. Many of the criticisms of the international solution were, he felt, justified. The "ultimate beliefs and desires" that created the problem were part of the capitalist system. In this system economic ideals dominated. Its essence was the profit motive: "the passion of buying cheap and selling dear." As long as Africa was seen simply as something to make profits out of, the economic struggle, the hostility, the exploitation, would continue. International control could be substituted for national imperialism, but if the ideas and beliefs of the European remained the same, the result would merely be the substitution of exploitation by international groups for the exploitation by national groups. Woolf gave the name "international imperialism" to what Hobson called "inter-imperialism" and Karl Kautsky, "ultra imperialism."[63]

Woolf was thus "forced to the conclusion that if the European State is to become an instrument of good rather than of evil in Africa, the economic beliefs and desires of Europeans must suffer a change." But he did not hold out much hope of such change taking place. A revolution would be required. The state would have to abandon the practice of using its power in the interests of Europeans and accept in its place the role of a trustee whose only duty would be to promote the interests of Africans. In practice this would entail a "definite political programme" involving such typically Fabian measures as: reservation of the land for the natives; "systematic education" to enable the natives to use it effectively; deliberate discouragement of the European wage- and labor-system; "gradual expropriation of all Europeans and their capitalist enterprises"; the "application of all revenue raised in Africa to the development of the country and the education, health, etc., of the native inhabitants"; a "return to the ['natural and native'] communal system, developed, improved, and organized by the European States"; and most paternalistically of all, the "absolute prohibition of alcohol."[64]

Where did this leave "internationalism"? Writing at the very time the issue of mandates was being discussed by the delegates at Paris, Woolf's answer was bleak. By itself it was no solution to the "African problem." Yet the "substitution of the idea of trusteeship for that of ownership and exploitation" was an essential part of that solution. Economic imperialism, Woolf seemed to be suggesting, could only be destroyed by a social revolution, that is, "a revolution in men's beliefs and desires." But the revolution itself required for its success rejection of the absolute right of ownership and acceptance of the idea of international trusteeship.[65]

This idea had always been the basis of internationalist proposals. But the most effective method by which it could be implemented—"administration by the League itself"—was commonly dismissed as "impossible and Utopian." Woolf repeated the claim made in *International Government* that the supposed failure of international government was deduced from examples, such as the Great Power condominia established in the New Hebrides and Somoa, not of international government but its opposite. International government had never been tried in Africa, "partly because people do not wish to try it—for it might succeed—and partly because those who do not wish it to be tried or to succeed, have induced the rest of the world to believe that it had been tried and has failed." Genuine international government would involve vesting the sovereignty over Africa in the League,

> which would delegate its powers of administration under a written constitution [embodying the "definite political programme" outlined above] to International Commissions in precisely the same way as the European Powers, with marked success, delegated their powers of administration over the Danube and its navigation to the Danube Commission.

Such a system, Woolf believed, would work. But it would not, he despaired, be tried: not because it was a failure, or impossible, or utopian, but because "the Western world has no belief in or desire for... trusteeship."[66]

There remained one other method. The League could "formally declare its trusteeship of non-adult races" and then hand over the administration "to particular States as its mandataries." Woolf was deeply suspicious of this idea. "The great advantage of this proposal," he mockingly declared, "lies in the fact that it will enable the world to introduce a new and noble system, and in reality to leave everything exactly as it was before." *The Times*, in a leader on the proposals emanating from Paris, had recommended that

> the system ought to mean nothing more hampering than the imposition upon the trustee of an obligation to give the beneficiary good government. It should bind them to the civilized world to administer subject

peoples in the interests of the governed; in fact, it should bind them in formal fashion to do exactly what, of their own accord, just nations do already.[67]

Woolf feared that, given the facts about economic imperialism, such a conception of the mandates system might easily be used to "throw a cloak of pseudo-internationalism" over the unjust acts of so called "just nations." It would be one more method of "soothing to sleep the unquiet conscience of just nations and just men."[68]

For these reasons Woolf found it "difficult to feel any great enthusiasm for this new mandatory system of the League of Nations." But it was arguable that it might at least be an improvement on the old system. Much depended on the League becoming "an effective force." This, in turn, depended on: (a) precise definition of the obligations of the mandatory in a treaty; (b) the creation of a permanent commission with "very considerable powers of enquiry and inspection"; (c) the guarantee of "absolute equality of commercial opportunity, by means of free trade and the open door"; and (d) the ability of the League to revoke a mandate if the mandatory was found to be in breach of its obligations. Fine sentiments, as the Final Act of the Congo Conference all too clearly demonstrated, were easily embodied in international declarations. The real test of the world's sincerity was whether such fine sentiments could be translated into actual deeds.

Later Confidence

Such uncharacteristic equivocation on Woolf's part soon gave way to a more confident position. In the steady stream of writings that followed, Woolf firmly pins himself to the mast of "internationalism." The other, more structuralist, camp hardly gets a mention. Soul-searching about the efficacy of internationalism in general, gives way to concern over the details of particular mandates—though his concern about the trustworthiness of the mandatory Powers persisted.

Within twelve months of the completion of *Empire and Commerce in Africa*, Woolf was boldly claiming that the mandates system was the "antithesis" of imperialism.[69] The core issue was sovereignty. According to Woolf:

> The whole system of imperialism is based on the claim of the imperial powers that, when they seized territory in Asia and Africa, they acquired sovereign rights over the territory and its inhabitants.

This meant that they had

> ...absolute power to do what they pleased with the lives and property of millions of the "subject races."[70]

Both Western civilization and international law, much to their discredit, upheld this claim. Consequently there was no right of interference, either by a national or an international agency, even in the face of mass persecution and repression.

Woolf argued that those who had devised the League's mandate system deliberately denied sovereign rights to the mandatory power. This was the clear implication of the principle underlying the whole system: that the "well-being and development" of subject peoples formed a "sacred trust of civilisation." Sovereignty ultimately rested with the League. Any authority the mandatory Powers possessed they possessed by virtue of the League and were always subject to conditions laid down by the League. In contrast to the doctrine of economic imperialism, therefore, the mandatory Powers had no right to exploit, only a duty to ensure the well-being and development of indigenous peoples.[71]

Woolf reiterated some of his earlier proposals for making the system effective, including granting the League Council: (a) "full and adequate powers" of "control, inspection, and supervision"; (b) the power to determine the form of government and type of constitution to be applied in each mandated territory; and (c) the power to "revoke" as well as amend a mandate. The scope of the Permanent Mandates Commission (PMC) needed to be widened to carry out these functions. Perhaps most importantly, Woolf advocated the extension of the mandates system to all subject peoples regardless of who their colonial overlords happened to be in 1918. The current arrangements were "illogical and morally indefensible" since some territories were to be administered in the interests of its inhabitants, while adjoining territories were "administered autocratically in the interest of imperialist European Powers."[72]

It should be noted at this point that Woolf accepted the distinction made in Article 22 between those peoples ready for self-government and those not. He agreed with the Covenant that African peoples fell into the latter camp. He felt, however, that as a step toward the eventual realization of this goal, local self-government should be immediately established everywhere. Woolf generally accepted prevailing assumptions about "the African" being "backward," "savage," and "primitive." Such things as war, slavery, mysticism, and cannibalism were, for Woolf, evidence, of this. But he firmly rejected the view that the "backwardness" of African peoples had anything to do with race or color. Indeed, Europeans were partly responsible for their condition since they had failed to introduce a proper system of education. Nevertheless, "backwardness" was a social fact and consequently full independence was not yet possible.

According to Article 22, the independence of "communities formerly belonging to the Turkish Empire" could be "provisionally recognised" subject to "advice and assistance from the more advanced nations." It further decreed that "the wishes of these communities must be a principal consideration in the selection of the Mandatory." Woolf not only approved of this article but also gave it a bold interpretation. In Woolf's opinion it granted an immediate right of self-government to the various peoples of the Middle East. The European Powers had no rights, only an obligation to provide, if requested, "advice and assistance." It is also the case, however, that Woolf felt such advice and assistance was vital if independence was to have real meaning. This was necessary because these peoples had been long subject to "the paralysing government of the Turk" and faced the prospect of fierce religious and racial dissent. They were also vulnerable to political disruption and economic destruction caused by the war and needed, like African peoples, time to "adjust their Eastern to our Western civilisation."[73] It is a curious fact, to be discussed in chapter 6, that Woolf completely ignored the word "provisionally."

Since the vanquished Powers did not possess a large empire in Asia, the Covenant lay silent on the stage of development and therefore readiness for self-government of Asian peoples. Woolf categorized them alongside the "communities formerly belonging to the Turkish Empire." This is an additional aspect of his bold interpretation of Article 22—the extension of the logic of paragraphs 3 and 4 to Asia. Woolf held that the ancient civilizations of India, China, Persia, and Japan possessed their own elaborate social, economic, and political systems, which differed from but were not necessarily inferior to those of the West. It was because of this that resistance to European penetration had been far more robust in Asia than in Africa. The development of various and increasingly powerful Asian nationalisms further reinforced the respect in the West for the civilizations of the Orient. Writing in 1928 Woolf asserted that it was unlikely that the European Powers would be able to hang onto their Asian colonies for much longer. The price of trying to do so would be violent confrontation, the scale and intensity of which was bound to grow the longer independence was postponed into the future.[74]

These two factors meant that, as with the Middle East, complete independence should immediately be granted to the Asian colonies. But, as with the Middle East and Africa, Asia still had the problem of adapting to Western civilization and the "modern world" of technology, industry, commerce, and finance. China especially would have to do this in the face of "economic chaos" caused by economic imperialism and foreign intervention. It was in this respect that the mandates system could help by providing expert advice and assistance. Given the history of Western subterfuge and exploitation, no independent Asian state would accept an individual or even a consortium of European states as a mandatory. But this role could be performed by "the League itself." This is significant for two reasons. First, it represents a departure from his earlier gloominess about the prospects for international administration. Second, it demonstrates that Woolf conceived the League as more than merely a "consortium of states," having, perhaps, a life of its own independent from its member states. The League could provide its "own" experts, administrators, advisers, and advisory commissions. These would be "disinterested" and therefore "free from the suspicion which naturally attached to similar 'advisers' provided by the great imperialist Powers."[75]

Thus Norman Etherington's claim that Woolf advocated either complete independence for colonial peoples or the transfer of power to "a truly international body which could look after their interests until they were 'ready for independence'" is misleading in two ways. It is true that Woolf's overriding goal was complete independence for all subject peoples. But only in respect of Asia did Woolf unequivocally advocate direct international administration. His recipe for Africa was "the mandates system honestly applied." Second, the Oriental dependencies, according to Woolf's interpretation of the Covenant, were already "independent," and the provision of administrative assistance was a right to be claimed rather than a duty imposed.[76]

Problem of White Settlers

When Woolf warned that in Africa immediate independence meant handing power from one exploitative group to one even more exploitative, the group he had in mind was the white settlers. In his earliest writings Woolf identified white settlers in Southern and East Africa as, collectively, one of the foremost villains of economic imperialism. He gave increasing emphasis to their treachery, *vis à vis* the treachery of joint-stock companies and/or the European state, as his work progressed. Indeed, as early as 1922 Woolf was attacking the government for "abandoning the path of a sound and moral colonial policy." This is a curious claim since the strong implication of earlier writings was that such a policy had never existed, and indeed could not exist given the nature of imperialism and the European state.[77] Increasingly Woolf called on the European state, the British state in particular, to thwart the dangerous ambitions of white settlers.

This group created a problem in four interrelated ways. First, they deceived and exploited indigenous peoples, having no regard for their welfare. Native land had been seized by various methods, none of them legitimate, and taxes imposed in order to force "native labour" to work it.[78] Wages barely reached subsistence level and attempts were consistently made to reduce them even further.[79]

Second, white settlers regularly managed to enlist the support of the British colonial administration in pursuit of their selfish ends. By exaggerating certain traditional festivals and ceremonies, for instance, settlers had been able to create the impression that certain tribes were endemically brutish and degenerate. This greatly assisted their campaign to induce the government to alienate the best land to them. The alliance between white settlers and certain colonial administrators was sometimes so close that the latter relied exclusively on information provided by the former in forming their view of "native interests." For example, a British Commissioner in East Africa, Sir Charles Eliot, recorded in his dispatches:

> The Masai and many other tribes must go under. It is a prospect which I view with equanimity and a clear conscience...Masaidom...is a beastly, bloody system, founded on raiding and immorality.

According to Woolf this view was largely a product of exaggerated reports drawn up by white settlers.[80]

Third, during the interwar period white settlers in East and Central Africa intensified their efforts to win self-government. This claim was based on the belief that such territories were "white man's country," and that consequently self-government should be granted just as it had been in Australia, New Zealand, Canada, and South Africa. Given the degree to which the nonwhite population far outnumbered the white population, however, such a claim was ridiculous. The white settlers, as Woolf unambiguously put it,

> are a menace not only to themselves but to the whole Empire. The notion is fantastic that a few thousand white men, possessed of the crude and narrow ideas which they openly display at what their papers call their "People's Parliament," can govern autocratically and exploit economically an African population which outnumbers them by hundreds to one, and also an Indian population which outnumbers them by four to one.[81]

The demands of this "gallant band of white democrats" must, Woolf insisted, be seen for what they really were: part of an attempt to gain complete control of the territories they inhabited in order to secure absolute freedom to exploit the land and the native as they saw fit.

Finally, and from the perspective of international relations, the foundations had been laid for an immense conflagration. In his earliest writings on the subject Woolf suggested that continued white exploitation and intransigence would exacerbate the already tense relations between the white overlords and their nonwhite vassals. This would inevitably lead to unrest and civil strife. A "tremendous catastrophe" involving a revolt of the "beneficiaries against their guardians and benefactors" was in the making.[82] In the late 1920s, noting the growth of African political consciousness, Woolf argued that although the white minority had the power to rule in the short term, "it is certain to end in a terrible catastrophe. The revolt against the European's political domination and economic exploitation, which we have already seen in Asia, will inevitably be repeated in Africa."[83]

Writing in 1952, Woolf applied the same logic to South Africa. Apartheid was a policy of "suicide," "despair," and "political nonsense." "Separate development" was an absurdity when the white economy depended so heavily on black labor. Moreover, the type of labor increasingly demanded was skilled, industrial labor, which presupposed a certain degree of educational attainment. Economic forces were creating "an economic class of African," which would inevitably claim political and social rights. The National policy of white South Africa thus contained within it the seeds of its own violent destruction.

In East and Central Africa these treacherous conditions had not yet been fully established. Such an eventuality, however, was certain unless the British government took firm action to thwart white ambitions. In particular, white demands for the creation of a Central African Federation, so bitterly opposed by all African groups, needed to be unambiguously rejected.[84]

Although it is true that Woolf gave greater emphasis to metropolitan than to peripheral developments, this synopsis shows that it is not entirely true to say that "[i]n an era before the emergence of radical black nationalism, Woolf envisaged the transformation of imperialism solely through political action in the European heartland and failed to imagine this occurring through initiatives within the colonies themselves."[85] Woolf was an early and perceptive observer of the rising tide of African nationalism, and had a firm appreciation of the implications of this development for the future political constitution and well-being of the continent.

The Education and Political Advance of "Backward Peoples"

In true Fabian style Woolf believed that education had a vital role to play in preparing colonial peoples for self-government. In its absence these peoples would be unable to understand and deal effectively with the forces of the modern world. This was particularly the case with the "non-adult," "primitive," or "backward" peoples of Africa. From the early 1920s through to the 1940s Woolf's view on education changed little. He envisaged education on Western lines—primary, secondary, and higher: academic and vocational—and unswervingly maintained that colonial governments had a duty to provide it. The implementation of a "deliberate and detailed educational scheme" was, he asserted, their "first duty," though it was one that they had nowhere fulfilled adequately.[86] Some facts regarding the "dismal" and inequitable record of the colonial authorities on native education have been cited in the section "Economic Imperialism: Effects." It may be added that in 1926 Woolf claimed that in many cases Europeans had

> ... deliberately kept the natives uneducated and ignorant in the hope that they may be more docile under economic exploitation. In Nigeria the revenue for 1923–24 was £6,260,561, the expenditure on education was £135,866 [i.e. 2.17%]. In Kenya the revenue was £1,839,447, and the expenditure on education £44,946 [i.e. 2.44%].[87]

In 1943 he pointed to the "extraordinary position" in Kenya where, after 50 years of British rule, only two of eighteeen members of the Legislative Council represented African interests, and these were Europeans nominated by the governor. The justification was that there were no Africans sufficiently educated to speak for their people: this in a country where the native population measured three million compared with 20,000 Europeans (electing eleven members to the Council) and 30,000 Asians (electing five). Woolf condemned this as an appalling state of affairs.[88] For many years he had been advocating, in classic Fabian style, periodic reform of administration "so that as the natives are educated, they may progressively be given a larger and larger share in the government of their country."[89] In the 1940s he added a sense of urgency:

> I suggest that after the war we must change our whole policy with regard to self-government in our African colonies. We must insist that the colonial administrations go all out deliberately to develop self-government and to train the Africans in it. This will require an enormous extension of

elementary and secondary education. But side by side with ordinary education there should be a continuous extension of self-government and self-governing institutions.[90]

The goal, both locally and at the center, should be the introduction of democratic self-government "at the earliest possible moment."[91]

Though Woolf's position on these matters did not change significantly over the years he did, later on, become more aware of the objections to his "Western" approach to education and political advancement, and sought to dispel them. To the modern-day reader these objections could be classified under the broad heading "cultural relativism." Woolf's chosen nomenclature was the "anthropological view," the "scientific view," or the "Africanizing attitude."

According to Woolf this view challenged the central liberal assumption about colonial policy: that "the African" was "ultimately ... as capable as the European ... [in] managing his own affairs and of enjoying the blessings of freedom and democracy" and that, consequently, African peoples "no matter how primitive" should be prepared, stage by stage, for eventual self-government.[92] The anthropological view held that it was a mistake to try to turn Africans, or Asians, into Europeans. Rather, native culture and ways of life should be preserved and Western ideas of progress encouraged only so far as they were compatible with the social customs and institutions of the particular "tribe, people or race."[93]

Woolf rejected this view not on theoretical but on practical grounds. The preservation of such customs and institutions "intact like a museum piece" was bound to fail given the "disturbing and disintegrating influences of western or European civilization." The following typically vivid and ironic passage neatly characterizes Woolf's position, and it is worth quoting at length:

> It is extremely doubtful whether such an attempt to isolate and mummify African society in the closely integrated and explosive world of the twentieth century can possibly be successful; it might have been possible to keep savage Africa virgin and savage—if that be a reasonable object of government—if the governments had not let in the copper mining companies, the soap makers, the gold diggers, the cocoa buyers, and the white planters, but those who think that in an Africa which has already been moulded for half a century by the apostles of civilization that Africans can be forced or cajoled into leading the life of noble savages—in the eighteenth century sense—are making the same mistake as those

well-meaning medievalist enthusiasts who think that by exhorting English villagers to use spinning wheels and do poker work an oasis of arts and crafts can be preserved in the desert of the machine age.[94]

Moreover, not only would such a policy fail in its objects, it would also, to the horror of its well-meaning proponents, produce results much the same as those desired by the white supremacists. In the sphere of education, the advocates of the Africanizing approach maintained that education on Western lines was unsuitable for Africans. They favored a policy that gave primacy to elementary education, made vernacular rather than English the main language of instruction, and concentrated on vocational rather than academic training. Higher education would be strictly limited. In Woolf's view such a policy would inevitably condemn the African to an "inferior" and "subordinate" economic, social, and political status—precisely the object of the self-proclaimed white "Herrenvolk" of Kenya, Rhodesia, and South Africa.

Similar dangers awaited the application of a new, highly fashionable, approach to indirect rule. The habit of using native institutions as organs of government had been an important feature of British colonial policy for many years. But in the past this policy had been opportunistic rather than systematic. The new approach was informed by the latest findings in the scientific field of Anthropology. It involved not only the use, if it was sensible to do so, of existing native institutions, but also the "deliberate preservation" of such institutions and the creation of new ones. Woolf had grave reservations about this approach. As with the Africanizing policy in education, it could "very easily become a powerful instrument of policy for those who hold that the African is incapable of democratic self-government of the western type and must be content indefinitely with an inferior political and economic status." Under the guise of an "advanced," "up-to-date," and "scientific" theory, such a policy could be easily used by Europeans to permanently frustrate African aspirations for self-rule. Whether indirect rule was used as an "instrument of progress" or "social fossilization and mummification" depended on the satisfaction of a number of conditions. The native authorities, for example, needed to be accountable to the people and fully integrated with the main organs of government at the center. If these conditions were not met the result would not be self-government but pseudo–self-government.[95]

At this point it should be noted that Woolf's position was not entirely free of ambiguity. As well as advocating education on Western lines he also asserted, "our object in Africa should be to produce good Africans, not tenth rate imitations of fifth-rate Europeans." Similarly he maintained that the purpose of self-government should be to enable Africans "to manage their own affairs in their own way."[96] "Good Africans"? "Own affairs"? "Own way"? Woolf gave no indication as to what he understood by these terms, a serious omission given the extent to which he felt Africa had been disturbed and reshaped by modern Western civilization. He also asserted that the universal value of political freedom could not be realized except by "some form" of democratic government. Yet he later insists that African political institutions "must be fundamentally democratic in the *western sense*."[97]

Nowhere does Woolf suggest that the Africanizing attitude or the anthropological view is empirically unfounded or ethically flawed. Rather, his position was that its implementation would be either impossible or harmful. That Woolf refrained from challenging the relativist position on empirical or ethical grounds is indicative of the fact that he had a sneaking sympathy for it. A subtle appreciation of and admiration for the naturalistic qualities of "traditional societies" is certainly a hallmark of his fictional works *The Village in the Jungle* and *Stories of the East*. Indeed, there is evidence to suggest that his dislike of imperialism was, at root, aesthetic rather than political.

This is a complex question as it concerns Woolf the man—his character, temperament, psychological make-up, and the effect of his experiences upon these things—rather than Woolf the political writer, therefore I do not propose to examine it in detail.[98] In his diaries and letters, and especially in his autobiography, however, there are strong indications that an aesthetic distaste for imperialism began to emerge and take form long before he began to work out a moral and political position. His starkly contrasting descriptions of Sinhalese society and the kind of society kept by the "white ruling caste" are particularly revealing. Woolf saw in the Kandian villages, for example, "a satisfying depth, harmony, beauty," which he felt the Western world "was losing or had lost."[99] He described his dealings with the Europeans in Kandy as "dull and irritating." By way of contrast

> ...everything to do with the Sinhalese seemed to me enchanting. The Kandyans, both the Ratemahatmayas, the feudal chiefs and headmen, and the villagers, were the most charming people I have ever come across. They were typically mountain people, independent, fine mannered, lively, laughing, in their enchanting villages hidden away in the mountains, and isolated, unchanged and unchanging.[100]

This enchantment extended to their religion. Woolf was not a religious man. His characteristic attitude toward it was one of suspicion and contempt. But in Buddhism he found much to admire: simplicity, gentleness, quietude, tolerance, reverence for solitude, and contemplation. Like all religions it was ultimately a dream. But it was, nonetheless, "a civilized and humane dream of considerable beauty."[101]

The beauty of the Sinhalese stemmed from their closeness to nature:

> The people on the verandah of the Jaffna and Hambantota kachcheries... are—or at least were in 1905—nearer than we are to primitive man and there are many nasty things about primitive man. It is not their primitiveness that appeals to me. It is partly their earthiness, their strange mixture of tortuousness and directness, of cunning and stupidity, of cruelty and kindness. They live so close to the jungle... that they retain something of the litheness and beauty of jungle animals. The Sinhalese especially have subtle and supple minds... [and] when you get to know them, you find beneath the surface in almost everyone a profound melancholy and fatalism which I find beautiful and sympathetic—just as something like it pervades the scenery and characters of a Hardy novel.[102]

Nothing provided more of a contrast than the life of the "white sahibs," whose assumed grandeur and constant refrain of "shop, sport, or gossip" Woolf found "strange and disconcerting." Whereas the Sinhalese lived in harmony with their natural environment, the Europeans in Ceylon lived in a social climate that was "unreal" and "theatrical."[103] It was his growing appreciation of the qualities of Sinhalese society allied to an awareness of the disturbing effects of European society, and a disdain for the form that that society took in Ceylon, that first led Woolf to suspect that the "Europeanizing of the non-Europeans" might be a mistake.[104]

CHAPTER 6

Imperialism: Analysis and Assessment

When the Labour Party came to power following its landslide election victory in 1945, it adopted a colonial policy that in broad outline Leonard Woolf had been advocating for more than a generation. Self-government would be progressively granted to all colonial peoples capable of benefiting from it. In practice this meant the gradual dismemberment of the empire, with only a few of the smallest and most vulnerable colonies remaining under Britain's protective shell. Full independence would be granted, however, only when it was deemed that the people concerned were fully able "to stand by themselves in the strenuous conditions of the modern world." The central job of the Colonial Office became to encourage the development of the social, economic, and political infrastructure necessary for the achievement of this goal. Woolf's warning from the 1920s, that immediate independence for native peoples would mean handing over their fate from the exploitative European state to the even more cruel exploitation of irresponsible white men, remained a plank of government policy—except that the "exploitative European state" had now been reformed, at least in Britain, along Fabian lines.

It was in the area of colonial policy, indeed, that the Fabians chalked up some of their biggest successes. Though less celebrated than in the fields of social welfare or education, the speed with and extent to which Fabian ideas permeated the Colonial Office in the 1930s and 1940s was remarkable. In no small part this was due to the research and propaganda work of such bodies as the Labour Party Advisory Committee on Imperial Questions, the

New Fabian Research Bureau Committee for International Affairs (which Woolf chaired), and the Fabian Colonial Bureau (which, with Margaret Cole and Rita Hinden, Woolf helped to found in 1940).[1] The latter body was particularly influential, winning the respect of MPs on both sides of the House of Commons and of many officials within a conservative and initially hostile Colonial Office, with its combination of careful empirical research and constructive policy analysis. The Webbian strategy of "permeation"—of "not making social*ists* but thinking persons socialistic"[2]— won its most visible triumph when the chairman of the Fabian Colonial Bureau, Arthur Creech Jones, became Colonial Secretary in 1946. Such an appointment, widely applauded, would not have been possible had not the Colonial Bureau and the Colonial Office been singing largely from the same hymn-sheet. Like so many Labour MPs of the time, Creech Jones entered Parliament knowing virtually nothing about colonial and international affairs. He later acknowledged that his education in these matters came largely from the Labour and Fabian advisory and research committees, which Woolf either ran or played a leading role in.[3]

Given that so much of what Woolf recommended in the 1920s became British government policy in the 1940s—and the imprint of Woolf's ideas is clearly perceptible in Creech Jones's introduction to the most influential volume on the subject[4]—the label "idealism," so often applied to Woolf's work on international politics, seems singularly inapt. This chapter seeks to systematically assess the extent to which it is fair to characterize Leonard Woolf's thought on imperialism in this way. In order to do this it first of all seeks to ascertain the standing of Woolf's work on imperialism in contemporary opinion.

Contemporary Opinion

Woolf's books on imperialism were published to widespread critical acclaim. A reviewer of *Empire and Commerce in Africa* opined,

> ...the labours Mr Woolf has undertaken...put all students of politics and economics under a great debt. His analysis is thorough, impartial and convincing, and if his book is painful reading—the record of all the Great Powers in Africa is a shameful and a terrible one—the pain is of the kind that moves not to hopelessness but to action.[5]

A further review in a later issue of the journal came to an even more favorable conclusion: "A clearer exposition of the relations between imperialism and finance has never been penned, and the whole book rests on a masterly marshalling of indisputable fact."[6] In the same vein, a reviewer in the *Commonwealth* remarked: "Great credit is due to the Labour Research Department and Mr Woolf for the issue of such a well-balanced and exhaustive work."[7] The founder of the Union of Democratic Control and fellow anti-imperialist, E. D. Morel, described the book as "a piece of historical research of great value... [which should] be widely read and deeply pondered."[8]

One might expect such enthusiasm from such eminently Left or Left-leaning publications. But *Empire and Commerce in Africa* was also enthusiastically greeted by publications without any obvious Left or radical bent. A Canadian academic journal described it as "a contribution to the literature of international relations of cardinal importance... [one] which all students should familiarize themselves and with which statesmen must reckon."[9] The *Nation* considered it "masterly," "thorough," "painstaking," "powerful," "courageous," and "conspicuously honest in the handling of facts."[10] The *Glasgow Herald* declared:

> Whatever one may think of the political standpoint of Mr Woolf, there is no doubt that he has given us a most fascinating book, packed full of information, brilliantly written, and sound alike in statistics and judgement... we question whether the whole field has ever been surveyed more boldly or with more advantage to the reader.[11]

Even the staunchly imperialist *Daily Mail* described it as "a penetrating study which no student of politics or history can afford to leave unread."[12]

No doubt because of their nature—*Economic Imperialism* is essentially a popular condensation of *Empire and Commerce in Africa*, and *Imperialism and Civilization* is a "bringing together" of a number of related themes within a single, easily accessible, conceptual framework—Woolf's subsequent works met with less critical attention. Such attention that they did receive, however, was generally favorable. A reviewer in the *New Statesman* described *Economic Imperialism* as an "extremely useful little book... admirably written... [and one which] ought to be in the hands of everyone who wants to understand the underlying causes of the foreign policy of the Great Powers."[13] A German reviewer similarly concluded: "Any person who wishes to have in a brief compass the facts about imperialism should consult this cheap and masterly summary."[14] Of *Imperialism and Civilization* the weekly newspaper of the Independent Labour Party, the *New Leader*, said: "Few wiser or more thoughtful books have been written on this problem";

a view echoed by an American reviewer who declared: "I know no clearer analysis of the nature of nineteenth century imperialism and its difference from previous movements of conquest than is contained in this little book."[15]

The judgment of contemporary critics was not, however, uniformly favorable. Morel, in the review cited above, criticized Woolf for accepting at face value the explanations given by capitalists and imperialists of their own actions. In Morel's view "sheer individual will-to-power" as much as greed for gain accounted for a good deal of what went on in modern Africa. The *Economist* congratulated Woolf for "brilliantly exposing" the mistakes and iniquities of Empire, but questioned his method of quotation without reference to context. In their view Chamberlain, his clever rationalizations notwithstanding, was essentially no different to Disraeli: both regarded commerce not as an end in itself but as a means to national greatness, power, and prestige.[16] The *Manchester Guardian*, while considering the work "really valuable," nonetheless felt that its author had been arbitrary in his choice of cases. Little had been said on Nigeria, Liberia, Nyasaland, and South Africa, but a great deal, inexplicably, on Abyssinia. Woolf had also been selective in his choice of quotations. Those emphasizing the motivating force of new investment opportunities were clearly significant, but statements and declarations of equal significance could be found emphasizing native welfare.[17] A reviewer for the *TLS* reached the same verdict. The book clearly contained evidence of much research, but it was

> ...always on one side and directed to proving what the author wants to prove.... The facts and figures may be accurate, as far as they go, but only one side is given or emphasized.... Authorities are regarded only so far as they square with preconceived opinions.[18]

Even the *New Statesman* had some critical words to say about the volume. In a lengthy review it praised Woolf for having produced a "very remarkable," "detailed," "thoroughly documented," and "fascinatingly readable" book. It also praised him for his "intense intellectual honesty," which not only prevented him [*pace* the *TLS*] "from distorting the facts to suit his thesis," but saved him "even from any suspicion of having overlooked facts which might be inconvenient." It concluded that it was "far the ablest and most stimulating book that has been written about the subject from the democratic point of view."

But it also criticized the book for being "too black." This was not because the facts were "wrongly or unfairly presented," but because the standpoint from which they were presented was "impossibly Utopian." It was impossible to question on general principles Woolf's moral indictment of European imperialism. But a "purely ethical judgement" of so great an episode seemed "curiously irrelevant": it was "as if one were to write a book showing that Julius Caesar had no moral right to invade Gaul or Britain."

Superior civilizations, the *New Statesman* claimed, would always dominate inferior ones when they came into contact with them. It was wrong therefore to put the new imperialism down to economic motives. Such motives were "for the most part merely camouflage." The key factor was "the development of transport which brought Europe in close contact with great areas over which an immensely lower civilisation prevailed."[19]

Finally, along with criticism of his method and his moral standpoint, more than one skeptical eyebrow was raised at Woolf's prescriptions. The *Nation* questioned his call for a change in men's beliefs and desires, from economic imperialism to humanitarianism. Such a change—"so simple, so reasonable, so commonplace"—was difficult enough for an individual to accomplish let alone a nation. To ask for such a change was to ask for nothing short of a miracle. Indeed, Woolf was in effect requesting "the old change of heart of the evangelist": to be saved the world had to "find salvation."[20]

The *Manchester Guardian* found Woolf's proposals for reform of the mandate system "suggestive" and "valid" but cautiously concluded that the system envisaged was a long way removed from current reality.[21]

Lewis S. Gannett was similarly skeptical. It was true that Article 22 had publicly recognized that the welfare of the backward peoples was a sacred trust of the stronger powers. But so had the Treaty of Berlin 40 years earlier. These pledges had to be taken with a large pinch of salt. "To paint a sweet vista of a League of Nations, led by France and Great Britain, resolutely fighting imperialism," was "arrant romanticizing." While Woolf's analysis was valuable, his suggestions for extending the role of the League, Gannett concluded, were "sheer mush."

From this overview of the critical reception of Woolf's work, three observations can be made. First, nearly all reviewers praised Woolf for his detailed enumeration of the facts. This alone should give us pause before reaching for the label idealist/utopian. Second, several reviewers had reservations, along much the same lines as those generic problems with interpretivism identified in chapter 5, about Woolf's methodology. Third, criticism was leveled at the overtly moral tone of Woolf's approach, and his tendency to marshal facts for the purpose of drawing-up a moral balance sheet. This betrayed an evangelical view of political change: the central task was a mass conversion of hearts and minds, a task made easier by a stark presentation of the errors of the past.

It also, perhaps, contributed to a set of proposals that were a long way removed from current reality. It is in this third sense that the label idealism/utopianism might be said to apply.

I will now analyze Woolf's thought on imperialism in terms of the three key characteristics of idealism/utopianism identified in chapter 2. I will proceed on the basis of the four areas of Woolf's work identified in chapter 5. Without wishing to anticipate the conclusion, it will be seen, in line with some of Woolf's early critics, that the aspect of his thought most vulnerable to the charge of idealism is his overtly "moral" prescription that the mandates system be "honestly" applied.

Theory of Economic Imperialism

The enduring value of a number of aspects of Woolf's theory—his clear definition, his combination of interpretive and empirical analysis, his balance sheet of the costs and benefits of empire—has been reaffirmed by a number of writers in the postwar historical literature.[22] But the cumulative effect of this literature has been to cast doubt on rather than corroborate the validity of Woolf's theory as a whole.

At the most general level, numerous detailed historical studies, based on documentary evidence not available until the 1940s, have demonstrated that what Woolf and others called the "new imperialism" was in fact an immensely complicated historical phenomenon—perhaps more accurately, *set* of phenomena—which cannot be reduced to a single set of factors whether "economic," "political," "strategic," or "technological." The issue is still highly controversial. The weight of opinion suggests, however, that the causal matrix of late nineteenth-century imperialism differed from one colonial Power to another and from one part of the world to another.[23]

The weight of historical opinion also suggests that both "peripheral" and "Eurocentric" explanations have their place in any general theory of why the pace and temper of colonial acquisition changed so suddenly in the final decades of the nineteenth century. The absolute superiority of one approach over the other, on which debate raged in the 1960s and 1970s, is now generally rejected in favor of a hybrid approach, which postulates that crises erupting on the outer reaches of empire, requiring some kind of metropolitan response, interacted in various complex ways with internal socioeconomic and political changes that were simultaneously occurring in the metropolitan heartlands. Woolf's explanation—like Hobson's, Lenin's, and all the classical theorists'—was exclusively Eurocentric. To that extent, in the eyes of modern scholars, it is flawed.[24]

Along with these general points a number of more specific points can be made. Woolf contended that the growth of monopoly—the big factory, the trust, the cartel, the syndicate, the multiple shop—was an important factor in generating, "around the year 1880," the new, "economic" imperialism. It has been shown, however, that this could only have been an important factor in two countries—Germany and the United States—and even in these countries the industrial and financial combines that were undoubtedly rising at this time did not reach the level of dominance suggested by Woolf until the final decade of the century, that is, at least ten years *after* the events that they allegedly caused had begun to occur. The countries with the largest empires—Britain and France—were the countries where the growth of monopoly was least advanced.[25]

Second, it has been shown that references to the commercial benefits of the extension of Empire—especially into the tropical zones—in the speeches of leading statesmen and politicians, only became pronounced in the final years of the century. Fieldhouse has shown that references to these benefits by Ferry and Chamberlain in particular were rationalizations of events that had already taken place or justifications for keeping hold of territories that were already under imperial control and had been acquired for quite different reasons. The issue at stake here was escalating administrative costs, and the feeling that newly acquired colonies were placing an intolerable strain on the public finances. If they were to be retained they must, it was felt, be made to pay. Hence the appeal by imperialists to their untapped economic potential.[26] In this respect Woolf got his primary and secondary factors back to front. Economics, rather than being a primary factor, were a secondary factor in the sense that they were not so much a cause of Empire as a justification for keeping and extending it.

Third, as Etherington has shown, Woolf played fast and loose with chronology. What is flagged as a more or less discreet historical phenomenon—the *new* imperialism—soon becomes indistinguishable, as Woolf's analysis unfolds, from European colonizing activity in the nineteenth century as a whole. Woolf gives at least five dates for the beginning of the new imperialism ranging from 1839 to 1890.[27] Ironically, this implicit recognition that the so-called new imperialism perhaps did not represent such a sharp break with the past as many at the time believed—Woolf included—is one that finds confirmation in one of the most important academic papers in the postwar literature.[28]

There are of course other problems with Woolf's, and similar theories of "economic" or "capitalist" imperialism, which professional historians have unearthed in what has been one of the most intensely excavated fields of historical scholarship of the postwar period. The problems outlined above and in chapter 5 are some of the more salient. It is a striking fact, however, that none of these problems—perhaps with one or two exceptions—have any bearing on the accusation of idealism. Of all the sins Woolf can be accused, having an idealist approach to imperialism is not one of them. He cannot be accused of ignoring facts: Woolf's contribution to theorizing about late nineteenth-century imperialism largely resides in the vast amount of statistical data he brought to bear on the subject. He cannot be accused of ignoring analysis of cause and effect: though his theory has clear normative underpinnings (the desire to discredit both commercialism and imperialism by linking them inextricably together), and though Woolf drew strong moral conclusions from it (that imperialism was an unqualified evil for both the colonized and the colonizers), the theory is a causal theory *par excellence*: it stands or falls not on its normative underpinnings, its normative implications, or its practical usefulness, but on its empirical accuracy, its conceptual clarity, and its internal coherence. Nor can it be said that Woolf was guilty, in Carr's quasi-Marxist sense, of peddling some kind of bourgeois ideology, the hidden but real purpose of which was to promote and defend a particular *status quo*. The whole thrust of Woolf's analysis was that the *status quo* was corrupt and dangerous and needed to be replaced as a matter of first importance.

There are two senses, however, in which the charge of idealism might apply. First, it is worth stating that in this context I am not using the term idealism to mean philosophical idealism or idealist epistemology, that is, the belief that knowledge and "reality" is a construction of mind. Interpretivism, the main method employed by Woolf in the first part of his analysis, is sometimes associated with philosophical idealism. To this extent, Woolf was an idealist. But it would be erroneous to suggest that interpretivism necessarily implies an idealist epistemology. It is possible to maintain that a concrete reality exists external to our consciousness regardless of whether or not we comprehend it, and still employ interpretivism as a means of acquiring at least partial knowledge of it. This is especially true of social reality since a significant part of it is constituted by the thoughts, feelings, and opinions of the appropriate social actors, as well as by more concretely observable phenomena. Ideas and beliefs for Woolf were deep and integral facets of social reality. But it would be wrong to conclude from this that Woolf was an epistemological idealist. For him there was one reality and it could be discovered, in typically Fabian fashion, by detailed examination of the relevant facts. Woolf, notoriously, was not in the habit of changing his mind and almost never did he admit that he might be wrong. Such epistemological confidence is more characteristic of positivism than philosophical idealism.

Second, it might be said that in exaggerating the importance of economic factors Woolf underestimated the role of power: power, that is, in the realist sense of political and military power. The problem with this assertion is that it comes close to suggesting that Woolf was an idealist simply because he was not a realist, that is, he did not accept the narrow—state-centric–politico-strategic—realist definition of power. It should also be pointed out that Woolf did not ignore *realpolitik* and the strategic factor: he emphasized, for example, that it continued to exercise a powerful influence in North Africa long after economic factors had become the dominant motive elsewhere on the continent. In sum therefore, although it is probably true—and key works by Langer and Fieldhouse certainly suggest it is[29]—that the power-political/strategic factor was more important in determining the European division of the African continent in the late nineteenth century than Woolf conceded, it would be unreasonable to cite this as evidence of idealism. Woolf did not ignore the power factor in general; nor did he entirely ignore the influence of the power factor conceived in this particular way.

Mandates

The charge has greater weight, however, when we come to Woolf's thought on mandates. In his bold interpretation of Article 22 can be seen: (a) a tendency to "ignore facts and pay little attention to analysis of cause and effect"; and (b) a tendency to "grossly underestimate the role of power and overestimate the role of law, morality, and public opinion in international politics." Woolf speaks of Article 22 as if President Wilson's views had been shared by the other delegates of the Allied and Associated Powers at Paris. But Article 22 was a product *not* of gentlemanly discussion, but of hard diplomatic bargaining—as was the actual distribution of the mandated territories. The following four points are salient.

First, President Wilson wanted the peace conference to reject the practice of annexation *in principle*. A number of delegations—Australia, New Zealand, Italy, and South Africa—strongly opposed this having already staked out claims for various territories of the German empire in Africa and the Pacific. The Smuts Plan, on which a large part of President Wilson's important second draft of the Covenant was based, did not include what later became known as the "B" and "C" mandates in its proposals for a mandates system. It recommended instead that these territories be dealt with in accordance with the fifth of President Wilson's Fourteen Points, which called for an "open, fair-minded and just settlement of colonial claims." It was only due to the insistence of the president that these territories were eventually included in the system. Article 22 was thus a compromise—a "residual alternative" in the words of one authority—the main elements of which clearly reflected these substantial differences of opinion.[30] The approach to colonialism embodied in the mandates system was, in the words of another authority, "determined by compromises among statesmen of the continental and extra-continental European world, including those who had troubled consciences or troublesome constituents with troubled consciences, those who had unsatisfied colonial ambitions, and those who had peace preserving aspirations."[31]

Second, those Powers desirous of adding to their stock of colonies became, unwittingly, the prisoners of their own rhetoric. In their wartime propaganda the Allies repeatedly contrasted the cruel and exploitative colonial record of the Central Powers with their more humane and altruistic record. They pledged not to engage, at the end of the war, in old-style annexation, making promises about self-government that turned out to be less than entirely sincere. William Rappard, the first secretary of the mandates system, commented:

> [i]t was impossible... once the peace was signed to return to the *status quo ante*. Such a solution could not be adopted for practical reasons, while annexation pure and simple would have been in contradiction with the principles which secured the victory of the Allies.[32]

Third, the compromises made during the negotiations are clearly reflected in the ambiguous language of Article 22 (4), which stipulates that the independence of "A" mandates "can be *provisionally* recognised *subject to the rendering* of administrative advice and assistance." Such ambiguous phrasing provided unreconstructed colonialists with the fog under which they could continue to indulge their imperialist tendencies. But it also provided Wilsonians with a weapon with which to attack them, and a platform in law for the advancement of their radical agenda. In particular, it provided the mandatory Powers with an official defense for doing what they invariably did until the 1940s: cling on to full sovereign control. Woolf was strangely blind to the euphemistic character of these phrases. He nowhere concedes that they were expressly designed to enable the Powers to retain their spheres of influence and continue to assert their hegemonic rights if they wished to do so.[33]

Fourth, the distribution of the mandates was conducted not by the League but by the Supreme Allied Council. Some of the most important territories—Palestine, Iraq, Transjordan, Syria, Lebanon—were shared out along the lines of the unashamedly imperialist Sykes–Picot agreement of 1916. The stipulation that "the wishes of these communities must be a principal consideration in the selection of the Mandatory" was not respected. In substance what took place was a division of the spoils of war in the interests of the victorious European and extra-European colonial Powers.[34]

It might be said that Woolf's recommendations made in 1920 for extending the scope of the system were idealist in the same senses. The mandatory Powers showed no willingness for granting a right of "control and inspection" to the PMC. Even petitions could only be considered by the PMC with the approval of the relevant governing authorities. A proposal of 1926 that petitioners should be granted a hearing before the PMC *de jure* was balked at an early stage of its proceedings.[35] The principle established, *contra* Woolf, was *accountability* not *control*.[36]

More generally, the mandatory Powers showed no inclination to give any outside bodies or Powers a say in the form of government to be applied in the mandataries. They did not express any desire for *all* colonial possessions to be brought within the remit of the system. Nor did they indicate any willingness to give the League Council the power to "revoke" a mandate.

Yet the picture is not entirely clear-cut. The principle of international accountability was conceded with: (a) acceptance of the "sacred trust" idea (Article 22 (1)); (b) the commitment to guarantee certain freedoms and erect safeguards against certain abuses (Article 22 (5)); (c) the obligation to furnish annual reports (Article 22(7)); (d) the creation of the PMC to examine these reports and advise the Council (Article 22 (9)); and (e) the inclusion of the, admittedly vague, "just treatment" clause (Article 23 (b)). In addition, the mandates system, and the sensitive way in which the PMC discharged its duties in particular, contributed to a general climate of opinion, which enabled a much wider-ranging regime to be created under Chapters XI–XIII of the UN Charter. This new regime contained many of the ideas championed by Woolf 25 years earlier. The Trusteeship Council, unlike its predecessor, was given powers of inspection (Article 87). The system was extended to cover potentially all colonial territories (Article 75). Provision was made, in certain circumstances, for direct international administration (Article 81). The "positive" duty to promote the political, economic, social, and educational advancement of colonial peoples was grafted onto the "negative" duty to guarantee certain freedoms (conscience, religion) and prevent certain abuses (the slave trade, the arms and liquor traffic) (cf. Articles 73 and 76 of the Charter, Article 22 (5) of the Covenant). The obligation was established that *all* trust territories, not merely "A" mandates, must be prepared, by their respective "administering authorities" (see Article 81), for self-government

(Article 76 (b)). In addition, the weaker obligation to "develop self-government" was established for *all* dependent territories whether trust territories or not (Article 73 (b)).

Significantly, however, the Trusteeship Council was not given the right to revoke a Trusteeship; or powers of "control" (Woolf never, incidentally, stipulated what he meant by this); nor the right to determine the form of government within a trust territory or its type of constitution.[37] "The Trusteeship System represent[ed], as did its predecessor, the very limited willingness of the colonial Powers to superimpose a formal trusteeship structure upon their administration of dependent areas."[38]

The evidence suggests that although aspects of Woolf's thought were idealistic in the sense of being insufficiently grounded in fact and analysis of cause and effect, and insufficiently cognizant of the factor of power, other aspects were considerably more concrete and astute, even prescient. In general, his belief that absolute sovereignty over colonial territories was no longer tolerable was one that soon became widely accepted. But he vastly overestimated the degree to which the imperial Powers would be prepared to set aside the principle of nonintervention in their colonial relations. For a number of complex reasons the imperial Powers created, for the first time, two international organs, the League Council and the PMC, charged with the responsibility of supervising a carefully and narrowly circumscribed sphere of colonial activity. But, the United States apart, they did not do so with any great enthusiasm. The structures erected had their foundations in a complex configuration of power between, within, and across states, which Woolf signally failed to analyze. Moreover, the nature and purpose of these structures was always highly contested.[39] The revolution in the relationship between the colonizers and the colonized would have to await further shifts in the configuration of power before its scope would become fully realized.

Two further points throw light on the degree to which Woolf's ideas on mandates were utopian. First, it is important to note that the bulk of Woolf's extensive, though repetitive, work on mandates is exhortatory in tone and purpose. His overriding concern was to get the colonial Powers, especially Britain, to take their obligations under Article 22 seriously. He frequently stated that until "translated into hard and unpleasant facts," inevitably involving self-sacrifice, these obligations would remain but "pious aspirations" and "noble gestures."

But Woolf was under no illusions as to the likelihood of success. He recognized from the outset that the behavior of the mandatory Powers was far from consistent with a strict interpretation of their obligations. In 1920 he castigated the British and French governments for behaving as if the "imperialist" Sykes–Picot agreement had greater authority than the League Covenant. A year later he reported on how the British were increasingly acting contrary to the spirit of the Covenant in Kenya Colony. By 1928 he felt compelled to accept that the application of the system had been accompanied by "subterfuge" and "hypocrisy." In effect, the mandates system had become merely a cloak to conceal the "nakedness of the older imperialism."[40]

Yet the fact that he spent so much time and energy trying to cajole the mandatory Powers into acting "honestly" betrays a belief in the practicability of such a goal. Indeed, Woolf's increasing cynicism did not lead to a corresponding decline in his enthusiasm for the mandates system, but rather to further restatements of its core principles and additional proposals for strengthening the executive power of the League Council and the PMC. Woolf's verdict 20 years later is illuminating:

> The mandate system was very far from perfect, but it did for the first time establish some very important principles of colonial policy regarding the rights and interests of African peoples. Though governments and statesmen did a good deal to nullify the principles in practice, they did not succeed entirely and I think it is incontestable that the administration of the mandate territories was on the whole better than that of non-mandated territories (from the African's point of view) in colonial policy and government. It also established the important and to many people inconvenient principle that the exploitation of African territories and peoples by imperial Powers was a matter of interest to the other nations of the world and might even be subjected to international supervision.[41]

This is a fair verdict and one broadly in line with recent historical opinion.[42] It also shows that Woolf's exhortatory and propagandist efforts to promote the principle of international accountability were far from *un*realistic. This is especially so if the radical shift in attitudes that occurred during the interwar period is taken into account. In the 1920s the notion that the chief job of British colonial policy was to systematically promote the social, economic, and political development of dependent peoples, and prepare them for self-government, was a minority view. By the late 1930s it had become much more widely accepted. In an address on changing attitudes to empire to the Royal African Society in 1939, Lord Hailey, distinguished Indian civil servant and successor to Lord Lugard as the British member of the PMC, declared:

> I think we no longer look on overseas possessions in the light of their material advantages to us. We are fully prepared to accept all the humanitarian principles that are embodied in the mandatory system...

It needed men like Lord Hailey to distil the radical ideas of the 1920s into a respectable form. But these ideas were pioneered by radical campaigners such as Woolf. Their stubborn refusal to be defeated by "reality," or to completely fall victim to its near-relation, cynicism, contributed profoundly to the more enlightened chapter in British colonial history, which opened in the 1940s.[43]

Second, there is some evidence to suggest that Woolf's view on the question of the status of the mandated territories was not entirely incorrect. Even as sober an observer as F. S. Northedge does not refute the claim that the so-called "A" mandates were, by virtue of Article 22, already sovereign. Moreover, while Woolf's claim that sovereignty for "B" and "C" mandates resided with the League can be doubted—after all, it was not the League that had distributed the mandates but the Supreme Allied Council, and the League *was*, to a large extent, the mandatory Powers—it can also be doubted whether sovereignty resided unambiguously with the mandatory Powers. The juridical status of the mandates was highly uncertain—a fact largely due to the revolutionary nature of the system the Allied and Associated Powers had created. Certain states, notably South Africa, argued that they "possessed" sovereignty over their mandates. The PMC in response argued that they "exercised" but did not "possess" "sovereign powers."[44] Woolf, of course, did not clear up this matter. But he did play a decisive role in nudging public opinion in the direction of the latter. Claude asserts that "gnawing doubts about the legitimacy of colonialism" within the colonial powers was an important reason for the crucial innovations of the Charter.[45] Woolf was an important gnawer.

White Settlers

The charge of idealism carries little weight with respect to this aspect of Woolf's thought. Much of Woolf's analysis of the white settler problem was both accurate and prescient. He was one of the first commentators to point out that government policy in British East Africa, under pressure from the white minority, was leading, however unintentionally, to even greater exploitation of the indigenous population. He skilfully and unequivocally exposed the democratic pretensions of the white minorities in Kenya, the Rhodesias, and Nyasaland. The "illusion" that these territories were "white man's country" was still widely entertained in Britain up until the Hola Camp incidents in Kenya and Harold Macmillan's subsequent "winds of change" speech. In the 1920s the dream, to use Ronald Robinson's words, of a great white commonwealth in tropical Africa stretching from Salisbury (and perhaps the Cape) to Nairobi, was one entertained not only by "unofficial" colonial opinion but by colonial governors and even some colonial secretaries.[46] Woolf demonstrated on simple demographic lines that it was absurd to regard these colonies as comparable to Australia, Canada, or New Zealand. It was an absurdity that unless checked was bound to lead to violent confrontation. In vigorously putting forward these views Woolf contributed to what Robinson has described as the "spectacular advance of the new moral order" in African colonial relations. For complex practical and political reasons—bureaucratic, parliamentary, and international—this new order, summed up by the notion of "native paramountcy," brought few immediate, tangible benefits to the indigenous population. It did, however, play a vital role in "holding the front" against white separatism until the time came, two decades later, when African (and immigrant Indian) political consciousness was sufficiently developed to hold these separatist ambitions in check. In doing so it prevented the emergence in east-central Africa of another Southern Rhodesia or even another Congo.[47]

It is true that Woolf was prone to exaggeration. In the 1920s, for instance, he argued that a storm of nationalism and conflict was gathering in Africa by comparison with which the Great War was "the mildest of evils."[48] This is undoubtedly Woolf the propagandist getting the better of Woolf the political analyst. But rhetoric aside, it is clearly the case that much of what Woolf predicted with regard to Kenya and Rhodesia did subsequently happen, and what he predicted with regard to South Africa was only narrowly avoided. As Noel Annan has observed, Woolf had been making the winds of change speech ever since the 1920s.[49]

Far from underestimating power in his analysis of the white settler problem, the role of power was central. But Woolf's conception of power was a broad one encompassing "ideational" as well as material and instrumental conceptions. He was impressed by the strength that a group attains when utterly convinced of the rightness of its cause. Such strength could not be reduced to power *over* public opinion, to cite Carr's formulation, since the power resided in the emotional and intellectual force of the ideas themselves rather than the skilful way in which they could be employed. Ideas like liberty and equality possessed a contagious quality that made them immune to control. They always transformed the political consciousness of those infected, with profound consequences for prevailing configurations of social power and communal political organization. As early as the 1920s Woolf noted the rapidity with which African political consciousness was growing. He drew the conclusion that imperialism, at least as it was known in the nineteenth century, was dead. The only question that remained was whether it would be "buried peacefully" or in "blood and ruins."[50]

In Woolf's view the notion that a small band of white men could rule autocratically in countries where the African and even the immigrant Asian population far outnumbered them, was one that simply went against the grain of the modern world: it was one, to use a favorite notion of his, that contradicted "the logic of modern ideas and beliefs."[51] Only through the use of force could true self-determination be resisted and then only temporarily. This was clearly a prescient observation and one rooted not only in his belief in the power of ideas but also in his empirical observation that the new imperialism contained within it the seeds of its own destruction:

> European civilisation, with its ideas of economic competition, energy, practical efficiency, exploitation, patriotism, power and nationalism descended upon Asia and Africa. But with it also carried, involuntarily perhaps, another set of ideas which it had inherited from the French Revolution and the eighteenth-century forerunners of the French Revolution. These were the ideas of democracy, liberty, fraternity, equality, humanitarianism. They have had a profound effect upon the later history of Imperialism, for they have led to the revolt of the subject peoples against it.[52]

This was one of the central conclusions of Woolf's analysis of imperialism. It is true that he failed to point out that the influence was not entirely one way.[53] It is also true that he tended to give the impression that Africans and Asians were passive recipients rather than active seekers of Western ideas.[54] But this does not diminish the clarity and precision with which he expressed what is now an almost axiomatic proposition: that the Asian and African revolt against Western imperialism was itself largely a product of the impact of Western imperialism.

Education and Political Advance of "Backward Peoples"

As the tide of war began to turn in 1942–1943, and attention began to turn to what the postwar world might look like, the BBC Home Service invited Woolf to give a talk on the future of colonial empire.[55] The talk elicited a highly critical response from Elspeth Huxley who accused him of being harsh, especially on the system of indirect rule, and "rather out of date."[56] She disputed Woolf's assessment of the record of the colonial administrations in the field of education and training for self-government. Far from being dismal, the record was a creditable one. In some provinces, Northern Nigeria for example, training in self-government was far advanced. The native authorities were now responsible for the performance of all but a few of the essential functions of government. Even in Kenya, *pace* Woolf, much had been achieved. When the British government took over in East Africa "they saw nothing but wilderness." There were no roads, or railways, or communications of any sort. Economic conditions were primitive. There was no money and no trade but the slave trade. The indigenous peoples were ravaged by disease. Warfare between them was endemic. It would have been impossible to set up schools in these conditions. First the "bare bones of civilization" had to be created: law and order established; the slave trade abolished; disease combated; railways, roads, and bridges built. Only then was it possible to think of education—and before teaching could take place in earnest all the different native languages and dialects had to be "put down on paper," schools had to be built, teachers trained, and so on. Given these facts, and the fact that the war put things back ten years, the record of the British government was far from the disgrace that Leonard Woolf made it out to be.

Huxley made two further points. First, she criticized Woolf for speaking of "Africans" as if they were part of an undifferentiated whole. This widely held but erroneous assumption failed to take into account the vast differences in language, custom, and religion between the many races and countless tribes of Africa. It was as accurate to assume that Africans constituted an undifferentiated whole as it was to assume that Europeans did. Second, such vast differences meant that one tribe would not necessarily agree to be represented politically by a member of another. It followed that "a very high degree of national unity and like-mindedness" needed to be attained before self-government had any chance of succeeding. But in the colonies lack of unity was rife. In Ceylon, for example, the key question was not, as Woolf supposed, whether or not the indigenous people were to be granted self-government, but "whether the Sinhalese majority are going to govern the very big minority of alien Tamils—or rather, how the very different ideas and customs of the Buddhist Sinhalese and Hindu Tamils are going to be reconciled." The key problem was to devise a democratic system that had some chance of working in a country divided on racial and religious lines. In Huxley's view, the striking thing was not so much that these problems had not been solved but that "often a solution barely seems in sight."

Huxley did not call Woolf utopian. It might be contended, however, that an implication of the first and third criticisms is that certain aspects of his thought in this area are utopian in the sense that they pay "insufficient attention to existing facts and to analysis of cause and effect." More precisely, it might be contended that in his desire to accelerate the pace of change he conveniently overlooked some important facts and failed to analyze with sufficient rigor the conditions under which meaningful self-government could be achieved.

These contentions are valid up to a point. Woolf was not an imperial historian. Nor was he a social anthropologist. He did not contribute to the detailed empirical work on African societies and the impact of the European world upon them that began in the 1920s and 1930s. He was, however, one of the first analysts to investigate the general nature of this impact and he kept abreast, through his work as a reviewer, of the latest developments in these new, highly specialized academic fields.

It is probably true that Woolf underestimated the difficulties involved in providing education and establishing the conditions for self-government in many parts of Britain's colonial empire. This is a curious fact given his radical conviction that the history of European penetration in Africa, particularly of private capital, was one of cruelty, exploitation, ruthlessness, and destruction. One would have expected someone with such a bleak view of the colonial past to have a pessimistic view of the tasks facing the reform-minded colonial administrator.

Yet Woolf's view of the colonial past was not an entirely negative one. Along with other radical thinkers he frequently held up West Africa as a model of what could be achieved. In one article, indeed, he speaks of the "relative excellence" of British policy and administration in the region.[57] In a later article he speaks of the conclusive evidence West Africa furnished of the ability of "the African" to "understand" Western civilization and "master the arts of government."[58] Huxley seems to have overlooked the sharp distinction Woolf made between colonial practice in East *vis à vis* West Africa. Her claim that Woolf's account was out of date is based on a skewed reading that equates his position on East Africa with his position on Africa as a whole. Woolf did not believe that the colonial record was uniformly discreditable and, *pace* Huxley, he too felt that big strides had been made in extending self-rule in the West Coast colonies. Similarly, Huxley failed to appreciate that Woolf's reservations about indirect rule were not directed at the idea *per se* but the particular form it had taken in practice.

But Woolf did overlook some important facts, which one would have expected a man of his knowledge and experience to recognize. He did not discuss at any length the lack of social cohesion and the lack of a sense of nationhood in the colonies. He did not seriously consider the possibility of postindependence interethnic violence. Such facts, as Huxley demonstrated, were of critical importance. The only kind of communal violence he predicted was interracial violence resulting from white minority rule. Other comments of a prognostic kind were limited to warnings about the dangers of premature independence: Africans, he repeatedly warned, would be at the mercy of exploitative white men until they had been educated to understand and control the economic and political forces that had been unleashed upon them by the modern world.

Woolf's failure to consider these facts is perhaps one of the things Huxley had in mind when she described him as "rather out of date." By 1943, the year of his BBC talk, the belief that the primary objective of British colonial policy should be to systematically promote the social, economic, and political development of dependent peoples, and prepare them for self-government was, as mentioned, widely accepted. Indeed, this belief had already received official sanction, at least in part, with the passing of the Colonial Development and Welfare Act in 1940. Under this act a substantial sum of public money was, for the first time, made available for colonial development. Although it did not formally commit the British government to complete self-government, the passage of the Act clearly presaged the readiness of the official classes to contemplate an end to colonial rule.[59]

In certain respects, therefore, the debate had moved on. Concern had shifted away from principles and objectives toward procedures, programs, and schedules. But even as late as 1945 Woolf was asking questions such as: "What is to be the political future of these [African] peoples? Is it our intention to keep them permanently in a state of complete tutelage or eventually to give them self-government?"[60] He was, in other words, asking questions that, in the opinion of Huxley and others, had long since been answered.

Yet there is another side to the story. First, Woolf was not *exclusively* concerned with questions of this kind. Most of what he had to say in the 1940s concerned means rather than ends, though his analysis, it is true, tended to be rather general in nature. Second, Woolf was perhaps right in thinking that the battle over objectives had not been completely won. Notwithstanding the arrival on the statute books of a second Colonial Development Act in 1945, and the handing back to its people of the jewel in the imperial crown a few years later, the absence of a clear position on the future of the Empire remained for some time a conspicuous feature of British colonial policy. No official "considered long-term assessment" was ever made of the likely course of decolonization.[61] Winston Churchill, among others, remained steadfastly committed to the continuance of "Britain's heritage."[62] The political and strategic expediency of acquiescing to the demands of the white colonists in east-central Africa continued to hold appeal for Colonial Office ministers and even some secretaries of state.[63] The special problems of this part of the continent led Creech Jones to confess in 1952 to Denis Healey that "Kenya will not be independent in my lifetime or in yours."[64] Many other men in and around the centers of power—not all of them "Tory diehards, aged Milnerites, or eccentric press lords"—remained firmly attached to the integrity of the Empire. Although they were prepared to accept, on balance, the wisdom of granting independence to India, they found it less easy to accept that Uganda or Borneo or Cyprus should go the same way.[65] As late as 1959, Lionel Robbins, hardly a reactionary figure, wrote in a letter to *The Times*:

> The predominance of the white man... must continue for at least another generation. Few black Africans of the central African tribes have yet developed the qualities of leadership or the education and experience to act without control.[66]

Even such a progressively minded observer as David Mitrany did not feel that the days of Empire were so firmly numbered as they now, with hindsight, appear to have been. Reflecting on his failure to consider nationalist pressures in the first edition of *A Working Peace System*, he wrote:

> ...no one felt that "decolonization" was smouldering so near below the surface, least of all in tribal Africa, the Africa which now asserts the liveliest temper and presents the most awkward problems for the international system.[67]

Clearly, Mitrany had not read Woolf on the subject.

These statements illustrate that for well over a decade after the war unconditional acceptance of self-government as the immediate and primary goal of colonial policy was far from a foregone conclusion.

Yet there is a sense in which Woolf did fail to keep pace with the debate in the 1940s, and some of his views, once new and radical, did begin to look rather jaded. P. S. Gupta has noted that Woolf's paternalism toward "backward peoples" long outlived its usefulness and never entirely lost a certain racial tinge.[68] This is a complex issue, especially given that Woolf, along with Barnes, Leys, and others, often went to great lengths to dispel the idea of racial superiority.[69] But it is true that Woolf never entirely kicked the habit of thinking in racial categories—a habit deeply engrained in men of his class and time, and an intrinsic part of the imperial bureaucratic outlook inculcated by the public schools, the ancient universities, and the colonial civil service.[70]

This habit was both cause and effect of Woolf's tendency to stereotype "the African." This, it will be remembered, was the brunt of Huxley's second criticism. Simplistic beliefs about African society were widely shared in Britain during the period. The dichotomy between "civilized" Europe and "primitive" Africa, and the concomitant assumption that all African societies were much the same, enjoyed near-universal acceptance. Woolf was no exception. He made no attempt to examine in detail the social structures, habits, myths, and customs of specific African communities—a remarkable fact given his sophisticated understanding of Ceylonese society. He tended, instead, to see them as uniformly undeveloped and "backward." This amounts to nothing less than acceptance of the easy nineteenth-century assumption that African societies occupied an earlier stage in a simple, linear process of social evolution. The robust rejection of this assumption as conjectural and biased by the new, functionalist, school of Social Anthropology seems to have entirely passed by Woolf.[71]

The evolution of Woolf's nomenclature regarding African peoples and societies provides an interesting footnote to this question. Throughout his writings Woolf unblushingly speaks of "the native" and "the African," although, significantly, the terms are rarely used in his last work, his autobiography, published in the 1960s. Here Woolf generally opts for the less condescending "Africans" and "African peoples." In his earliest works written around 1920, Woolf used the terms "non-adult races," "primitive peoples," even "African savages."[72] Later in the 1920s his preferred term was "backward peoples" and, significantly, he sometimes enclosed it in inverted commas or qualified it with "so called."[73] When he returned to the subject in the 1940s his preferred term was "backward peoples" (with "primitive peoples" coming a close second) but, contrary to what one would expect, it is rarely used in inverted commas or in qualified form, though "the African" is softened in places to "the Africans."[74] I have no explanation for this curious linguistic pattern, except perhaps encroaching old age and the impatience with social niceties that sometimes accompanies it.

Conclusion: Radical Dissent and Fabian Paternalism

While it is true that in certain senses of the word there are clear elements of idealism in Woolf's thought, the above analysis shows that these elements are part of a broader and much more complex whole. Historical research has shown that Woolf's theory of economic imperialism greatly exaggerates the role of the economic factor and underestimates the role of "peripheral" factors. But he could not be accused of "ignoring facts and analysis of cause and effect" nor "underestimating the role of power and overestimating the role of law, morality, and public opinion" nor "espousing universal interests that amount to promotion and defence of a particular *status quo*." The same could be said of his analysis of the white settler problem though this was, in relation to economic imperialism, a subsidiary concern and one, therefore, where one finds less empirical analysis of a detailed kind.

His work on mandates and the political education of backward peoples is more contentious in this regard. Yet even here one finds that the label idealist/ utopian can be applied only at a high Procrustean price. Woolf's work on mandates was for the most part exhortatory and admonitory but it was not bereft of factual analysis nor did it entirely discount the factor of power. Woolf may have underestimated the extent to which the Article 22 was a product of *raison d'état*, and also the extent to which the colonial Powers were prepared to set aside the principle of nonintervention in their colonial relations. As a consequence his exhortation to the mandatory powers that they act "honestly" does seem utopian in the sense implied by the *New Statesman* cited above. The statesmen of Paris did not have the slightest intention of complying with their ambiguous obligations. That is precisely the reason why they kept them ambiguous. In not appreciating this fact Woolf was at least to some extent guilty of mistaking rhetoric for reality. After saying this, however, it must be emphasized that Woolf's assertions about the far-reaching *implications* of the mandates system with respect to sovereignty and international accountability were in the main both accurate and prescient.

The same is true of Woolf's work on the political education of backward peoples. He may have underestimated the difficulties involved in providing such education and establishing the conditions for meaningful self-government in many parts of Britain's colonial empire. He also may have held some simplistic beliefs about "the African" that he clung on to long after they had become outmoded. But his assessment of the current position of native education in the colonies, and their unpreparedness for self-government, was supported by extensive empirical evidence; his constant warnings of the need for such education and preparation if colonial peoples were to have any chance of "standing by themselves," was informed by a highly pessimistic account of the motives of the white man in Africa and an acute appreciation of the extent of his power; and he was probably right to assume in the mid-1940s, *pace* Huxley, that the battle over the ultimate objectives of colonial policy had not yet been completely won.

To label Woolf an unqualified idealist, therefore, is to belittle his contribution to the construction of a more intelligent and realistic policy toward Africa and Asia. Woolf imbibed from the classics and from his mentor at Trinity, the philosopher G. E. Moore, a great love of and faith in reason. But it was not blind faith. It was not based on shallow optimism in abstract human nature. Nor was in a product of the high-Victorian belief in inevitable progress. Rather it was a product of an understanding and appreciation of what the carefully tutored human mind was capable of achieving.

It was this faith in the capacity of the tutored mind, together with dedication to public service, that made Woolf a natural Fabian. It is the paternalism characteristic of early Fabianism, allied with evangelical zeal of English radicalism, which together most aptly characterize his thought on imperialism.

Radical Dissent

By radical dissent I have in mind that tradition of political thought described by A. J. P. Taylor in his masterly *The Troublemakers*.[75] It is united by what it is against more than what it is for. Dissenters are vehemently critical of the orthodoxy of British foreign policy. They oppose the use of force, intervention, and power politics. They are deeply skeptical of the balance of power. They argue that war is little more than the sport of kings in which the vast majority of people have everything to lose but nothing to gain. They see diplomacy as an elitist and undemocratic activity, distant to the needs of ordinary people. They deplore the unprincipled conduct of international affairs and demand greater attention to morality. They view the military as militaristic and advocate either complete (or very substantial) disarmament or the concentration of armaments in the hands of a world authority.

The term "dissent" must be qualified by the term "radical" for three interrelated reasons. First, orthodox foreign policy is not only criticized, but also rejected root and branch. Second, the cause of international ills is located not at the international level but primarily at the domestic level. War and other forms of "dysfunctional" political behavior are seen, at root, as products of corrupt or unjust or obsolete or irrational domestic political structures. Third, the alternative policies prescribed by dissenters represent a fundamental challenge to the *status quo*. Cobden, for example, advocated a policy of pure nonintervention; Morel recommended open diplomacy and democratic control of foreign policy; Wells proposed the abolition of the wasteful system of interstate competition and its replacement by a world society based on rational scientific organization.

Taylor rightly cites Woolf as a prominent dissenting voice in early twentieth-century British history. The purpose of much of Woolf's work was to discredit orthodox or conservative policies and ideas. Throughout his career he arraigned them as variously irrational, myopic, immoral, stupid, deceitful, and impracticable. His tone was sometimes cool and skeptical but more often impassioned, indignant, or sarcastic.

These facets are highly pronounced in Woolf's thought on imperialism. The following three quotations are illustrative.

Woolf compared the open and explicit acquisition of colonies in Africa with the complex and shadowy exercise of imperialism in Asia. Imperialism in Asia was characterized by "tortuous subterfuges of diplomacy":

> We have sovereign States which are no longer States or sovereign, independent rulers who are neither rulers nor independent, a network of "protectorates," "spheres of influence," "perpetual leases," "peaceful penetration," concessions, "diplomatic pressure" or "advice," all of which are designed to conceal the powerful but often clumsy, movements of that Leviathan, the European State, in its encroachments on Asia.[76]

In similar style:

> The European went into Africa... desiring to exploit it and its inhabitants for his own economic advantage, and he rapidly acquired the belief that the power of his State should be used in Africa for his own economic interests. Once this belief was accepted, it destroyed the idea of individual moral responsibility. The State, enthroned in its impersonality and a glamour of patriotism, can always make a wilderness and call it peace, or make a conquest and call it civilization. The right of Europe to civilize became synonymous with the right of Europe to rob or exploit the uncivilized.[77]

Woolf was at his most mischievous when commenting upon the astonishing arrogance of the Victorian imperialists. The following is a typical parody of their views:

> Until very nearly the end of the nineteenth century, Europeans... regarded... [their colonial conquests] with complacent pride as one of the chief blessings and glories of Western civilization. The white race of Europe, they held, was physically, mentally, and morally superior to all other races, and God, with infinite wisdom and goodness, had created it and developed it so it might be ready, during the reign of Queen Victoria of England, to take over and manage the affairs of all other peoples on the earth and teach them to be, in so far as that was possible for natives and heathens, good Europeans and good Christians.[78]

Woolf saved most of his dissenting venom, however, for the white settlers. The following quote is a particularly striking example. In 1912 the complaints of European farmers in British East Africa about shortages of labor prompted the Colonial government to set up a Native Labour Commission. The farmers demanded *inter alia* that native taxation should be increased in order to force the natives to work on their farms. The Commission declared that increasing taxation for the purpose of forcing the natives to work was not justifiable. It then went on, however, to recommend an increase in taxation in order to meet the various other expenses of its recommendations (e.g. the reorganization of native reserves). According to Woolf this amounted to sophistry and cant *par excellence*:

> The casuistry of the Jesuit is famous, but, surely, it was never equalled by this casuistry of imperialism. For the recommendations of the Commission are not intended to promote the interests of the natives; the re-demarcation of the Reserves, etc., are recommended as a means of increasing the labour supply, of promoting the economic interests of the white settler. The Commission admits that increased taxation will "bring natives into the labour market," it holds that increased taxation in order to bring natives into the labour market is unjustifiable; and then it finally recommends increased taxation (which will bring natives into the labour market) not in order to bring them into the market, but in order to pay for other recommendations the whole object of which is to bring natives into the labour market.[79]

There are many such passages in Woolf. Their indignant and sarcastic tone, and their antiestablishment intent, clearly mark Woolf as a dissenter. In face of them, the term "idealist" is decidedly limp and inapposite.

Fabian Paternalism

By "Fabian paternalism" I have in mind that approach to government and political change, central to early Fabianism, which assigned a special role to a highly trained and dedicated technocratic elite. The object of government was to maximize national efficiency and the collective good, and this could only be achieved paternalistically from above, not "naturally" from below. Social progress was seen as broadly analogous to technical progress. Both depended on the careful accumulation and disinterested analysis of "the facts." Through disinterested analysis of physical facts, the scientist was able to discover the causes of physical phenomena, and use this knowledge in order to harness and control them. Through disinterested analysis of social facts, the social scientist would be able to discover the causes of social phenomena and use this knowledge in order to control and shape them.

It was thus to the scientific and social scientific "experts" that the communal good was entrusted. Her special knowledge allied to unswerving commitment to the public good put her at the vanguard of progress. In this way the general material, ethical, and spiritual welfare of society could be advanced without it falling prey to the "factional materialism," to use Beatrice Webb's infamous phrase, of the "average sensual man."[80] In the modern world the expert knew best. Politics in the ideal Fabian state would, to quote Beatrice and Sidney Webb, consist of little more than a "stream of reports" from independent and disinterested experts. The authoritativeness of these reports and the public spiritedness of their authors were not matters the Webbs saw any reason to question.[81]

An example of Fabian paternalism is the "paternal imperialism" of George Bernard Shaw described in chapter 3. Shaw did not see imperialism as iniquitous *per se*. Imperialism could be either iniquitous or "sound." If it brought the ideas, values, habits, and institutions of "higher" civilizations to those parts of the world dominated by "lower" civilizations, it was perfectly justified. Advanced persons such as Fabians would judge.

A further hallmark of Fabian paternalism was belief in gradual change. This had both a positive and a normative dimension. On the one hand, gradual change would inevitably occur if society chose to be governed by reason and "the facts" rather than by prejudice and opinion. Hence the Fabian motto, coined by Sidney Webb, "the inevitability of gradualness." On the other hand, change was best—more permanent, more just, more beneficial—if gradual. Only through gradual change could the evils of social turmoil, social injustice, and political reaction be avoided.

Fabian paternalism, in substance and in tone, is strongly evident in Woolf's thought on mandates and the political advancement of backward peoples. For the most part, as we have seen, Woolf wrote about African peoples as if they occupied a much lower level of civilization and were helpless in the face of the superior civilization of the West. As mentioned, he fully subscribed to the presumption of Article 22 that, unassisted, they would not be able to "stand by themselves under the strenuous conditions of the modern world." The native was "no match" for the European and was unable to cope with the European's economic and political system. It was consequently the job of the colonial authorities to "educate the people so that they may gradually take their place as free men both in the economic system and in the government of their country."[82] Accordingly:

> The end in view is an African population, with its own institutions and civilization, capable of making the most economic use of its land, able to

understand Western civilization and control the forces it has let loose on the world, governing itself through organs of government appropriate to its traditions and environment.[83]

The implication of this is clear: it was the job, indeed duty, of Europeans—with the aid of expert bodies such as League Committee for Intellectual Co-operation—to work out the general lines of economic and political development in Africa.

The paternalism of the following passage, written as late as 1943, is particularly striking. Responding to the "extreme left" opinion that full independence should be granted immediately, Woolf stated:

> In my opinion to do that would be disastrous—disastrous for the Africans. Most of them are ignorant and uneducated, terribly poor, ravaged by tropical diseases. To think that they are capable of suddenly taking over the government of their countries under the political and economic conditions of the modern world is just nonsense. They would fall victims to the first private profiteers and exploiters and the first imperialist government who crossed their path.
>
> No, the right way to deal with our African colonies... is to begin at once to educate the Africans to govern themselves.[84]

African peoples needed the paternal guidance of enlightened Europeans if they were to achieve real independence. They needed to be "gradually trained" in democracy and "the art of self-government." Only with such guidance would they ever be capable of "standing by themselves."

CHAPTER 7

Liberal Internationalism, Anticapitalism, and Consumers' Co-operation: Toward a Nonstate, Nonmarket Approach to International Economic Organization

Unlike a number of other progressive writers of the time, most prominently G. D. H. Cole, J. A. Hobson, and Maynard Keynes, Woolf did not have a grounding in economics. At St. Paul's School he was force-fed Latin and Greek until he was turned, to use his own phrase into a "classical pâté de foie gras."[1] He continued his classical education at Trinity, and there is no evidence to suggest he ever formally studied economic questions, or political ones for that matter. The Apostles, the focal point of Woolf's social and intellectual life at Cambridge (he cultivated a lofty disdain for such mundane things as the curriculum, examinations, and essays for his tutor), rarely discussed social or economic issues—at least not directly. Art, culture, aesthetics, ethics, conduct were their line of country. Discussions tended to be highly abstract and unconcerned with socioeconomic or political context. The central Apostolic figure of the time and Woolf's mentor, G. E. Moore, preached the aesthetic doctrine of intrinsic truth and beauty, a doctrine that his gifted protégés—Keynes, Strachey, Foster, and Woolf among them—fully absorbed and, indeed, never completely abandoned.[2]

Woolf's introduction to economics, as with other social subjects, was practical. On appointment as Assistant Government Agent in the Hambantota district of Ceylon, he at once set himself the task of raising the prosperity of its people, reducing poverty and disease, and making his district "the best administered in the island."[3] In particular he set about increasing the prosperity of the peasant farmers of the district, nearly all of whom relied on the unproductive and economically and environmentally shortsighted "chena" method of slash and burn; improving the efficiency of the government-owned salt industry; improving the safety of the seasonal activity of pearl diving; and ensuring that the pearl trade was regulated fairly and efficiently. In the performance of these tasks, and in the overarching task of making his district the best administered in Ceylon, he later said: "I do not think that I deceive or flatter myself when I say that I succeeded."[4]

On leaving Ceylon, Woolf's education in practical economics continued with his work in the London East End district of Hoxton for the Women's Co-operative Guild, and by way of contrast, in his stewardship of the newly founded Hogarth Press. Woolf originally conceived the Press not as a business venture but as a hobby for his wife. In 1915 Virginia suffered her first mental breakdown. Immersion in a practical activity like printing and publishing, Woolf felt, could have therapeutic value, and might succeed in putting her more firmly on the road to recovery than the simple rest prescribed by her physicians. In spite of his avowed amateurism, and the stringent criteria he and Virginia applied in drawing up their lists, the press soon became a considerable commercial success—a testimony both to Woolf's artistic judgment and his business acumen.

Woolf's induction to the *discipline* of Economics came with his research work on the Co-operative Movement and in particular on the relationship between consumer Co-operation and the structure of industry.[5] It is doubtful, however, whether he spent much time mugging up on economic theory. He was, indeed, rather skeptical of what he called "Theoretic Economics." This and other "academic" subjects, for example, were excluded from his syllabus for a "Co-operative College" in preference for practical topics such as "Decasualisation," "The Minimum Wage," "Management in Industry," and "Trade Unionism."[6] There is no evidence to suggest that Woolf ever seriously studied Smith, Ricardo, Mill, or Marshall. Most of Woolf's academic training in Economics came from the writings of fellow Fabians and radicals—the Webbs, Angell, Cole, Hobson, and Keynes.

If one includes Woolf's writings on economic imperialism, his output on economic issues is extensive. As well as four books, he wrote more than a dozen pamphlets and many articles. To these must be added a number of works not specifically concerned with economics but in which the economic factor, in true Fabian fashion, is never far from the surface. In his three-volume study of "communal psychology," for example, Woolf gave a great deal of weight to the influence of economic factors in the development of communal ideas about democracy, liberty, and the state. As we observed in chapter 3, economic and technological factors were fundamental to Woolf's theory of international government.

Along with his two books on economic imperialism Woolf's main writings on economic issues are: *Co-operation and the Future of Industry*, first published in 1919; *Socialism and Co-operation*, published in 1921; his only single-authored Fabian Tract (though he edited and/or wrote introductions for many others) *International Co-operative Trade*, published in 1922; the Labour Party pamphlet *International Economic Organization*, published in 1923; and his long essay on the relationship between Co-operation and peace, "The Way of Peace," published in 1928.

The 1920s was, therefore, a period of considerable activity on the economic front particularly on the issue of Co-operation. Indeed, despite the "massive inattention," in Margaret Cole's words, which greeted his books on Co-operation, Woolf acquired a reputation as one of its leading theorists.[7] But it is precisely this inattention that explains why Woolf wrote so little on the subject after this initial period of activity. Even the economic crisis of 1929 failed to rekindle Woolf's enthusiasm for things economic, and by the time the crisis had abated in the mid-1930s, Woolf's attention had turned to an even darker and more pressing set of world problems.

The main purpose of this chapter is to explicate Woolf's thought on international economic organization, and assess the extent to which it can be deemed idealist/utopian. In doing so it gives an account of: (a) the legacy of liberal internationalism in Woolf's thought; (b) his basic understanding and critique of capitalism; and (c) his "democratic" Co-operative alternative. In the process it provides an insight into how one, fairly typical, Fabian thinker viewed such politically contentious early to mid–twentieth-century issues as free trade, protectionism, and international economic planning.

Co-operation, Democracy, and Peace

Woolf's basic thesis was that capitalism was based on "the psychology of competition," which generated and intensified hostility among nations and generated a zero-sum view of the world. The prevalence of imperialism and protectionism were evidence of this. Its logical conclusion was war.

Woolf rejected, however, most of the radical solutions put forward by liberals and socialists alike. He rejected the orthodox liberal solution, free trade, in much the same terms that Carr was later to do. Free trade engendered a form of social Darwinism where the strong prospered and the weak went to the wall. It was also an impracticable doctrine given the tendency of modern capitalism toward monopoly and the instrumentalist way in which capitalists viewed and used the state. Under such conditions trade could never be truly free.

He rejected socialist solutions as embodied in syndicalism and guild socialism. In the final analysis, Woolf claimed, these solutions amounted to nothing more than the substitution of one kind of producer control for another. There was no reason to think that an oligopoly of socialist producers would not be just as inclined to fleece the consumer as an oligopoly of capitalist producers. Producer control of the economy would inevitably lead to the exploitation of the consumer since producer control *in any of its forms* was ultimately based on the psychology of competition or, as he frequently called it, the "psychology of capitalism." Producers would always seek to maximize their own interests, both against other producers, and against the community of consumers. They had no interest in the welfare of the whole.

But Woolf also rejected the state socialist solution, then the dominant model of socialism on the British Left, and along with it the municipal socialist solution as championed by his mentor Sidney Webb. For Woolf, the state both at the national and at the municipal level was essentially a political institution. It could not be assumed that it would always and everywhere be in tune with the economic interests of the people. Nor could it be assumed that it would be an effective economic manager. Periodic elections ensured a degree of popular control. But in elections many issues were at stake, not just the economic needs and desires of the people. There was always a danger, as a result, that these needs and desires would be pushed to one side or ignored.[8]

In this connection it is also significant that even as early as the 1920s Woolf feared the rising power of the state, whether in its capitalist or its socialist form. He argued that the all-powerful modern state could easily succumb to tyranny. At the time Woolf was a lonely voice in opposing the growing power of the state. Many socialists saw it as a social and economic panacea. The notion of an omniscient and beneficent state is strongly implicit in the founding text of Fabianism, *Fabian Essays in Socialism*.[9] As Rodney Barker has commented, "the State, with a capital 'S,' strides through [its] pages like a romantic hero, regulating and controlling, and replacing the anarchy of individualism with the good sense of collective social responsibility."[10] It is due to the prevalence of the state, so conceived, in early Fabian writings that Fabian socialism soon became synonymous with state socialism. It was not until the late Edwardian period that mavericks such as H. G. Wells and G. D. H. Cole began to question the efficiency and fairness of the Fabian state, hitherto taken for granted. Rather than promote the welfare of the whole it was conceivable that it could be partial, promoting the interests of a select group, or even self-interested. It was also conceivable that it might try to govern too much, thus making it oppressive. The huge growth in the centralization and power of the state during the First World War planted a few seeds of doubt in the minds of the Webbs. Their answer, however, was simply to call for an even stricter self-denying ordinance on the part of any future governing Fabian elite, to govern well in a disciplined, moral, and selfless fashion.[11] Woolf's voice was one of a few that cautioned against such a simple solution. There were deep structural and psychological reasons why too much faith should not be placed even in the most disciplined of the Fabian states.

The Legacy of Liberal Internationalism

Woolf's thought on international economic organization was largely a product of two distinct bodies of thought: liberal internationalism and consumers' Co-operation. One of the most important points to note about this is that whereas the former is a doctrine primarily concerned with the international context, especially the questions of international peace and prosperity, the latter was a doctrine almost exclusively concerned with the domestic context, especially the British context, though the model was later widely exported. In a sense Woolf was bringing together two bodies of thought in order to build a democratic and pacific alternative to power politics.

On the surface, however, the two bodies of thought seem diametrically opposed. Was it not the instability and inequity of free trade and *laissez faire* that the Co-operative Movement sought to supplant? Did not Co-operation involve the regulation and control of the very forces that liberal internationalists saw as the surest guarantee of liberty and peace?

By liberal internationalism I mean that body of thought, developed by Cobden and the Manchester School, which maintained that free trade was the key to a prosperous and peaceful world. G. W. Shepherd has described the central tenets of liberal internationalism succinctly:

> The free traders always regarded the world as a unity bound together by the mutual interdependence of national economies. They shunned the burden of armaments and sought to settle international disputes by

arbitration and conciliation, and they believed peace would be the natural result of ever increasing prosperity arising from the mutual advantage accruing from increasing trade and intercourse.[12]

Woolf shared these tenets but gave them negative rather than positive expression. He did not so much argue in favor of free trade as against its opposite, protection. This is explained partly by his socialist convictions, and partly by the economic and political context of the time: Europe was still struggling to recover from the destruction and economic dislocation of the First World War and many countries were still suffering from extreme economic hardship. The working class bore the brunt of this hardship through unemployment. Import protection was called for in many countries in order to get domestic production going again. Woolf, however, was strongly opposed to such a move because he felt that protection never benefited the working class in any lasting and substantial way.[13]

But protectionism not only conflicted with the *interests* of labor, it also conflicted with its general social and international *aims*. The general social aim was the maintenance and improvement of the standard of life of the "non-capitalist classes." This entailed a redistribution of national income, an increase in wage rates, a decrease in the working week, protection against unemployment, and "increased efficiency in the organization and management of industry." The general international aim was "peace and co-operation between nations," involving "the development of international co-operation in the League of Nations."[14]

A policy of protection, Woolf claimed, had the following effects: an increase in the profits of the protected industry; a rise in price of the protected good or commodity on the home market; and the encouragement of "capitalist rings, combinations, and trusts."[15] All these things, he claimed, were contrary to the interests of labor and, indeed, *all* consumers (of which labor constituted the majority). Increased wages would not inevitably spring from increased profits even in cases where workers were well organized: experience proved that "the major part of the tribute levied upon the consumer goes to the small group of capitalists in the protected industry."[16] A rise in prices or scarcity always hit the poorest classes hardest. In addition, selective protection tended to give way to generalized protection since governments found it difficult to deny to one sector of the economy that which it had granted to another. Powerful interests, according to Woolf, would inevitably compel the government to extend its policy, leading to the weakening of the worker *vis á vis* the capitalist, and a general increase in income inequality.

In accordance with the teachings of classical political economy, Woolf also contended that protection would lead to general impoverishment. This was so because even in the event of increased profits, wages, and employment, such increases would not be "equivalent to the quantity of goods kept out."[17] Higher prices would depress demand and eventually lead to unemployment. In addition, higher prices in one sector would raise costs and thus prices in another, this effect multiplying in cases where protection was the norm. The outcome would be a general reduction in purchasing power and thus a general fall in the standard of living.

The only thing that labor should do with regard to foreign competition was to make sure that the cheapness of foreign goods was not due to sweating. If it *was*, the correct course of action would be to get international agreement on labor legislation aimed at its abolition. The "indiscriminate" way in which states usually dealt with the problem almost always lead to "indiscriminate" retaliation.

The effect of protection on the international aims of labor was similarly dire. According to Woolf, protection was both a product and a cause of international hostility. It was based on the assumption that international trade was a zero-sum game, an assumption that the *practice* of protection merely confirmed:

> The policy of Protection is... based upon a theory of the divergence of interests among nations and upon international hostility; it actually, by a vicious circle, creates this divergence of interests and hostility.[18]

Protectionism resulted in a kind of economic warfare that, under modern conditions, had become "one of the most powerful engines of international enmity." In parallel with Cobden's contentions about the landed aristocracy, and Hobson's about financiers, Woolf further contended that the problem was fuelled by a small but powerful group of capitalists who alone stood to profit.

Hostility was particularly fierce when protection was discriminatory:

> For such "hostile discrimination" naturally channels the hostility bred by tariffs into a particular hostility between two nations, and the tariff becomes an economic weapon to be used in and to embitter and sometimes even to create political differences and disputes. Bad as a tariff is, its evil is greatly increased if it allows of differential duties and discrimination between different nations.[19]

Nor was the need to safeguard "key industries" a credible defense. According to this view, industries producing goods essential to the war-fighting potential of the nation needed to be protected during peacetime in order to avoid reliance on foreign sources of supply during war. In Woolf's view the relevance of this argument, like the doctrine of contraband in war, had been long lost. Its central assumption, that it was possible to distinguish in the abstract between "strategic" and "non-strategic" goods, was no longer tenable. It was no longer possible to say with any confidence which items would be essential and which nonessential to the waging of war. In principle practically all items were "essential." Hence practically all industries were "key industries." The logic of the key industries argument was, therefore, the logic of self-sufficiency and self-containment. Such a policy undermined rather than improved national safety since it generated a psychological environment of constant fear and preparation for war.

In any event such a policy was impracticable given the wide range of goods that could under no circumstances be produced at home. Bearing these factors in mind, the best policy was diversification of supply.[20] The only justification for impeding the flow or raising the price of foreign goods was in order to safeguard against accidents and prevent the spread of diseases.[21]

The arguments against domestic protection also applied to imperial preference—in fact even more so:

> ...even in the limited area of the home territory anything like a general tariff must prove disastrous to the interests of Labour. Still more disastrous would be an attempt to draw up a tariff to satisfy all the different interests of the Empire which includes not only the highly industrialised home territory but Australia, Canada, India, South Africa, and immense tropical possessions.[22]

Furthermore, due to the links between protectionism and imperialism, and the role of imperialism in causing war, the international implications of imperial preference were even more fearful than the domestic implications. The imperial rivalry of the late nineteenth century was largely fomented by the mutual fear that colonial possessions would be used as exclusive fields of economic exploitation. Every player in the colonial game feared being dealt a mortal economic blow. This fear was a major cause of the war. In light of these facts Woolf concluded that imperial preference was "completely incompatible with any kind of lasting peace." He recommended that all states adopt without hesitation the Open Door policy.[23]

Nowhere does Woolf advocate free trade in name. But in his rejection of protectionism, notwithstanding the working-class spin he put on it, the imprint of liberal internationalism is clear. He rejected the inherently conflictual, zero-sum, world of the protectionists, and implicit in his argument is the notion that the world, or at least a large part of it,[24] is in some sense unified by being "bound together by the mutual interdependence of national economies." Protection did not increase the wealth of any nation but brought conflict upon them. In places Woolf even suggests that international trade is in fact a positive-sum game:

> The form of society developed from the industrial revolution requires for its continued existence, both politically and economically, an international framework. Nations and peoples are so intimately knit together, one part of the world is so seriously dependent upon all other parts, that, in actual fact, one nation's loss is practically always every other nations loss, and one nation's gain every other nation's gain.[25]

As well as looking back to Cobden, Woolf here looks forward to Brandt.[26] He opposed the exploitation of colonial labor not only on moral grounds but also on economic grounds. Exploitation was not only bad for the exploited but also bad for the exploiters. He rejected what Lenin called the "labour aristocracy." Cheap colonial labor, he asserted, was "directly contrary to the interests of Labour, of industry, and of the world." He continued:

> It is to Labour's interest in Europe that the standard of living in Africa and Asia should be raised to the highest possible point in order that increased demand and consumption in those parts may encourage an exchange of commodities between Europe and Asia and Africa. The low wages of the African negro and the system by which he is forced to work for them make the fortune of the individual exploiter; they strike a blow at Labour in Europe by consolidating the power of capital and by restricting the possible market for European manufacturers and the free exchange of commodities throughout the world.[27]

Anticapitalism

At this point, however, Woolf parted company with Cobden and his twentieth-century free trade brethren since by "free exchange of commodities" he did not have in mind free exchange between *private* enterprises but simply the absence of state interference. Woolf was unbending in his rejection of all capitalist methods and institutions—indeed he both shared and helped to entrench the deep anticapitalist assumptions that until recently have dominated the thinking of the British Left.

Woolf's understanding of capitalism was unorthodox. In some respects he drew from the Marxist tradition in seeing capitalism as inherently exploitative. But he did not adopt Marx's definition of capitalism as a system of generalized commodity production in which labor itself is a commodity. Nor did he see capitalism in terms of the perfect competition model of classical economics—though he did share with Adam Smith the view that the interests of the consumer were paramount. Like Smith, Woolf was highly critical of economic systems that put the interest of the producer above the interest of the consumer. He endorsed Smith's claim that "consumption is the sole end and purpose of all production."[28] He would, however, have qualified the word "production" with the word "industrial." By "industrial production" Woolf meant efficient, mass, factory production of the basic commodities of life. The things that made life worth living—art, literature, science, learning, drama, recreations—ought not, Woolf believed, be produced by "industry" since the value of these things derived from their production as well as their consumption. Industry was necessary because it was efficient, but the good things in life tended to be corrupted once mass produced and/or commercialized.[29] To this extent, a technical account of the character of capitalism inherited from Marx was enjoined in Woolf's thought with a philosophical and aesthetic critique inherited from Robert Owen, John Ruskin, and William Morris.

Woolf did not systematically set out his understanding of capitalism. It contains, however, four particularly important features.

First, in sharp contrast to the classical model of perfect competition, Woolf understood capitalism in terms of monopoly, oligopoly, combination, and price rigging. Through these methods the capitalist, whether financier, manufacturer, wholesaler, or retailer, sought to drive up prices, the burden of which always fell on the consumer.[30] Second, following Robert Owen, capitalism meant production for profit rather than production for use. Under capitalism things were produced because the producer felt he could make a profit out of them rather than because they were individually or socially useful:

> Capitalist industry does not... produce things because they are beautiful, good, or useful, but because someone thinks that he will be able to induce other people to buy them and that thereby he will make a profit for himself.[31]

Profit was not the vital ingredient in the efficient working of an economy, as the classical economists maintained, but a "toll upon society."[32] Underlying this view is the assumption that the market is an inadequate mechanism for balancing supply and demand. According to Woolf, the question the capitalist asked was not "How can I best make things that people want to buy?" but "How can I best induce people to buy the things I produce at the highest price?" Contrary to the assumption of perfect competition that all participants had complete knowledge of the price, quality, and quantity of goods for sale, Woolf contended that under capitalism it was in the interests of all participants to keep all other participants as much in the dark as possible.[33]

Third, according to Woolf capitalism was an oligarchic system. Under capitalism sovereignty resided in the producer not the consumer and, therefore, with the few not the many. Over the last 100 years various aspects of social life had been democratized, but industry remained untouched. The producer still decided "what is to be made; how, where, and when" and consumers and workers had little if any influence on their decisions.[34]

Finally, as well as a system, capitalism was a way of thinking, a set of ideas and beliefs consciously or unconsciously held, a "psychology." Accordingly, "capitalist psychology" meant the attitude that one should pursue one's own interest regardless of the interest of the community. This pursuit of self-interest was most obviously manifested in the pursuit of profit but it was also evident in the struggle for wages:

> The capitalist, in pursuit of his own profits, will defraud the State, ruin his fellow capitalist, and join with his fellow capitalist to exploit the worker and the consumer, while the worker, in his struggle for wages, again and again finds that in order to protect his own interests he has to sacrifice those of his fellow workers or of the whole community.[35]

Indeed it affected (or "contaminated" as Woolf sometimes put it) many aspects of society from art and literature to the professions to trade unionism and even socialism itself. It might be said that by "capitalist psychology" Woolf essentially meant egotism: self-gain, self-promotion, self-interest, and the disregard of the welfare of the community.

Woolf's critique of capitalism was wide-ranging. First, and most basic, capitalism was exploitative. Workers were exploited as capitalists constantly strove to drive down wages in order to increase profits. They were assisted in this task by the fact that the supply of labor almost always exceeded demand.[36] The consumer was exploited through commonplace practices of deception—misleading the consumer being a perfectly legitimate means of making a profit—and price rigging. *Laissez faire* meant merely the liberty to "snatch according to the rules of the game from the community of fellow men."[37]

The art of the capitalist was buying cheap and selling dear, something he showed no compunction in doing even in times of hardship, often taking advantage of scarcity and consumer ignorance of market conditions in the process. In this he was greatly assisted by modern advertising, which enabled him to further hoodwink consumers into buying things they did not need.[38] Woolf shared the general contempt of the Left for private capital and profit-making that the First World War did much to aggravate. It was widely believed that the mutual hostility and fear that led to the outbreak of hostilities had been deliberately whipped-up by private armaments manufacturers. In addition, the shortages that the war generated—especially the food shortages resulting from the German submarine campaign—gave rise to the notion of the "profiteer." It became widely believed that a small number of traders, manufacturers, and capitalists were making enormous profits from the war and were engaged in a fiendish conspiracy to keep it going. Allied with the success of government in controlling virtually all aspects of the economy, the equation of profit-making with "profiteering" that arose from this conjunction of events did much to undermine the legitimacy of the free-market conception of economic organization that dominated before 1914. Individualism, competition, and the pursuit of profit, came to be seen, especially among working men, as intolerable and iniquitous.[39]

Second, capitalism was undemocratic. Capitalists wielded enormous power in the political system. As well as controlling production, capitalists and "a small group of property owners" effectively controlled the state—a control strengthened by the near-monopoly capitalists had over the media, and by the readiness of the law, the army, and the police to defend property rights and the "capitalist weapon of starvation" against the worker.[40] Here Woolf's analysis is decidedly Leninist except for the fact he believed that socialists, too, were capable of capturing the state. They too, he believed, were capable of ruling the state in the special interest of the few rather than the general interest of the many. Already by 1921 he had reached this conclusion with respect to the Soviet Union.[41]

Third, capitalism was inefficient. This was confirmed by the existence of "chronic unemployment in one part of the world and acute shortage elsewhere of the commodities for which the unemployed cannot find purchasers."[42] Capitalist psychology led to the failure to differentiate between what was socially valuable and what was not: whether sewers or champagne were produced was of no great moment to the capitalist since all that mattered was profit. Capitalist psychology also begot the "ca'canny worker" who did as little as he could get away with knowing that the fruits of his labor went not to himself but to his boss.[43]

A further aspect of the inefficiency of capitalism was its constant output of "shoddy, ugly, and useless" goods. It is here that the aesthetic dimension to Woolf's analysis is most pronounced. Like Ruskin he was appalled by the "unintelligent repetition" and "ceaseless mechanical or laborious operations" that characterized life in the modern factory. Like Morris he felt that capitalism had "debauched and debased our taste for material commodities." One of the central tasks of socialism, Woolf held, was to rid society of its materialism and crass commercialism. Nowhere does he unambiguously state, however, that these evils are exclusively the product of capitalism. The fact that he felt socialism could produce like evils suggests that his target was not capitalism but industrialism. The problem is much complicated, however, by Woolf's eccentric definition of capitalism and, in particular, his insistence that socialists too were not immune to capitalist psychology.[44]

Finally, in addition to being exploitative, undemocratic, and inefficient, capitalism was bellicose. The egotism of capitalist psychology produced a combative perception of international economic relations. Trade became "a struggle for existence or profits." This struggle "gave a new depth and colour to men's fear of other countries and the love of their own." Capitalist psychology thus both intensified international rivalry and was reinforced by contact with it.[45]

Capitalism as Scapegoat

There are a number of problems with Woolf's understanding of capitalism and his critique of it. These can perhaps best be analyzed by looking at the label anticapitalist, which suggests an element of dogmatism on Woolf's part.

Woolf can be described as an anticapitalist for two reasons. First, he makes no attempt to consider sympathetically the liberal case for capitalism. He focuses his attention entirely on its weaknesses without any consideration of its strengths. In saying that capitalists think only of profits and shareholders, for example, he dismisses too casually the mechanism by which the market enables demand to be balanced with supply. He does in fact admit that capitalists may occasionally have to think of consumers and workers since they need to produce things that the former will buy and offer wages that the latter will work for. But he then dismisses this as a trifling fact. For the classical economist, however, it is a fact of immense importance. In automatically requiring the producer to think of a wide range of such factors the market enables resources to be allocated efficiently thus precluding the necessity of employing a large and expensive body of experts to do the job administratively.[46]

Woolf also too readily accepts that the dynamism generated by capitalism is wasted in the mass production of shoddy, useless goods. There may be something in this—it has been a consistent line of critique since the time of Morris and Ruskin—but in not considering the ostensible benefits of capitalist dynamism—constant process and product innovation, the extension of consumer choice, the maximization of factor output and aggregate incomes—Woolf is at best providing only a partial picture. Similarly, he sometimes too readily assumes that economic change has generally been for the worse—for example in his request that

> the civilised capitalist ought somehow to explain the undoubted fact that all the great scientific discoveries of the last 100 years have contributed more to the sum of human misery than to the sum of human happiness.

Or in his assertion that

> If without sentimentality or prejudice we were to estimate in terms of human happiness and social progress the chief results of all industrial inventions of the eighteenth and nineteenth centuries we should be compelled to say that they are summed up in the difference between the slums of Manchester and the slums of Constantinople and in the difference between the battle fields of the Somme or Flanders and the battlefield of Waterloo.[47]

Again, there may be something in this, but it is, at best, a sketchy picture.

In addition, Woolf uncritically assumes that monopoly and oligopoly are unavoidable features of capitalism. As well as not being entirely consistent with his assertions about "unfettered capitalism" and capitalism being a "competitive system,"[48] such an assumption fails to take account of the ability of the state to dismantle monopolies as had already been powerfully demonstrated in the United States with President Theodore Roosevelt's "trust-busting" legislation.

Second, by defining capitalism in such a broad way—in terms of competitive psychology as well as in terms of monopoly, private profit, and oligarchy—Woolf was able to associate capitalism with a wide range of domestic and international ills. This suited his propagandist purpose. It enabled him to blame capitalism for bellicosity and even some of the defects of socialism as well as for the standard ills of social injustice and working-class poverty. His conception of capitalism was, therefore, a weapon at least in part fashioned to bring capitalism down. But in equating capitalism in effect with egotism, Woolf was blaming it for evils that, even according to the most extreme interpretations, considerably predate the emergence of capitalism as a distinct mode of economic organization. One can only conclude that Woolf's capitalism is something of a scapegoat.

Yet it is one that he was unable to sustain fully. He suggests in one place that the impulse of self-interest is "part of human nature." He suggests in another that "the motive of profit-making has probably always existed in human beings," with industry transforming it into "the most universal and perhaps the strongest of all the streams of individual and social psychology."[49] Capitalism, it turns out, is not the root of all evil, though *qua* industrialism it does have a large hand in its modern promotion.

Co-operation and Democracy

Much of what Woolf wrote on Co-operation concerned the democratic control of industry. For our purposes it is important to note his central argument, and also those aspects that may be regarded as *un*democratic. These are important because they help to explain why Woolf's ideas about international economic organization took little account of the liberty of states to define and pursue their own economic interests. They also help to explain why even such a democratically minded socialist as Woolf could sometimes suggest things of a highly authoritarian nature.

Woolf conceived democracy in terms of government for the whole people by the whole people, and he felt, at least until the late 1920s, that the only way of achieving this was through consumers' Co-operation. Woolf was critical of certain types of socialism because he felt they would lead to government for part of the people by part of the people: that is, government for and by a special interest. This special interest might comprise the majority of the population, but it was still, in Woolf's view, a special interest since large numbers of people would be excluded (most notably, women, who were far outnumbered by men in industrial production).[50] It was this conception of democracy that prompted Woolf's reservations about the Soviet Union: government by Soviets was, regardless of the elaborate institutional mechanisms designed to make them democratically accountable, government by the Party, and the Party was only a small minority of the whole population. Similarly, syndicalism, guild socialism, and other types of "producer socialism" could not be considered democratic since producers constituted only one part, albeit a large one, of the whole population. Calculated in straightforward utilitarian terms, the substitution of producer socialism for capitalism would, no doubt, be a big step in the right direction. It would not necessarily result in real democracy, however, since government *by* producers would inevitably mean government *for* producers. In this regard Woolf's observations were highly prescient, at least as far as the British industrial scene is concerned, in that he accurately predicted what would happen if producers gained political power. The "trade union syndicalism" of the 1970s, which involved the imposition by a small number of powerful unions of, in effect, a rent on the rest of society, would have not surprised Woolf in the slightest.[51]

The answer to the problem of the democratic control of industry and the economy lay not in the Soviet, the guild, the state, or the municipality, but in the consumer. And the beauty of the consumer was that everyone was one:

> The owners of capital will always be only a small minority of the whole community, and industrial workers can never be more than a large majority. But every one, man, woman and child, is in the nature of things a consumer. In a sense therefore... consumers represent the whole community in a way in which the capitalists or the workers could never represent it.[52]

Through the dividend on purchase and quarterly and annual meetings of the whole society, consumers' Co-operation, Woolf claimed, was the optimum, most democratic form of industrial organization. Unlike capitalism and producer socialism, Co-operation gave consumers control of what was to be produced, in what quantities, to what standards, and at what price. Co-operators also had control over investment decisions by being able, at the annual meetings of their respective societies, to set the level of dividend. Co-operators decided who they wanted as managers; they also chose their delegates to the Co-operative Wholesale Society (CWS).

In characteristic Fabian style Woolf argued that one of the advantages of the Co-operation over other forms of socialism was that it was already a real and living thing that had proven its abilities. By the 1920s the Co-operative Society had a membership of over four million and was in the process of becoming the country's largest commercial concern. Woolf ardently believed that socialism could be best achieved by the progressive development of Co-operative organization until it became conterminous with society as a whole—at which point all citizens would be members and all production Co-operative production.

Woolf enthusiastically welcomed the growth of international Co-operative trade—trade between the Co-operative movements of several countries— which had begun to take root in the early years after the war. He saw this as a means by which gains to trade could be maximized and natural endowments exploited without the need to enter the international struggle for markets and profits. Each national society would become a member of all the other societies with which they conducted business. Each would be entitled to receive, as with domestic Co-operative organization, a dividend on purchase. The welfare of each would thereby be intermeshed with the welfare of all.

In Woolf's view, Co-operation in Britain, Germany, and several other countries had reached a stage at which its "ordinary business of supplying its members' demands and its normal development" would be hampered unless "the co-operative system and co-operative control" could be extended to international exchange. This was a fact of "immediate and practical importance" but also one of "wider significance." There were many Co-operators who saw Co-operation as an alternative to the capitalist system. Woolf was the first major figure in the Co-operative Movement to stress that Co-operation would only replace capitalism in a very limited sphere if it did not adapt itself to international trade:

> Industry, commerce, and finance tend to become ever more and more international, and the basis of the capitalist's strength is more often than not to be found in his control of foreign markets, the foreign supplies of raw materials, and the channels of foreign trade. The co-operator will never oust capitalism and its evils unless it can oust the capitalist from foreign trade.[53]

Democracy of Ends or Means?

Three interrelated problems with Woolf's thesis on the relationship between Co-operation and democracy merit emphasis. The first has to do with Woolf's conception of democracy; the second with his notion of the "spirit of democracy"; the third with the relationship between coercion and democracy.

Woolf's rejection of producer socialism was based on the assumption that democracy meant "rule by *all* the people." Since producers formed a group that fell well short of all the people, producer control of industry could not be described as democratic.

There is a problem with this conception of democracy that Woolf recognized but never fully addressed. Even if Co-operation became conterminous with society as a whole, decisions would inevitably have to be made by a group smaller than society as a whole, since involving every member of society in all important decisions (and who determines importance?) would in any large society be impracticable. Even in the unlikely event that this group constituted a majority, control of industry would still be "in the hands, not of all the people, but of the majority of the people."[54] Woolf recommended the setting up of committees in order to protect the rights of minorities and suggested that clearly identifiable minorities within the Movement, such as employees, should have permanent representation in them. But he never managed to convincingly square democracy with the need for executive action—though it might be said that this is a flaw in the notion of direct democracy *per se*, certainly as applied to large and complex societies, as much as it is a flaw in the particular brand that Woolf was advocating. One solution, of course, would be to define democracy in terms of universal suffrage, periodic elections, and representation rather than rely, as Woolf does, on a literal definition. This would satisfy his criterion of universality (government by the *whole* people) without having to concede that failure of *all* the people to participate in *all* important decisions meant that democracy was deficient. Yet for some reason Woolf was reluctant to go down the "representative democracy" (*vis á vis* "direct democracy") road. In one of his most substantial and, indeed, highly sophisticated treatments of the subject, he defines democracy in terms of "politically equal rights and socially equal opportunities" involving "equal rights to happiness" and the treatment "politically" of everyone as an individual rather than as a member of a particular class or social group.[55] This is a remarkably broad definition. It is also eccentric in making no reference to the process of government or the basis of representation in government. Perhaps one reason for this is that he could not stomach the idea that if a *majority* chose capitalism, fascism, or communism, that decision would, by virtue of that fact, be democratic. In the same volume Lord Eustace Percy accuses Woolf of confusing what democracy is with what he would like it to do. Defining democracy in terms of an abstract political good such as "liberty" or "equality" has been described by one shrewd commentator as a "socialist escape clause."[56]

Second, Woolf contended that democracy could not be achieved by democratic machinery alone: democratic machinery had to be accompanied by "democratic spirit." By this Woolf had in mind a cluster of things such as a sense of social responsibility, "a wide and real interest in the machinery of government and administration," a willingness to actively participate, and a sense of the good of the whole.[57] With respect to Co-operation, Woolf argues that "half the good of democratic control of industry" would be lost if the level of dividend became the main object:

> Co-operators ought always to remember that they are controlling industry for the people, and that they are in a society not in order to make a profit, but in order to supply themselves with goods.[58]

While one can sympathize with certain elements of this view, it can be objected that it rests on a particular conception of the purposes of Co-operation and leaves little room for Co-operators to define these purposes themselves. What if the majority of Co-operators in any given Society decide that their main objective should be to maximize the dividend? For Woolf this would suggest a lack of democratic spirit. But the implication of this is that the existence of democratic spirit becomes contingent on the pursuit of Woolf's conception of the good of the whole. Pursuit of a different conception becomes "undemocratic" regardless of how many citizen-members support it: a perverse and dogmatic position.

Third, Woolf's conception of democracy is not entirely coercion-free. There are two striking illustrations of this. While the first, concerning Co-operative education, might be described as a form of paternalism; the second, concerning the organization of industrial production, is almost certainly a form of authoritarianism. Woolf believed that education was central to the proper working of democracy. In particular he believed, as mentioned, that "a wide and real interest in the machinery of government and administration" was a major ingredient of the democratic spirit. The implication of this for Co-operation was that members *inter alia* would have to study and understand the business of the Society, study and understand its balance sheets, and regularly attend its meetings. But what if they didn't? What if they were happy to leave all this to their managers and delegates?

Woolf argued that lack of interest was "the most serious danger to all democracies... it is certainly the most serious danger to the Co-operative movement." If a citizen or member did not feel responsible for the actions of the institutions that governed him, "real democratic control" was absent. His solution was, however, somewhat alarming:

> I often think that one of the most urgent needs in the movement is an organisation which will take this matter in hand. For instance, in every society there might be a democracy committee possibly of the Women's and Men's Guilds. This committee should see that every new member of the society is visited personally by someone who would explain the democratic nature of the movement, and impress upon him or her the importance of attending meetings and understanding the business of the society. The committee should have pamphlets explaining these things and also the meaning of balance sheets, and the visitor should leave these pamphlets with every new member. Further, the committee should watch the attendance at meetings, and note the names of those members who do

not attend, and they should then call personally upon such member [sic] and try to persuade them to take an active share in the control and affairs of the society.[59]

While Woolf's intentions—his desire to create an "active democracy"—are admirable, his methods, witnessed from a post-*1984* and *Darkness at Noon* world, seem rather like the Fabian equivalent of "sending the boys round."

Woolf's somewhat sinister paternalism is, moreover, sometimes accompanied by overt authoritarianism. This is best exemplified by his scheme for "national service in industrial production."[60] The way he arrives at this scheme is impeccably logical but the outcome is disturbing. He contended that capitalism combined with industrialism produced shoddy, useless goods that consumers were cajoled into buying. He also contended that industrial production was a miserable activity, which delivered not a shred of job satisfaction. Given these facts he argued that industry should concentrate on producing a smaller range of basic, but well-made goods. More elaborate and luxurious goods should be produced in a traditional, noncommercial way. He also argued that no one should be forced to spend their entire working life in "industrial slavery." A return to a medieval system of arts and crafts was not, however, feasible. Industrial production was by far the most efficient way of producing goods with mass demand. It was also the case that industrial production held such a grip on communal psychology that it would be impossible to abandon. It was in these senses "necessary." Since, however, industry would in future only be devoted to provision of the basics, less manpower would be needed to work it. Consequently the most appropriate way of organizing industry would be to introduce a scheme whereby every ablebodied citizen would be required for three months of the year to make themselves available for industrial work. For the remainder of the year their time would be free to concentrate on producing more intrinsically valuable goods. Such a system would be egalitarian in that everyone would spend an equal amount of time engaged in the horrible but necessary job of industrial production; it would be efficient in that the best means available for producing the necessities of life would be utilized; it would be materially enriching since nobody would be forced to consume the shoddy products of capitalism; and it would be spiritually enriching since everybody would be free for most of the year to engage in more satisfying work. The parallels with Holyoake's view of consumers' association as "a moral art as well as a new form of economy" are considerable.[61] Similar schemes of compulsory industrial labor, justified on similar grounds, can also be found in the writings of Marx, Bukharin, and Preobrazhensky.[62]

The problems with such a system are legion. To be minimally effective it would require almost complete acceptance by all sections of society and, most probably, either the organization of the economies of other countries on similar lines, or the closing down of frontiers to foreign trade. The latter, of course, would be unacceptable to Woolf for the "liberal internationalist" reasons outlined above. The international problem is a crucial one, however, because unless all countries more or less simultaneously sign up to the new system, those within would be vulnerable to the cheaper, mass-produced imports of those without. This would have profound implications for domestic economic stability.

But what is also striking about the system is its reliance on compulsion. What would be done with those who refused to perform their democratic duties? Is not dissent inevitable in the absence of severe, perhaps Draconian, measures to prevent it? At what point in one's life would the requirement to engage in industrial production begin and when would it end? How would "able bodied" be interpreted, and by whom? Would there be special exemptions, for example, for university students, health workers, soldiers, emergency service personnel? Is it, from society's point of view, an efficient use of resources to force a highly and expensively trained physician, or philosopher, or fighter pilot to do menial labor for three out of eleven months per annum? Given his persistent and trenchant criticisms of the Soviet model for its reliance on compulsion, Woolf's endorsement of such a system is surprising to say the least.[63]

Co-operation and Peace

Woolf contended that the best way of creating a peaceful and prosperous international economic system was through the expansion of intentional Co-operative trade. What was it about Co-operation that Woolf believed led to peace?

Despite the boldness of his claims Woolf's explanation was brief. Essentially he put forward three related arguments. First, he maintained that in contrast to the producer, and especially the capitalist producer, "[t]he psychology of the consumer is economically and internationally pacific."[64] The need for the capitalist to make a profit meant that he was in constant competition with other capitalists, and given the prevalence of nationalism, patriotism, and social Darwinism, international trade almost always degenerated into international economic conflict. Even though trade was undertaken by firms and businesses rather than states it came to be regarded as a measure of national profit and loss. For example:

> The sale of Lyons silk to a German purchaser in Dresden...naturally came to be regarded as a gain of France at the expense of Germany, and in this crude economic psychology the statistics of a nation's imports became the measure of its international economic loss.[65]

Co-operation, by contrast, did not involve the pursuit of profit since its purpose was to satisfy the needs of its members. Consequently, there was no need to compete (though Woolf did recognize that until the Co-operative transformation of the economy was complete, Co-operatives would have no choice but to compete with capitalists[66]) and the dangers of such competition degenerating into open hostility would be avoided.

Second, Woolf maintained, "[t]he consumer is your only real internationalist and true citizen of the world."[67] Consumers, he felt, were essentially indifferent to the country of origin of the goods they bought. What mattered to them was the satisfaction of their needs in the most effective way possible. Thus, for consumers, international trade was not a zero-sum game but "a vast and intricate co-operative enterprise, the sole object of which is to supply the world's needs."[68] The consumer was not, in consequence, prey to the patriotism and nationalism that so accentuated competition among producers. In the interests of peace, trade should therefore be organized from the point of view of the consumer rather than the producer.

Third, Woolf argued that the world was becoming more interdependent and that Co-operative organization was more in tune with this world than capitalist competition. One of the reasons why capitalism, and the economic nationalism that went with it, led to international hostility and war was that it attempted to force the actual growth of international society into a mold that could no longer contain it. Consumer Co-operation, by contrast, was a type of economic organization in keeping with this growth. Essentially Woolf was saying was that the development of "cosmopolitan international government" (see chapter 3) meant that economic organization, to be effective, needed to be increasingly inclusive and transnational rather than exclusive and national.

The Shift to NonCo-operative International Economic Organization

In Woolf's post–Second World War proposals for international economic reconstruction, the Co-operative Movement does not get a mention. This is striking because, as described above, Woolf was utterly convinced that international Co-operative trade (and not only trade, but eventually finance too) would be the most effective way of organizing the world economy in the interests of peace and prosperity. Woolf's relegation of Co-operation is in a sense evidence of his realism. His proposals of the 1920s were largely ignored by the Labour Movement. The extensive development of inter-cooperative trade he recommended did not materialize. In recognition of these facts Woolf shifted his attention to more orthodox ideas about international economic reform.

An Economic Council of the League

Yet it should be noted that this was more a stepping-back than an about-turn since from the outset there had been more than one strand to his thought on the subject. In *International Government* Woolf advanced, as we have seen, a highly eclectic vision of international economic cooperation (see chapter 3). As early as 1919 he had advocated an "International Commission of the League" for Africa to protect the natives from white exploitation and "guarantee" free trade and the Open Door in Africa.[69] In 1923 he proposed the formation of an "Economic Council of the League" with functions remarkably similar to what later became ECOSOC, the IMF, and the World Bank.[70] This kind of prescription for the treatment of international economic ills—the setting up of international institutions with research, regulatory, supervisory, and sometimes redistributive functions—was a consistent strand in Woolf's thought.

In his important 1923 pamphlet Woolf argued that a "negative" international policy of opposing protectionism should be accompanied by a "positive" or "constructive" international policy of cooperation to settle economic differences and develop common interests. This could be achieved by developing the existing Allied Supreme Economic Council into a World Economic Council of the League. This would have seven permanent functions. First, the maintenance of credit to ensure the supply and "fair allocation" of important materials and to provide against "unnecessary disturbance of world conditions through a breakdown of purchasing power in a particular country owing to preventable causes." Second, the "development of international lines and means of communication either where the interests of two or more nations are concerned, for example, the Baghdad Railway, or where a supply of raw materials or a market of world importance could be opened up by the co-operation of nations in providing credit or labor or technical skill or other resources." Third, the "regulation of loans and concessions in undeveloped countries" and "the safeguarding of such countries from unfair exploitation or monopolisation by particular interests of nations." Fourth, the "co-ordination and development of the work of public international unions" and cooperation with them in "schemes having as their object world economic interests" (e.g. concerning the international organization of agriculture, the international insurance of crops, and the collection and publication of "accurate international economic statistics"). Fifth, the "promotion of international economic conventions based on the widest measure of international co-operation, e.g. commercial treaties, Labour conventions, traffic agreements." Sixth, the "[s]upervision and enforcement of international economic conventions" and the "prevention of exploitation by trusts...operating in the world market." Seventh, the "promotion and creation of international conferences or councils in various industries and economic groups, in order to secure the greatest possible measure of co-operation in each group."[71]

Although novel, indeed revolutionary, at the time, the idea that responsibility for the performance of such functions should be entrusted to international institutions is now a part of the epistemic fabric of international relations. Many of these functions, though not by a single overarching body, and not always in the decisive way envisaged by Woolf, are now performed by such institutions as ECOSOC, the IMF, the IBRD, the FAO, the ILO, the OECD, UNCTAD, and the WTO—to name only a few of the more illustrious bodies in the field. Although this may not be testimony to Woolf's direct influence on the creation of the postwar economic order, it is undoubtedly testimony to the influence of a group of Left-leaning, progressive thinkers who consistently argued for this kind of "welfare" or "constructive" internationalism. Here I have in mind, along with Woolf, such thinkers as Angell, Cole, Hobson, Keynes, Mitrany, Arthur Salter, and, indeed, in his reformist mode, E. H. Carr.[72]

Although most of the reforms Woolf proposed at this time were reformist in nature, not all of them were. In places Woolf goes beyond constructive internationalism and explicitly advocates central international planning. In Wight's terms this is a form of revolutionism.[73] Whereas constructive internationalism leaves the society of states more or less intact, central international planning presupposes or implies something that goes beyond it—a community of all mankind perhaps with a single world government. To illustrate, as well as recommending the maintenance of credit to ensure the supply of important commodities, Woolf also advocates the allocation of "supplies and credit according to need." He advocates not only the "co-ordination and development" of public international unions such as the Institute for Agriculture, but also "the international organisation of agriculture and the distribution of agricultural products." He speaks not only of the "supervision" of international economic conventions, but also of their "enforcement." He talks not only of "preventing exploitation" by trusts, international firms, and combines, but also of "controlling their operations."[74]

These ideas assume a degree of central control (though Woolf left open the composition and decision-making procedures of his World Economic Council), which according to some definitions would spell the end of state sovereignty.[75] They also assume a degree of human solidarity and cohesion greatly exceeding that which pertains in the society of states, both then and, for that matter, now.

A Central World Authority

It was Woolf's revolutionism rather than his reformism that informed his proposals for international economic organization in the 1940s. He argued that the primary postwar task was to "establish an economic and political authority as the nucleus of international government" adding that this would not be possible in the absence of "a radical change in the attitude to and form of what is known as national state sovereignty." He contended that the world had become "so closely integrated" that the claim of states to "economic sovereignty"—"unregulated and irresponsible control of their economic relations and power"—must inevitably lead to economic chaos. Sovereignty had become an "unworkable anachronism": "a dead fossil which must give place to a living organism adapted to the new conditions." This meant that the state "must enter and subject itself to a wider order and organisation."[76]

But this organization would not take the form of a superstate or a federation. It did, however, involve the renunciation by states of their right to make decisions irrespective of their impact on the rest of the world. The scope of the authority would be worldwide, though regional organizations would have an important role to play, particularly in the fields of economic development and transport. So too would functional organizations. Woolf applauded the creation of UN Relief and Rehabilitation Administration, and the FAO, and called for "bold experiment" along the lines of the Tennessee Valley Authority and, somewhat paradoxically, the trans-Europe system of heavy industry developed by the Nazis. The latter, if controlled by an international commission, would "solve the difficult problem of preventing the great German monopolists, if they again controlled the heavy industries, from once more providing the weapons for aggressive war." Echoing the functionalism then being advanced by David Mitrany, Woolf contended:

> It is, perhaps, through such cooperation for economic purposes that Europe may learn most easily to forget some of its fatal obsessions with national frontiers and learn to cooperate politically.[77]

But this said, he firmly maintained, *contra* Mitrany, that regional and functional organizations could not work effectively without a "central world authority." Such an authority was needed

> ...both to co-ordinate the activities of regional or functional international organs and to deal promptly and authoritatively with any action or situation which may threaten the world's peace or prosperity.[78]

Woolf did not spell out what he meant by "deal promptly and authoritatively with" but it would not be unreasonable to conclude that he had something far-reaching in mind: the "first political task" of the authority would be establishment of a "general system of law and order" and the creation of an "effective system of collective security." This in turn would entail "effective control of international force adequate to meet the threat of national force" and the establishment of the necessary procedures and machinery to ensure "prompt decisions and decisive action."[79]

The economic aim of the authority was no less far-reaching: "to enable eventually production, trade, distribution, and consumption to be organized and controlled internationally in the common interests of nations and peoples." Although vague, this statement is significant in two respects. First, it shows that Woolf did not contemplate much of a role for market forces. This is confirmed by his belief that "the economic and international principles of Socialism are the only sound ones and that unless European society is rebuilt on them, there can be no prosperity and peace" and that "Labour's policy for the international post-war settlement must be founded uncompromisingly on Socialist principles." It is further confirmed by his belief that the move from "economic anarchy" to a "system of international government of the world's production and consumption" could not be fully achieved until all states were socialist.[80] Second, it shows that Woolf did not expect the implementation of his scheme to be immediate. By the same token, however, he did not say implementation would be gradual. The probable explanation for this ambiguity is that he did not want to give the impression to his largely socialist readership that they would have to wait an eternity before their international socialist commonwealth could be created. Similarly, in the spirit of Fabian inclusiveness, he did not want to give the impression to his nonsocialist readers that this radical, perhaps revolutionary, transformation in the economic organization of the world could be made overnight, that there were not many severe practical obstacles to be overcome.[81] He added that because of the shortage of socialist states, immediate implementation was "improbable," perhaps even "impossible." To this extent his revolutionism is qualified.

The vagueness of Woolf's proposals is highlighted by his estimation of what the authority would be capable of doing immediately. He specifies three things: most radically, the "encouragement" and "direction" of "production and consumption on a world scale"; less radically, the removal of "uneconomic barriers against international trade" (thus, it may be asked, permitting "economic" barriers such as the protection of infant industries, and "emergency" protection to deal with balance of payments crises?); and less radically still, the making of rules and regulations to "promote international economic cooperation and prevent economic aggression by, e.g., the restriction of supplies, the depreciation of exchange rates, or the abuse of monopoly powers." In the absence of a detailed examination of means it might be concluded that such suggestions amount to little more than broad declarations of intent.

NonCo-operative Economic Organization: Four Weaknesses and some Strengths

There are a number of problems with Woolf's proposals for nonCo-operative economic organization. First, the institutional character and mode of operation of his "central world authority" is unclear, as is the source of the considerable power he granted to it. Second, Woolf made no attempt to define or clarify such key terms as "organize," "control," "direct," and, indeed, "plan." The exact nature and scope of his scheme remains therefore uncertain—although all the evidence points in the direction of substantial collective planning on a worldwide scale. For some, of course, this was the road to serfdom. Third, many of his proposals presuppose the existence or immanence of a world community of mankind, a presupposition that Woolf makes no attempt to lay bare or empirically demonstrate. Finally, in parallel with his vision of a "Co-operative Commonwealth," Woolf strongly implied that some degree of compulsion would be needed in order to achieve the common good, but he failed to examine in any detail whether the compulsion of the new system would in any way be an improvement on the compulsion of the old.

Yet some of these weaknesses may also be strengths. It might be argued in particular that his ambiguity is largely due to reluctance to indulge in the business of drawing up constitutions or detailed blueprints for future world orders. Woolf, like Carr, believed this to be a rather futile exercise. He saw great virtue in the "trial and error" approach to institution building.[82] Having clear goals was important. So too was some idea as to how these goals might be accomplished. But elaborate theories did not always work in practice. Flexibility and a willingness to experiment were needed. So too was a willingness to accept progress in increments. The important point was to begin the move away from the political and economic *laissez faire* of the old nationalist, competitive, conflictual order, toward a new order based on cooperation, organization, and rational planning.

The Question of Idealism

The degree to which Woolf's thought on international economic organization can be regarded as idealistic is no small matter. A comprehensive analysis would have to consider not only his proposals for a "World Economic Council of the League," the expansion of "inter-co-operative trade," and a postwar "central world authority," but also his anticapitalism, his antiprotectionism, his analysis of the relationship between Co-operation, democracy, and peace, and his (highly optimistic) evaluation of Co-operation as a mode of economic organization. To do this properly would require the skills not only of the international relations theorist but also of the economic and social historian—perhaps those of the economist and the political theorist, too.

This being said, there are several aspects of Woolf's thought in this area that are prime candidates for the epithet idealist and which the IR theorist is in a good position to assess.

First, it might be said that Woolf is an idealist to the extent that he embraced free trade. In Carr's view, free trade was an "imaginary condition that has never existed." The *doctrine* of free trade was based on the erroneous belief in a natural harmony of interests. Most damning of all, as highlighted in chapter 2, free trade was not an absolute or universal principle but merely "the unconscious reflection of national policy based on a particular interpretation of national interest at a particular time."

The simple equation, free trade = liberalism = idealism, however, glosses over the fact that the importance of free trade in liberal internationalism shifted over time. The Cobdenite association of free trade with civilization, prosperity, and peace, was not something that later thinkers uncritically accepted. Woolf is interesting from this point of view because he accepted many of the assumptions of nineteenth-century "free trade" liberalism but in a negative form—as a bastion against the evils of nationalism and mercantilism and as a stage in the transition to a more stable and peaceful international order based on Co-operation, regulation, and planning. If some of his assumptions were liberal, his vision was essentially Owenian and Fabian. He shared Owen's goal of "the complete elimination of profit and the profit-maker."[83] He also shared Owen's "New Vision of Society in which all would work together in a rational manner for the common good, without need of a violent revolution."[84] He joined the Fabians in viewing free markets—even if preferable to capitalist "controlled" markets—as essentially the freedom to exploit. In connection with all these things he shared Wallas's hope that cooperation could be substituted for competition as the fundamental principle of social organization.[85]

So, while Woolf borrowed from liberalism in his repudiation of mercantilism, his constructive policy derives from the British socialist tradition. Indeed, Woolf was one of the first thinkers to apply some of the doctrines of mainstream British socialist thought to international questions. And it is striking that despite Woolf's reputation as an idealist and Carr's as a realist both men attempted to do this—as will be seen in chapter 8—in their proposals for postwar international economic organization.

Second, it might be said that Woolf's proposals for nonCo-operative international economic organization were idealistic in the sense that they ignored certain facts—such as the limited degree of solidarity in international society—and they failed to take proper account of the role of national power. Here a distinction needs to be made between Woolf's reformist and revolutionist proposals. The former proposals—those pertaining to international bodies with research, regulatory, supervisory, and limited redistributive functions—are not so vulnerable to the charge of idealism since, despite jealously guarding their sovereignty, states have shown themselves to be consistently willing to set up such bodies in order to manage common interests. Woolf's reformist proposals are only idealistic to the extent that the FAO, the ILO, and the IBRD are idealistic. Woolf's revolutionist proposals—those involving central "direction," "distribution," "enforcement," and "control"—are more vulnerable to the charge. In the main, states have been unwilling to invest international bodies with such powers—the Court and Commission of the European Union and the European Convention on Human Rights being notable exceptions. This is basically due to insufficient solidarity between the members of international society with respect to core economic interests, values, and goals. While states have seen advantages, for example, in setting up and funding international financial bodies to help countries in balance of payments difficulties, or with short-term liquidity, or longer-term structural problems, they have not seen advantages in setting up bodies with far-reaching powers to "direct" or "control" production and distribution. This is partly due to the hegemonic status of "embedded" or "managed" liberalism in international economic relations, which, in turn, is largely due to the reluctance of the major economic Powers to relinquish to "outsiders" formal control over those areas of their economic lives they deem central to their economic, social, and political well-being. To the extent, therefore, that Woolf overestimated the degree of solidarity between states on these core matters, or the prospects for achieving such solidarity in the near future, his proposals are idealistic—though no more so than Carr's proposal for a European Planning Authority with ultimate responsibility for "vital decisions on European economic policies."[86]

Carr claimed that during the utopian stage of the political sciences "investigators...pay little attention to existing 'facts' or to the analysis of cause and effect, but...devote themselves whole-heartedly to the elaboration of visionary projects for the attainment of ends which they have in view." It might be said, finally, that Woolf's plans for the expansion of international Co-operative trade constitute such a "visionary project." Woolf conceived international Co-operative trade as a genuine alternative to the faltering "capitalist system of foreign trade."[87] He asserted that the potential for developing international Co-operative trade was "almost unlimited."[88] Yet capitalism has not only survived but has arguably gone from strength to strength. By contrast, international Co-operative trade never really got off the ground and Co-operation itself has all but vanished as an alternative mode of economic organization.

Yet the failure of Co-operation does not prove that Woolf's ideas at that time and in this respect were utopian. This is a complex matter but the following facts about Co-operation during the interwar period are important to state.

First, the Co-operative system experienced rapid growth both vertically and horizontally. The CWS built or acquired factories in a range of industries including shoemaking, pottery, textiles, furniture, cutlery, building, bread making, and fish curing. It became a major dairy producer and arable farmer. In 1914 it owned less than 3,000 acres of agricultural land. By 1921 it owned nearly 35,000 acres. It became one of Britain's biggest wheat-growers and its biggest flour-miller. Since before the war it had been her largest grocer. Due to its growing involvement in the building trade, it soon became one of her largest timber importers. Also by 1921, 5,550 trade union organizations and friendly societies were banking with the Co-operative. This was all part of an ambitious strategy to radically reduce the dependence of the Co-operative Movement on capitalist manufactures, finance, and sources of supply.[89]

Second, the CWS rapidly extended its operations overseas. In 1920 alone it acquired an additional 30,142 acres of tea plantations in India and 1,769 in Ceylon. New palm oil depots were opened in West Africa. In Canada 10,000 acres of wheat fields were acquired.[90]

Third, the CWS traded with national Co-operative wholesale societies in 19 European countries. In addition trade took place between the CWS and local Co-operative societies in Australia, Canada, South Africa, India, Egypt, Palestine, Brazil, China, and Soviet Russia.[91]

Fourth, an international meeting of wholesale societies in 1919 agreed on various measures to expand international Co-operative trade including the establishment, in Manchester, of an International Central Bureau for the gathering of statistics and the dissemination of information.[92]

Fifth, membership of Co-operative societies in Britain reached 1 million in 1905, 3 million in 1914, 4.5 million in 1920, and 6.5 million in 1938.[93]

Sixth, if the Co-operative Movement itself did not appreciate its strength and potential, Capital and the state certainly did. Small businesses and their spokesmen in Parliament had expressed concern about the growth of the Movement as early as 1900. During the war the government kept the Movement, as well as other actual or potential oppositional bodies, under surveillance, as did a number of semiofficial and private bodies such as the Engineering Employers' Federation and the Economic Study Club.[94] With the onset of the Depression, small shopkeepers in the industrial North began a political campaign to halt the growth of the Co-operative Movement. By 1932 they had the support not only of the multiple-shop companies and department stores, but big business and the Rothermere and Beaverbrook press. They saw the ability of Co-operatives to trade without profit as a major threat to their livelihoods, which, since the war, had come to depend on the control of free competition through a system of price-fixing and boycotts. (According to one study, 3% of consumer spending went on price-fixed goods in 1900. By 1938 the figure had reached 30%.)[95] Bodies such as the National Chamber of Commerce, the National Traders' Defence League, and the explicitly anti-Co-operative National Organizations Co-ordinated Committee, vigorously lobbied the government to tax the "divided" and the "trading surplus" of Co-operative societies and introduce other measures to curb their growth. The Treasury's Ritchie Committee had looked at this question in 1905, as had the Royal Commission on Income Tax in 1919, and a further Treasury investigation of 1927. All these bodies concluded that the dividend on purchase was not "profit" or "unearned income" but a "rebate" or "discount." Co-operative societies were not therefore benefiting from the "special treatment" alleged by the shopkeepers. By the early 1930s, however, and despite a counter-campaign by the Movement, opinion in the Treasury and among Conservative MPs had hardened. The shopkeepers largely achieved their legislative objective in 1933 when the government adopted the report of a further specially established committee—the 1932 Raeburn Committee—which recommended that for tax purposes mutual societies should be treated as joint-stock companies (though much to the consternation of the shopkeepers it also recommended that the dividend should be treated as a nontaxable trading expense). This "weakening of mutuality," according to one author, did much to thwart the development of the Co-operative Movement.[96]

Seventh, two government enquiries into restrictive trade practices were conducted. By comparison with the repeated investigations into the tax position of the Co-operative Movement they were halfhearted affairs. No action was taken. The *status quo* was effectively vindicated.[97]

Though this is a big subject these facts go some way toward showing that the idealism/utopianism of this branch of Woolf's thought is far from total. Co-operation did not decline spontaneously because it was inherently less efficient than capitalism. Rather it was deliberately and successfully attacked and its progress was deliberately and successfully thwarted. Woolf provided numerous facts from a variety of primary and secondary sources to demonstrate the strength of Co-operation and the potential of international Co-operative trade. He was not indulging in wishful thinking. His basic position, indeed, was a sober one. He did not maintain that international Co-operative trade would *definitely* expand or *definitely* achieve its potential, but rather that a "peculiarly favourable" moment existed for such expansion since "the failure of the capitalist system to right itself" left the field open to Co-operators in so many markets.[98]

He added, however, that "it is characteristic of moments, and particularly favourable ones, that they pass." The possibilities were "not theoretical or utopian, but extremely practical and immediately attainable." Everything depended, however, on whether the Movement had the desire, knowledge, energy, and confidence to actively pursue them.[99]

Nor was Woolf indulging in "the elaboration of visionary projects for the attainment of ends which he had in view." His main work is not "visionary" in the sense of a "blue-print" or a "grand plan" but an empirical and theoretical analysis of the various forms of international Co-operative trade and the ways in which they might be developed. His principal recommendation was not the creation of new institutions such as a "vast" International CWS with "vague and general powers," but wider and more effective use of the methods and machinery—the "depot system," joint international purchase, the "agency system," the new Central Bureau—already in existence.

In conclusion it might be said that Woolf provided a vision of a nonstate, nonmarket approach to international economic organization, based on an optimistic though not utopian reading of existing conditions and tendencies. By the early 1920s it was already clear that the traditional recipe of orthodox economic policy and market forces was proving an inadequate means of recovery in the face of the vast economic problems generated by the war. The economic disasters of the late 1920s and early 1930s compounded the view in the eyes of many that the unregulated market was spent, and that new means of economic organization, based on new principles, were needed to meet the challenges and requirements of a new era. But for some radicals and socialists searching for these new means, the traditional Marxist, Social Democrat, and Fabian remedy of an omniscient and omnipotent state was no longer feasible or morally acceptable. G. D. H. Cole was the first prominent Fabian to breach the Webbian orthodoxy with his proposals for a model of socialism based on producer guilds. But Woolf, too, broke ranks with his plan for the extension of consumer Co-operation. While he may have underestimated the extent to which the success of Co-operation would provoke a counterattack by the twin forces of conservatism and Capital, it is nonetheless true that it acquired a strength and influence in British society that is difficult to fully appreciate in the much changed market-oriented and capitalist-dominated world of today.

CHAPTER 8

The Idealist Counterattack: Mr. Woolf versus Professor Carr

The established order of things received more than one deadly blow in 1939. The European political order based halfheartedly on the League received a devastating, though hardly disguised, blow in the shape of Hitler's invasion of Poland. That part of the European order based equally halfheartedly on the venerable concept of the balance of power, received a sudden and unexpected blow in the form of the Molotov–Ribbontrop Pact. The relatively calm though far from harmonious world of IR received its own blow in the form of ex-Foreign Office official and newly ensconced Aberystwyth professor, E. H. Carr. If on analysis it transpires that Carr's onslaught consisted less of a series of well-timed and accurate intellectual punches, than an indiscriminate throwing of fists at a none-too-sure academic target, then this served his polemical purpose admirably. Carr's seminal and infamous text knocked the fledgling field of IR to the ground. It succeeded in discrediting the thought of a whole generation. Though not wholly his intention, Carr succeeded in getting virtually the whole field of IR as it had evolved during the interwar years labeled utopian, and therefore by implication foolish or wrong.

Until recently the response of the so-called idealists/utopians to Carr's onslaught has languished almost entirely hidden from view.[1] This is a tribute not only to the brute intellectual power of Carr's attack—why bother with the utopians, it was felt, if their arguments are so palpably false?—but also to its usefulness to a new generation of IR scholars facing a very different, Cold War–dominated, world. It is also, importantly, a tribute to Carr's sheer rhetorical brilliance.[2]

Yet Carr's book was met with anything but acquiescence. It drew a wide and for the most part hostile response.[3] Even Carr's admirers, Professor Morgenthau in Chicago included, had more than a few bones to pick with him.[4] Chief among both Carr's critics and admirers was Leonard Woolf. This chapter tells a story long overdue in the history of international thought: the response to Carr's "devastating critique of utopianism" (as it is conventionally portrayed) by one of the leading Center-Left commentators on international affairs of the time.

Woolf's Response to Carr

The Twenty Years' Crisis is widely regarded as a comprehensive attack on "idealist" or "utopian" thought. In one sense this is true. It was aimed not only at the League of Nations, but at all those "devoted and energetic intellectuals"[5] who supported it, at all those who believed that peace was indivisible and that free trade was a universal interest, at the Union of Democratic Control, at proponents of a United States of Europe, at defenders of the principle of national self-determination, and much else besides. The attack is not, however, comprehensive in the sense of being a detailed and systematic analysis and critique of the principal standard-bearers of "utopian" thought. Indeed, of all the figures Carr might have chosen to examine only four—Norman Angell, Arnold Toynbee, Alfred Zimmern, and Woodrow Wilson—are dealt with in any detail. Carr does not refer to Woolf. But given that Woolf was not only a staunch supporter of the League, but in an indirect way one of its architects, and also given that he shared many, though not all, of the ideas and aspirations Carr condemned as utopian, it is not surprising that Woolf viewed the book, at least in part, as an attack on his own position. Indeed, as the following pages will reveal, Woolf was so incensed by the book that he wrote two acerbic replies.[6]

Woolf recognized that Carr was a man of extraordinary intellectual and literary gifts. Only a few years before the publication of *The Twenty Years' Crisis*, he praised Carr's study of the nineteenth-century anarchist Michael Bakunin in the highest terms. It was, he said, "a model biography," written with "remarkable impartiality."[7] By contrast Woolf regarded *The Twenty Years' Crisis* as anything but impartial. Like Angell, Toynbee, and other critical respondents, he considered the book to be negative and damaging. It amounted to little more than a rationalization of intimidation and violence in the vein of Nietzsche, de Gobineau, Spengler, and other continental romantic disparagers of reason.[8] With a good measure of Bloomsburyite condescension he even condemned the book as "superficial," "vulgar," and "absurd."[9]

Before moving on to a detailed exposition of Woolf's response it may be worthwhile to indicate its general direction. Woolf did not counter Carr's objections to collective security and the judicial settlement of international disputes despite the fact that he was a staunch advocate of both. Similarly, Woolf did not, directly at any rate, challenge Carr's conception of international morality, despite the fact that Carr claimed that the utopians completely misunderstood the nature of this morality.[10] It is also significant that although Woolf gave a lot of attention to the "twin conceptual pillars" of Carr's analysis—utopia and reality—he failed to appreciate their mutually supporting, even dialectical, character.[11] Instead, Woolf gave most of his attention to Carr's construction of realism and his realist critique of utopianism.

Woolf's main gripe with Carr's thesis was its underlying determinism. Like many other writers of the period, Woolf believed in the power of reason properly, intelligently, and humanely applied. He was a voluntarist. He believed that change, perhaps fundamental, was possible if enough people had the intellectual and moral courage to pursue it. Woolf found Carr's thesis, especially as stated in Parts I and II of the book, particularly distasteful because it suggested, not without a certain diabolical relish, that good intentions meant nothing, that everything that happened was bound to happen, and that nothing could be done to improve a miserable world.

Woolf's counterattack consisted of four prongs. Carr's concept of utopia was unclear and confusing. Contrary to Carr's belief it was "realism" that was utopian not "utopianism." Carr's assumption of the immutability of conflicting interests was damaging and factually wrong. Finally, "realism" was not an objective account of political reality, but a bitter and twisted ideology, the function of which was to rationalize violence.

In the following I set out these four prongs in more detail before moving on to assess their validity. I then compare the Woolf–Carr debate with the conventional understanding of the so-called "First Great Debate" of IR, and ask to what extent our understanding of the latter should be modified in light of a renewed awareness of the former.

The Meaning of Utopian

Carr claimed that his analysis laid the foundations for a science of IR. In Woolf's view this claim was spurious since Carr's principal concepts were ambiguous, and no enquiry could claim the status of science if it rested on insecure conceptual foundations. In particular, the concept of utopia was used to mean two very different things. On the one hand, it was used to mean "false beliefs" or "falsehoods." On the other hand, it was used to mean "impossibility of attainment." When Carr described the doctrines of nineteenth-century liberals or the ideas of League supporters as utopian, it was as a consequence difficult to be sure what exactly he meant. Did he mean that their ideas and arguments were false? Or did he mean that their objectives and policies could not be attained? According to Woolf, Carr said a good deal about the falseness of their beliefs, "but he never clearly demonstrates to us why their objectives and policies were impossible of attainment."[12] This failure to distinguish between the two meanings of the term utopian led, in Woolf's view, to considerable confusion.

The Utopianism of Realism

In an attempt to rhetorically outflank his adversary, Woolf accepted Carr's terms but turned them on their head. Rather than so-called utopianism being utopian, the real utopianism was realism. First, Carr had asserted that whereas realism was concerned with "facts," "realities," and "cause and effect," utopianism was concerned with "principles," "ideals," and "ends." Unlike realists, utopians did not analyze political problems, they merely proposed solutions to them believing they would work simply because they had to, the consequences of them not working being unpalatable.[13] Woolf refuted the claim that so-called utopians pay no attention to "facts." He referred, for example, to his own analysis of the facts of the nineteenth century (in *International Government*), which demonstrated that the organization of human society was becoming increasingly international rather than national. It was also a fact, Woolf maintained, that national self-determination—the logical conclusion of nationalism—was incompatible with an international system based on power politics: if power and force were to remain the principal determinants of international relations the independence of small states could never be more than temporary.[14] He also referred to another set of facts that Carr ignored: the massive swell of opinion at the end of the war calling for "no more war" and demanding "never again." During this time there was a deeper and more widespread hatred of war among European peoples than ever before. According to Woolf,

> Their aspiration may or may not have been utopian ... but their convictions, the state of their minds were a political reality which was having profound effects all over Europe and which not even the most realist statesman, general, or historian could afford to neglect.[15]

Moreover, the fulfillment of such an aspiration was not without precedent. There had, after all, been a similar swell of opinion immediately after the previous Great War. Just as public opinion had declared war intolerable in 1918, so it had declared slavery intolerable in 1815, and to considerable effect. In Woolf's words:

> Their [the common people's] demand was so insistent that, although many practical men and professors proved that it was utopian to attempt to abolish slavery, it was in the face of considerable opposition and with some difficulty abolished.[16]

Carr was mistaken, therefore, to assert that "utopians" ignored facts.

Carr was also mistaken to claim that only so-called utopians were concerned with principles, ideals, and ends. In Woolf's view *all* statesmen pursue ends and even base their actions on principles. Bismarck, for example, pursued the end (perhaps even the ideal) of German unification. Hitler pursued the ideal of a New Europe based on German supremacy. Both these statesmen pursued ends that were probably ideals, yet neither of them was deemed utopian as logic required. On the contrary they were deemed realist.

In addition, realism itself might become a principle if statesmen believe it with sufficient conviction, particularly so if realism was equated with "the ends justify the means." In Woolf's view, Carr's realism could be interpreted in this way. Even if the validity of the assertion that utopianism is concerned with principles whereas realism is concerned with facts was accepted, there remained the problem that Carr sometimes implied that the terms "morality" and "power" could be substituted, respectively, for "principles" and "facts." This, Woolf argued, came very close to saying that whereas utopians took morality into account in the enactment of policy, realists did not. This, in turn, was tantamount to suggesting that ends justify means. The problem here was that, in Woolf's words: "If this is realism, it is itself a 'principle' and based upon morality, for the judgement that the ends [state power, national interest] justify the means is itself an ethical judgement."[17]

Carr's claim that realism was not concerned with ends, ideals, principles, or indeed, morality, did not, therefore, stand up. Moreover, this way of looking at things led to some very odd conclusions:

> According to Professor Carr, we should have to say that Hitler is utopian in so far as he has ethical ends and a realist in so far as he uses power to attain them, and that the means, even though they attain the ends, are incompatible with the ends. There must be something very wrong with a theory and a definition which lead to such conclusions.[18]

But there was a second sense in which realism was utopian. Along with its inevitable harboring, however covertly, of ends, principles, and ideals, realism was utopian due to its inability to achieve its goals. In Woolf's view

> ... nothing is more "utopian" than the idea that you can create a stable and permanent society by power and the pursuit of conflicting interests; the ideal is unattainable because it involves an attempt to use two of the most unstable and disintegrating of all social forces, violence in the service of cupidity, as the primary ingredients in the cement which is to hold society together.[19]

Perhaps realism did not aim to create a "stable and permanent society." Even so, the problem was a deep one because realism could not achieve its *own*, stated, goals with any degree of permanence. The Great Powers who had provoked war in 1790, 1815, 1870, 1914, and 1939 had not gained from their actions; they had not gained from their "ruthless pursuit of conflicting interests."[20] The *realpolitik* of Germany toward Czechoslovakia, for instance, could only, at best, achieve temporary gains. If the hallmark of realism was success, then what was to be made of the "realism" of Napoleon I, Napoleon III, Bismarck, Wilhelm II, the Russian Czars, and the British imperialists? If success was the criterion, these "realists" were, in fact, "utopians." As Woolf contended in typically acerbic and dissenting style:

> Five hundred years of European history have proved that the "realist" system of power politics, war, and the conflict of interests is grotesquely utopian. Its purpose is to ensure stability of national power, glory, prosperity, and peace; its result has been a kaleidoscope of loud voiced jingoism and national glory alternating with war, defeat, misery, and impoverishment.[21]

Such a view of power politics was at the time far from an uncommon one, nor indeed one confined to radical circles. On the creation of the United Nations, President Roosevelt declared: "It spells—and it should spell—the end of the system of unilateral action, exclusive alliances, and spheres of influence, and balances of power, and all other expedients which have been tried for centuries and always failed."[22] Though one should never discount the rhetorical element in public statements such as this, it is also important not to underestimate the extent to which Woolf's contempt for power politics, his belief that they were futile in an ever-more interdependent world, was widely shared at the time.[23]

Immutable Interests

Carr argued that there was something intrinsic to states and their relations that gave their power and conflicting interests a peculiar reality over and above cooperation and common interests, and made a harmony of interests impossible.[24] Interests, Woolf contended, had become the political and social shibboleth of the twentieth century, just as utility had been in the nineteenth century, and rights in the eighteenth. The doctrine that certain *national* interests possessed a peculiar reality was one among several twentieth-century doctrines in which

> interests are treated just as natural rights were regarded in the eighteenth century, as fixed and immutable "natural" elements in society, hard facts or realities, like climate or navigable rivers or the sun and planets, and therefore causes whose effects upon history are naturally inevitable and outside human control.[25]

But in Woolf's view interests in general were not natural and immutable. On the contrary, they were unstable and fluid. They could change as a consequence of broader changes in society. Moreover, interests often possessed a "chameleon character." This was even true of so-called "vital national interests" that in theory were concerned with the continued existence of the state, but in practice meant "any interest which the government of a state considers important."[26]

To illustrate his counter-thesis Woolf cited several cases. Carr maintained

> To internationalise government in any real sense means to internationalise power; and since independent power is the basis of the nation-state, the internationalisation of power is really a contradiction in terms.

Exactly the same argument had been deployed in the mid-nineteenth century against socialism when many philosophers later sympathetic toward the doctrine, notably J. S. Mill, viewed it as an "ideal standard" but distant from "reality." Socialism was utopian, so the argument ran, because society was based on the institution of private property; in abolishing private property, socialism would only succeed in undermining society and thereby itself. Socialism and society were therefore incompatible; the interests of private property were immutable; the idea that society could be based on socialism was a contradiction in terms.

But as the nineteenth century unfolded, Woolf noted, such convictions began to lose their weight. By the first decade of the twentieth century many ideas previously considered utopian were widely entertained as sensible and correct. Woolf cited, *inter alia*, the public provision of primary and secondary education, municipal control of utilities, the extension of the franchise to the non-propertied classes, and state provision of old age pensions. Private property had not been abolished, but the view that the state had a vital role to play in curtailing and regulating the free play of private interests in service of the public good had become widely accepted. This example, Woolf felt, clearly demonstrated that interests were not natural and unchanging, and he concluded

> one must hesitate to accept sweeping statements about interests, conflicts of interests, and power being such immutable social or political "realities" that they inevitably determine the structure of society and make any attempt to alter it ... utopian.[27]

While it would be an overstatement to suggest that Woolf was putting forward a philosophically idealist conception of interests—note his frequent references to "the facts"—it is certainly true that in places his notion of interests resembles the type of interpretive analysis characteristic of C. A. W. Manning.[28] He compared, for example, the case of the conflict in the Balkans during the years 1900–1913, with the conflict in Scandinavia, over the desire of Norway to secede from Sweden, which occurred at the same time. The former conflict resulted in violence and war, whereas the latter was settled peaceably. Woolf insisted that it would be wrong to suppose that the Balkan states only had conflicting interests, whereas the Scandinavian states had only common interests. The states involved in both conflicts had common *and* conflicting interests. The key difference was that the Balkan states "believed that they had irreconcilable interests which could only be settled by power. And because that was the way in which they regarded their interests, their interests were, in fact, irreconcilable."[29]

In support of this point he gave the further example of Anglo-French relations between 1890 and 1904. This is a curious example since it is often cited as evidence of the realist claim that interests are defined in terms of the configuration of power. The Entente Cordiale, so the realist (and conventional) wisdom goes, was made possible by the rising power of Germany, and British and French fear of it. Woolf offered a fascinating account of how it became almost axiomatic in Britain during the 1890s that France was the "natural enemy."[30] The enmity between the two countries was seen as immutable. Then, quite dramatically, they began to foster closer relations and their mutual enmity began to subside. In Woolf's view this was entirely due to the sudden realization that Anglo-French differences, though considerable, could be settled by cooperation and compromise instead of competition and conflict:

> Lansdowne and Delcassé did not suddenly see that the conflicting interests had suddenly become "unreal" and the common interests "real"; they came to the conclusion that in general and in the long run the two countries would gain more by pursuing common interests and attempting to compose conflicting interests by compromise than by continuing the pursuit by each of its own interests at the expense of the other.[31]

Thus it was a "psychological" change that had occurred, not a realization that certain interests previously considered "real" had suddenly become "unreal."

The realist response that mutual fear of the rising power of imperial Germany was the major factor was dismissed by Woolf in the following rather cavalier way. If one held that fear was the key, one was in effect admitting that psychology, not material reality, determined international relations. If this was true, the notion that states could gather together in an association for the purpose of eliminating war was not utopian, as the realists claimed, but realistic. Fear of mutual destruction would provide the necessary incentive. If fear of Germany could induce Britain and France to settle their "immutable" interests, then why could fear of mutual destruction not induce all states to follow the same path?

However, although Woolf refuted the existence of immutable interests, and asserted that interests are fluid and changeable, he also strongly implied that real, permanent, interests do, in fact, exist. He asserted that the previous 100 years had demonstrated that not a single nation had gained anything permanent from war and that the vast majority of individuals lost out. Indeed, the history of Europe since 1815 showed that all nations had a common interest in peace and preventing war.[32] He clarified this point by making a distinction between immediate and long-term interests. The conventional view that conflicting interests are "more real" than common interests sprang from the fact that most people are more conscious of their own, immediate interests than their common interests, since the latter always involve the sacrifice, usually painful, of some immediate individual interests. Both conflicting and common interests therefore exist but whereas the former are immediate and superficial, the latter are long-term and substantial. Thus, Woolf suggested, "even the potential murderer is better off in the end if he refrains from cutting the rich man's throat." Similarly, "a class which ruthlessly pursues what it considers its own interest at the expense of other classes nine times out of ten digs its own economic grave."[33] And, taking an example from international relations, it was not the case that the interest of Germany in "cutting the throat" of Czechoslovakia was "more real" than the interest of both in living peacefully and composing their differences by compromise and conciliation.[34]

At root Woolf was saying that there is a long-term *objective* interest in peace. But for whom? Clearly he did not believe that this objective interest applied only to some states but not others. The key to a clear understanding of Woolf's thought on interests, and to understanding his dispute with Carr over them, lies in his notion of the state. In common with many of his contemporaries, Woolf did not have a sophisticated notion of the state. He commonly used the term "state" interchangeably with "nation" and conceived it as largely coterminous with its people.[35] Thus in his discussion of state interests in peace and war, Woolf often had in mind the people or society of the state rather than the "coercive/institutional" state.[36] When Woolf said that it was not in the interests of Germany to "cut the throat of Czechoslovakia," he had in mind the interests of the German people rather than the interests, as defined by those in power, of the "notional entity" "Germany." Two points must be made in this connection. First, when Woolf and Carr referred to state interests they were referring to different things. Carr, at least in his "realist critique," was referring to an abstracted state, reified, but in effect, personless. Woolf, by contrast, was for the most part referring to the people who constitute the *society* of the state. Second, Woolf was ultimately making what many would consider the rather banal point that human beings are generally better off when they are living in peace than when they are fighting wars.

The Rationalization of Violence

Woolf's most damning judgment was that Carr's theory amounted to little more than a rationalization of conflict and violence. It was one among a number of currently fashionable theories ("ex post facto consolatory explanations"[37]) that sought to prove that the increasing frequency and intensity of violence in interwar domestic and international political life was inevitable. It amounted, more generally, to the worrying view that nothing could possibly happen except in the way that it did. This view was particularly evident in Carr's treatment of the League. Carr asserted, "The first and most obvious tragedy of [the] ... utopia [of the League] was its ignominious collapse." Woolf angrily retorted that failure was not *ipso facto* ignominious, and it was not the case that just because the League failed it was bound to fail. There was a striking inconsistency in Carr's logic: after all, appeasement had failed but this did not lead Carr to the conclusion that this policy was utopian—nor indeed that its failure was "ignominious." Similarly, Hitler's policy of creating a new European order based on German supremacy would in all probability fail but neither did Carr reject this as utopian.

Implicit in Woolf's discussion here is the assumption that the whole matter turned on the question of "attainability." It was true that the League had aimed at the unattained objective of preventing war. But the policies of Hitler and Chamberlain had aimed at the unattained objectives of, respectively, German hegemony and "peace in our time." If the criterion of utopia was unattainability, Carr should have reached the conclusion that "the policies of Hitler and Mr. Chamberlain [were] no less utopian than the League policy."[38] But, aided by selective use of evidence, he had come to the opposite conclusion.

All this led Woolf to conclude that the central problems of contemporary international politics could not be understood or solved through a reliance on the distinction between utopias (or "illusions," or "shams") and realities. Whether the question was the survival of democracy, the validity of liberalism, the relevance of internationalism, or the efficacy of the League, this fashionable distinction was of no value. *The Twenty Years' Crisis* may have been the most sophisticated analysis to date to have been framed in these terms but, Carr's brilliance notwithstanding, it failed to specify with any degree of precision the criteria by which the utopianism or realism of any given idea or project could be gauged. In particular, Carr failed to demonstrate why the League of Nations was utopian except for the fact that it had failed.[39]

Woolf's Critique: An Evaluation

How valid are Woolf's criticisms of Carr? Before addressing this question, a brief qualification should be made. Woolf touched on a number of fundamental questions in his response, for example, the nature of interests, the meaning of utopianism and realism, and the practical and moral value of realism as a doctrine of IR. It is not my purpose here to confront these questions directly, and certainly not to give answers to them. Instead I will examine Woolf's response with the aim of identifying the most important respects in which his assertions are accurate or inaccurate.

Objection 1: The Meaning of Utopian

Woolf was right to contend that a major shortcoming of Carr's analysis was the failure to clearly define the term utopia. To demonstrate this it may be helpful to draw a distinction between Carr's general elaboration of the concept of utopia, as explicated in chapter 2 of *The Twenty Years' Crisis*, and the specific examples of utopian doctrine that he cites at various points in the text. The essence of Woolf's contention is that Carr's concept of utopia is highly ambiguous.

This judgment is not without merit with respect to Carr's general elaboration of the concept. But it is not the most apposite criticism that can be made. It is certainly the case that ambiguities exist, not least in Carr's failure to be explicit as to his understanding of the meaning of "theory." It is far from certain whether by "theory" he has in mind explanatory or normative theory, though it seems to be the case that he usually has the latter in mind. A more incisive criticism, however, is that Carr's exposition was simplistic. In his efforts to clarify what he considered to be the fundamental antithesis in political thought—between utopia and reality—Carr makes a number of sweeping generalizations that would, in his own terms, be worthy of the most utopian of utopians.

These generalizations are highlighted by what Hedley Bull has called Carr's "breathtaking equation" that utopia : reality = free will : determinism = theory : practice = the intellectual : the bureaucrat = Left : Right (to which might be added "generalization : observation = universal : relative = morality : power").[40] The boldness of the characterization is only matched by its artificiality. Marx, for example, is interpreted along with Engels and Lenin as a seminal modern realist, since he historicized and made dynamic the ahistorical and static realism of Hobbes, Spinoza, and Bodin. It is difficult, to say the least, to square this with the assertion that "the radical is necessarily utopian, and the conservative realist." Indeed, Carr's reading of Marx, the most cited figure in *The Twenty Years' Crisis* along with Hitler, is an interesting case in point. Marx was a realist because of the importance he attached to historical cause and effect, to the impact of material factors on history, and to the "relativity of thought to the interests and circumstances of the thinker." But he was also a utopian: (a) because he assumed "just as firmly as did the *laissez-faire* liberal" that "economics and politics were separate domains, one subordinate to the other"; (b) because of his *moral* condemnation of the bourgeoisie; and (c) because of his belief in the immanence of proletarian revolution and the culmination of the historical process in the creation of a worldwide classless society. In Carr's view, therefore, Marx was, in a number of respects, both realist *and* utopian. But this was not unusual. According to Carr, *all* realists are to some extent utopian since consistent realism is psychologically unsustainable. The notion of politics as an infinite process with no ultimate goals or final destination, says Carr, is "in the long run uncongenial or incomprehensible to the human mind." Mankind as a whole, he adds, is not prepared to accept Hegel's dictum that "World history is the world court." "The belief that whatever succeeds is right... must, if consistently held, empty thought of purpose, and thereby sterilise and ultimately destroy it." The conception of history as a rigid sequence of cause and effect, in which independent thought and action are, if possible, futile, is "plainly repugnant to the most deep-seated belief of man about himself." "The human will," Carr concludes, "will continue to seek an escape from the logical consequences of realism." For these reasons realists cannot, in practice, avoid positing a finite goal, engaging in moral judgment, assuming a normative ground for action, and appealing to human emotions. Indeed, although "utopian" Carr deems these four things "essential ingredients of all effective political thinking." In this way utopianism inevitably "penetrates the citadel of realism."[41]

Given this, Woolf's claim that Carr's realists and utopians are, to say the least, somewhat curious political animals, is a valid one. Given what Carr himself says, such creatures do not and could not exist, at least not in pure form. They are artificial creatures, creatures perhaps of the imagination, at best "ideal types," at worst crude caricatures.

But Woolf's charge of conceptual ambiguity has most weight when directed at the specific examples of utopian doctrine that Carr gives. In a sense this is not surprising since it is this aspect of Carr's analysis that Woolf had in mind when he claimed that Carr used the term utopian in at least two different senses. One of Carr's primary examples of utopian doctrine is classical political economy and, in particular, free trade. Carr makes three observations: (a) that classical political economy was founded upon the "negation" of existing, mercantilist, reality; (b) that it was predicated on "certain artificial and unverified assumptions about the behaviour of a hypothetical economic man"; and (c) that universal free trade—"the normal postulate of economic science"—was an "imaginary condition which has never existed." Just as no one had ever lived in Plato's republic or in one of Fourier's phalansteries, no one had ever lived in a world of universal free trade.[42]

It is clear that Carr's three observations correspond to three different meanings of the term utopian. Thus a utopian doctrine may be one that: (a) rejects an existing state of affairs in preference for a more desirable, but not yet existent, other; (b) is based on unverified and perhaps false assumptions; and (c) postulates as an economic, political, or ethical benchmark a condition that has no historical precedent. Whether or not Carr was aware of the fact that he had not one but several concepts of utopia, and that he was thus guilty of good deal of conceptual slippage is a moot point.

The example confirms, however, that Woolf was right to contend that his use of the term is ambiguous.

Woolf was also right to contend that while Carr had much to say about utopianism in the sense of "falseness of beliefs," he had little to say about it in the sense of "impossibility of attainment." Carr argued that classical political economy was based on certain false or at least unproven assumptions. But did this mean that its prescriptions were always and everywhere unattainable? In Woolf's view, the doctrine of free trade as conceived by the classical economists may have contained certain falsehoods, but this did not mean that the goal of free trade was a logically absurd or futile. Much more needed to be said to prove such a claim.

A second example Carr gave of utopian doctrine is Benthamite liberalism, in particular the Benthamite doctrine of "salvation by public opinion."[43] According to Carr,

> The belief that public opinion can be relied upon to judge rightly on any question rationally presented to it, combined with the assumption that it will act in accordance with this judgement is an essential foundation of the liberal creed.[44]

The pursuit of the good was a matter of "right reasoning," and "right reasoning" would soon come within everybody's reach with the spread of education. Although it was true that this doctrine had been a brilliant success in a limited number of countries, its advocates committed the fundamental error, Carr claimed, of assuming that it was an *a priori* principle of universal validity. In fact, its validity was strictly relative to material circumstances. Its success derived not from "certain *a priori* rational principles" but from "a balance of forces peculiar to the economic development of the period and the countries concerned." To assume otherwise was "essentially utopian."[45]

Even before the end of the nineteenth century, serious doubts had been cast on the assumptions of "Benthamite rationalism."

> Yet [Carr continues], by one of the ironies of history, these half-discarded nineteenth century assumptions reappeared, in the second and third decades of the twentieth century, in the special field of international politics, and there became one of the foundation-stones of a new utopian edifice.[46]

Through *The Great Illusion* and other books, for example, Sir Norman Angell sought to end war by convincing the world that war never brought profit to anyone. War was simply a failure of understanding that could be rectified by the correct application of reason:

> Reason could demonstrate the absurdity of international anarchy; and with increased knowledge enough people would be rationally convinced of its absurdity to put an end to it.[47]

But despite its easy appeal, this assumption was not well founded. It was not long before even the most optimistic utopian thinkers were forced to recognize that rather than being right and compelling, international public opinion was "almost as often wrong-headed as it was impotent."[48]

Again, two possible meanings of utopia can be detected in this example, which broadly corresponds to the two senses of the term identified by Woolf. On the one hand, Carr casts doubt on the Benthamite faith in public opinion by suggesting that its underlying principles were not only inapplicable to the international sphere but were also "false" or "untenable" *per se*. On the other hand, Carr criticizes Bethamite rationalism for imputing universal validity to principles strictly limited in their application. The success these principles generated in the nineteenth century was due to a special set of circumstances—Victorian prosperity, technological progress, British hegemony—which could not easily be replicated elsewhere. Benthamism, contrary to the assumptions of the interwar utopians, could *not* be transplanted.

Thus the doctrine was utopian: (a) in the sense that its assumptions were false or untenable; and (b) in the sense that its principles were only applicable within a particular socioeconomic context.

Free trade and Benthamism are Carr's prime utopian suspects. He does, of course, similarly berate a number of other things, chief among them being (a) the assumption that peace is indivisible; (b) the assumption that disarmament is a universal interest; (c) the assertion that war can be abolished through legal prohibition; (d) the idea of collective security; (e) the idea of an international police force; and (f) the idea of a United States of Europe.[49] In none of these cases are the grounds on which they should be considered utopian precisely and unambiguously laid out.

One may conclude, therefore, that although Woolf's analysis was incomplete, his argument was broadly speaking correct. Utopianism, rather than a precisely defined scientific concept, is a protean term used by Carr to cast in a bad light a range of ideas that he happened to find disagreeable.

Objection 2: The Utopianism of Realism

In common with many other radicals of the period Woolf was concerned to show that his outlook on international relations was accurate and practicable. In the second line of response identified here, Woolf took this concern to extremes. He sought to demonstrate that it was not utopianism that was utopian but, on the contrary, realism.

Although not without merit, the arguments made by Woolf in this connection are somewhat suspect. Woolf's most cogent claims turn out to be leveled at the weaker aspects of Carr's thesis. Woolf's characterization of realism is at best unsophisticated and at worst deeply flawed. Here, once more, the propagandist element is uppermost. He was not addressing a highly specialized IR audience on a rarefied theme of academic discourse but a general audience, comprised mainly of "the intelligent reader," on a theme of tremendous practical importance. He was eager to win narrowly defined political points as well as to uphold his conception of the political truth. In consequence, he was not averse to oversimplifying complex arguments, or even downright misrepresenting them, if it suited his propagandist purpose.

Taking the merits first, Woolf was correct to question Carr's distinction between realism defined in terms of a concern with facts, realities, and cause and effect, and utopianism defined in terms of a concern with principles, ideals, and ends. Such a distinction gives a crude impression of the ideal-type realist *vis à vis* the ideal-type utopian. But it grossly exaggerates the differences between actual, flesh and blood, realists and utopians—or more precisely those who have been described as realists and utopians. Clearly, as Woolf pointed out, it is nonsense to claim that utopians are unconcerned with facts and realities, though it is true that those so labeled emphasized different kinds of facts. Indeed, as we have seen, Woolf is a good example of a thinker conventionally labeled utopian who engaged in a good deal of factual analysis, though not of the kind necessarily valued by realists. Similarly, it is nonsense to claim that realists are unconcerned with principles and ends. After all, the notion that a statesman should act in accordance with the national interest is a principle—if not a particularly helpful one—and even the most pragmatic statesmen pursue ends in the sense that they have some sort of image of a desirable world—albeit one limited in ambition and heavily contingent on concrete historical circumstances. Indeed, "turning the weapons of realism on realism itself,"[50] it might be argued that pragmatism is the principle of action of the satisfied Powers. A pragmatic foreign policy involves keeping ethical principles at arm's length, continually modifying foreign-policy goals in the light of prevailing circumstances, privileging practicability over ambition, and concrete short-term interests over abstract long-term ones. It presupposes general satisfaction with the way things are. To this extent it embodies no less of an "end" to the desire to radically change things.

This, of course, receives some recognition by Carr. He rejects the sharp separation of fact and value that a "consistent and thorough-going realism" presupposes. He says, for instance, that "the distinction between the analysis of what is from the aspiration of what should be can never be absolute" and that "political scientists can never wholly emancipate themselves from utopianism." In this sense pure realists and utopians do not actually exist—all political thought, perhaps action too, contains elements of both realism and utopia, with some thinkers and practitioners giving more emphasis to one and others to the other.[51]

Woolf was the first of Carr's critics to point out that lack of precision in this respect constitutes a serious theoretical flaw.[52] Indeed, it leads to some heroic inconsistencies. Carr asserts, for instance, that a "pure" utopian or realist cannot exist. But this does not stop him from presenting certain figures as unequivocally utopian (Wilson, Angell, Toynbee), and others as unequivocally realist (Hobbes, Machiavelli, Marx). He contends that all policies contain the "mutually antagonistic" elements of reality and utopia. But he also asserts that certain ideas (democratic control of foreign policy, an international police force, a United States of Europe) are "purely utopian." He strongly implies that the antagonism between utopianism and realism is rooted in human nature (an unverifiable proposition and therefore utopian?). But he also insists that all knowledge is socially constructed.[53]

Woolf's second and more polemical claim was that realism is utopian not only in the sense that ideals and goals, *pace* Carr, are pursued by "realist" as well as "utopian" statesmen, but also in the sense that these goals cannot be achieved by realist means. According to Woolf, the goals of realism are stability of national power, glory, prosperity, peace, and a "stable and permanent society." The methods of realism are violence, war, power politics, and "pursuit of conflicting interests." The failure of these methods to achieve these goals was, in Woolf's view, amply demonstrated by the historical record. The historical evidence actually provided by Woolf is, however, rather thin. Not only does he give few examples, but also those he gives are undeveloped and leave considerable room for interpretation. For instance, though we may be comfortable with the proposition that Napoleon I and Wilhelm II failed to achieve their objectives, the proposition that Bismarck and "the British imperialists" failed to achieve theirs can be doubted. So too can the proposition that the "Great Powers who provoked war" in 1790 and 1870 did not gain by their actions. As for the 1914 War, the question who provoked it and who is to blame—not of course the same question—is still a highly contentious matter.

Woolf's line of attack here is too general to be of value. The postulated goals of realism are so broad that it is impossible to assess, in the absence of further clarification, whether they had been achieved or not (or, perhaps more pertinently, to what extent). After all, what is to count as "prosperity," "glory," "stability of national power," and indeed "peace?" Further clarification of these notions is needed before anything like an accurate appraisal can be made.

Woolf's depiction of the instruments of realism is similarly broad. He strongly implies that realism has a monopoly on the methods of "violence" and "war." But this is a fallacy. Woolf himself believed that the use of these methods was necessary and justifiable in certain circumstances, even though, as we saw in chapter 4, he tended to give them different names. "Power politics" and the "pursuit of conflicting interests" are notions generally associated with realism but again Woolf fails to indicate precisely what he means by them. "Pursuit of conflicting interests" is, to say the least, tendentious.

One must conclude, therefore, that although Woolf clearly demonstrates his prejudices against realism he fails to enhance our understanding of it, or throw much light on its shortcomings. Like Carr's utopian, Woolf's realist is a straw man. He did not seriously confront Carr's more intellectually robust realist claims regarding the self-interested character of thought and the inescapable ethical relativity of the international domain.

Objection 3: Immutable Interests

Woolf claimed that Carr attached a peculiar reality to power and conflicting interests over and above cooperation and common interests. The clash of interests, in the world according to Carr, was immutable and a harmony of interests impossible.

There is plenty of evidence for this claim in Carr's text. Carr asserts,

> realism tends to emphasize the irresistible strength of existing forces and the inevitable character of existing tendencies, and to insist that the highest wisdom lies in accepting, and adapting oneself to, these forces and tendencies.

Moreover,

> the outstanding achievement of modern realism ... has been to reveal, not merely the determinist aspects of the historical process, but the relative and pragmatic character of thought.

The intellectual assumed that his theories were objective and universal. Realism demonstrated, however, that they were in fact historically conditioned, "being both products of circumstances and weapons framed for the furtherance of interests." This was the sense in which all thought was "pragmatic": it was not only relative to the circumstances of the thinker, but also consciously or unconsciously directed at the fulfillment of his or her purposes.[54]

Those thinkers who postulated a harmony of international interests, Carr continued, were in reality merely the unthinking proponents of a particular conception of national interest at a particular time. The doctrine of a harmony of interest in free trade and peace was merely the doctrine of the economic and political top dog. Count Walewski's maxim that "it is the business of a diplomat to clothe the interests of the state in the language of universal justice" was amply confirmed by utopian intellectuals who clothed their own interests in the guise of universality for the purpose of imposing them on the rest of the world.[55] At disarmament talks Britain and the United States condemned the submarine and submarine warfare as "uncivilized" and sought to secure a worldwide ban. It so happened, however, that they were speaking from a position of surface fleet supremacy, and the invocation of "civilization" failed to resonate with Italy, France, and Japan who viewed the submarine as a valuable weapon that they could use to challenge such supremacy. Similarly, throughout most of the nineteenth century, and in the twentieth century until 1931, tariffs and other protectionist measures were generally regarded in Britain as not only counterproductive but immoral. But this attitude dramatically changed as Britain's economic fortunes worsened. As with the submarine, the tariff revealed itself as the weapon of the weaker Power. When Britain resorted to a range of protectionist measures with the onset of the Depression in the 1930s, the moral response was "curiously muted."

This summary of Carr's "realist critique"[56] certainly suggests that his rejection of international or universal interests was absolute. In reality, such interests were nothing more than cleverly disguised national interests. Indeed, given the rigid determinism of realism this was inevitably so. All thought was consciously or unconsciously self-interested.

In Woolf's objection to the "peculiar reality" that Carr attaches to conflicting interests over and above common interests, one can detect, therefore, the beginnings of a critique of what is the central plank of Carr's thesis: that the "supposedly absolute and universal principles [of the utopian] were not principles at all, but the unconscious reflexions of national policy based on a particular interpretation of national interest at a particular time."[57] The only real interests are selfish interests. The notion of a harmony of interests is merely an ideological device.

It could be countered, however, that the validity of Woolf's argument is limited to the extent that it is confined to Carr's "realist critique." This critique, as set out in chapter 5 of *The Twenty Years' Crisis*, may not be *his* critique, that is, a position that Carr himself fully subscribed to. One of the big problems in making sense of the book is that Carr, whether consciously, for rhetorical purposes, or not, does not take care to distinguish his own voice (whatever, precisely, that might be) from the realist voice (however idiosyncratically portrayed), which is set out in Parts I and II of the book and makes intermittent appearances thereafter. This accounts for the tendency in IR to erroneously interpret *The Twenty Years' Crisis* as an unambiguous realist text.[58] Carr beguiles the reader into thinking that the realist voice in Parts I and II of the book is his voice. But in the final chapter of Part II and throughout the rest of the book it dawns on the reader, at least the careful reader, that this might not be the case. Carr in his typically subtle way begins to distance himself from the realism that he had initially presented as incontrovertible fact. Realism was a "necessary corrective to the exuberance of utopianism." It was essential for "counteracting" the dangerous neglect of the factor of power in utopian thought. But it did not have a monopoly on political truth. On the contrary, realism could be "carried to a point where it results in the sterilization of thought and the negation of action." It contained a number of severe limitations, lacking, as we have seen, four essential ingredients of effective political thought: a finite goal; an emotional appeal; a right of moral judgment; and a ground for action.[59]

It could be argued, therefore, that Carr was not so much presenting a manifesto for political realism as restating and redefining the case for one of the two elements of politics irreconcilably locked together in an endless dialectical relationship.

Although Woolf recognized that *The Twenty Years' Crisis* was more than just an explication of realism, he did not fully appreciate the dialectical nature of Carr's approach. However, his view that Carr assumed that there was a peculiar reality in conflicting interests does not hinge exclusively on his "realist critique." For example, Carr challenges the notion, frequently espoused at the time, that war was irrational or immoral and that all states had a common interest in peace. According to Carr, this notion "in reality" was a reflection of the special interests of the *status quo* Powers, particularly Britain and the United States. He asserts,

> The common interest in peace masks the fact that some nations desire to maintain the status quo without having to fight for it, and others to change the *status quo* without having to fight in order to do so.[60]

There was a "fundamental divergence of interests" between the *status quo* Powers and the revisionist Powers. The world interest in peace was a "utopian assumption" based on "a peculiar combination of platitude and falseness." "The fact of divergent interests is disguised and falsified by the platitude of a general desire to avoid conflict."[61]

Similarly, Carr refutes the *laissez faire* belief, manifest in numerous official pronouncements during the period, that international economic conflict was unnecessary and illusory. He asserts, on the contrary, that a policy of economic nationalism may not be detrimental to the states that pursue it. The presumption of a world economic interest disguised the "true nature" of the problem. The harmony of economic interests was the doctrine of the economically strong; protectionism the defensive doctrine of the economically weak. "The clash of interests," he concluded, "is real and inevitable; and the whole nature of the problem is distorted by an attempt to disguise it."[62]

These examples are significant because they illustrate the difficulties that Woolf and subsequent readers have faced in accurately interpreting the text. Since they are not taken from Carr's explicit realist critique it is initially and naturally assumed that they are Carr's opinions, and not merely the opinions of one among several abstract voices woven into the text for pedagogic or heuristic purposes. Whether intentionally or not Woolf discounted the possibility, here as elsewhere, that these opinions were not precisely Carr's but those of a purposefully constructed abstract realist. They thus provide grist to Woolf's mill that Carr attached a peculiar reality to conflicting interests over and above common interests.

The confusion that Carr's rhetorical style and analytical method (which together have led some observers to dismiss the book, unfairly, as merely a polemic) provoked was considerable, especially on the matter of common versus conflicting interests. Writing a year after Woolf, the moral philosopher Susan Stebbing commented:

> [Carr] usually speaks as if he thought that power and conflicting interests of nations were the sole realities. In the latter part of the book he seems to admit that there really are some common, international, interests. It is very confusing.[63]

Stebbing interpreted Carr's antonyms (to which she added "conscience : coercion = goodwill : enmity = self subordination : self assertion") in the same way as Woolf. Not only were these antonyms confounding and misleading but they also helped Carr to believe that "conflicting interests are significantly 'real' and goodwill and common interests importantly 'unreal.' "[64]

Given the slippery nature of Carr's analysis, Woolf was being far from unreasonable in equating Carr's voice with the realist voice, and in particular, in attributing the cynical realist position on common and conflicting interests to Carr himself.

Objection 4: Rationalization of Violence

Carr's assertions about real interests and cause and effect led Woolf to conclude that *The Twenty Years' Crisis* amounted ultimately to little more than a rationalization of violence. He took particular exception to Carr's assertion—as he saw it—that the League was utopian as proved by its failure. The logic of this kind of argument was that success was the sole arbiter of practicability. To Woolf and other critics this was grossly deterministic. As Stebbing put it: "To make success the criterion is to fall into the mistake of supposing that whatever has in fact happened inevitably happened."[65]

Most worrying was the implication that Fascist bullying, dictatorship, intimidation, and violence, was a necessary and therefore inevitable part of the historical process. Woolf considered this an outrageous claim—especially in an age in which the corollary of "inevitable" violence and conflict was recurrent totalitarian war.[66]

The determinism of Carr's conception of realism is certainly striking. He describes the following three suppositions as the foundation stones of political realism: (a) that history is a sequence of cause and effect; (b) that theory does not create practice but practice theory; and (c) that politics is not a function of ethics but ethics politics. "On the 'scientific' hypothesis of the realists," he continues, "reality is thus identified with the whole course of human evolution, whose laws it is the business of the philosopher to investigate and reveal." He cites Spinoza: "every man does what he does according to the laws of his nature and to the highest right of nature," and adds the famous phrase of Hegel: "World history is the world court." He amends the popular but "misleading" paraphrase "Might is Right" with the more refined formula: "History creates rights, and therefore right."[67]

However, as we have seen, Carr did not fully subscribe to the doctrine of political realism he so vividly explicated. This is implicit, among other things, in his use of inverted commas around the word "science" in the sentence quoted above. Woolf's claim that Carr's determinism resulted in the rationalization of violence is therefore only partly true. Carr was no bellicist or militarist, though Woolf sometimes gives this impression. His later, lesser-known, works contain far less of the "ruthlessness" and "detached relish in the supremacy of things evil."[68] As will be seen in the next section, Carr's

Conditions of Peace is markedly progressive, even utopian. In addition, it should be remembered that the principal policy recommendation of *The Twenty Years' Crisis* is appeasement, conceived as a process of give and take between satisfied and dissatisfied Powers, an act of "prudential yielding" (to use W. T. R. Fox's helpful phrase) on the part of the former to the latter, involving both "essential elements" of politics: power and morality. It was for Carr a relatively peaceful means of securing necessary adjustments to the *status quo*.

Nevertheless, after saying this, some of Carr's pronouncements on appeasement and peaceful change do lend credence to Woolf's claims. To describe such events as Mussolini's successful conquest of Abyssinia, and Hitler's successful seizure of the Rhineland, Austria, and Czechoslovakia, as instances of *peaceful* change does seem to be stretching language to an absurd degree. It involves in fact a limitation of the concept of peace to "absence of armed conflict between the Great Powers." Also, as W. T. R. Fox has demonstrated, although Carr stated that he did not substantially revise anything in the second edition of *The Twenty Years' Crisis* he had said in the first, one revision at least is highly significant. In the second edition the following passage was omitted:

> If the power relations of Europe in 1938 made it inevitable that Czecho-Slovakia should lose part of her territory, and eventually her independence, it was preferable (quite apart from any question of justice or injustice) that this should come about as the result of discussion round a table in Munich rather than as the result either of a war between the Great Powers or of a local war between Germany and Czecho-Slovakia.[69]

The omission of this passage suggests that by 1946 Carr was conscious of the fact that some of his pronouncements could be interpreted as callous, perhaps even apologetic. It would, however, be only half the story to interpret this passage as a rationalization of violence, since the clear implication is that accepting a certain amount of intimidation may be a necessary price to pay in order to secure something much more valuable: peace between the Great Powers.

Ultimately, whether or not the deterministic elements in Carr's thesis amount to a rationalization of violence depends on the extent to which such a rigid theory of historical cause and effect is true. Woolf believed it profoundly *un*true. He was, as I have argued, a voluntarist. He placed great store by the role of reason in human affairs. He also attached great importance to what he called the psychological dimension, by which he meant the influence on events of consciously or unconsciously held assumptions, values, and beliefs. He believed that there was no reason why a body like the League could not work as long as the necessary "internationalist psychology" existed to back it up. This psychology had been steadily building up for a century or more. It was driven by the onward march of technological progress and the inexorable demands of modern commercial life. It had received a huge boost with the mass revulsion against war that had occurred in the wake of the First World War. Until 1933 Woolf felt that for these and other reasons, that the prospects for an effective League based on a strong and widely shared internationalist psychology were encouraging.[70] Thus radical progressive change was possible in international affairs and it was a product of sometimes rapid, but usually gradual, changes in people's ideas, attitudes, and beliefs. For Woolf it was a travesty to suggest that international conflict was "more real" than international cooperation, that conflicting interests were immutable, and that the League was doomed to fail.

Woolf and Carr Compared

Despite Woolf's root and branch rejection of Carr's analysis, and despite the fact that Woolf himself noticed little common ground, it can be argued that the two thinkers had a great deal in common. Indeed, it might be argued that they were coming not from the opposite poles of utopianism and realism, but from a very similar perspective. This perspective was, broadly speaking, socialist, functionalist, and collectivist. They shared the belief that nineteenth-century liberal democracy and *laissez faire* were obsolete, that the nation-state was obsolescent, and that the future lay in economic and social democracy and cross-border functional and collective organization.

Like so many commentators both at the time and since, Woolf did not notice the functionalist and collectivist aspects of *The Twenty Years' Crisis*, even though they are fairly explicit. This is primarily due to the fact that he gave all his attention to the first half of the book and largely ignored the second. If he had paid more attention to the latter, he would have realized that the book was far more than an *apologia* for violence and unbending political realism. This is certainly true of Carr's work as a whole. The diversity and indeed eclecticism of his thought is clearly revealed in subsequent works, *Conditions of Peace, Nationalism and After,* and *The New Society* in particular. To some extent Woolf remedied his omission when he reviewed *Conditions of Peace*.[71] He welcomed much of what Carr had to say about postwar reconstruction and organization, especially the idea that democracy needed to be reinterpreted in predominantly economic terms, and the view that the right to self-determination needed to be placed within a wider framework of international obligation. Woolf insisted, however, that these ideas were far from new, having long been central to radical and socialist thought. Such a reinterpretation of democracy had been called for in *The Communist Manifesto* and it had for many decades been the policy of the Labour Party. Similarly, what was the League, asked Woolf, if it was not an attempt to place self-determination within a wider framework of obligation? He was astounded that Carr failed to acknowledge this, and he boldly concluded that Carr "has always misunderstood and misinterpreted the years between the wars, and particularly the history of the League of Nations."[72] Woolf's general view was that although *Conditions of Peace* was in the main correct, it was essentially a naïve book since it failed to recognize that its central arguments had been made before.

The common ground in the thinking of Carr and Woolf is most striking in the following five areas.

First, they both argued that nineteenth-century liberal democracy had become stale and hollow, and that, if democracy was to remain meaningful in the age of mass production and mass participation, narrow "political" democracy needed to be supplemented with economic and social democracy. According to Carr, political equality needed to be supplemented with "a progressive advance towards social and economic equality." The will of the ordinary citizen, he contended, must be made to prevail against the "organised forces of economic power." This could be done by "draw[ing] the ordinary citizen more and more into the processes of administration," thus "kindling a fresh sense of obligation," making democracy "his affair," and dissolving at last the destructive antithesis of "we" and "they" in social life. Similarly, Woolf argued that democracy could not survive unless vast differences in wealth were reduced, education improved, and "socially equal opportunities" established.[73]

Second, they both argued that the right of self-determination was not an absolute right. It did not permit states to do whatever they wanted within their borders regardless of the impact on the wider world. So conceived the right of self-determination was destructive of all that was good in international life. It made any "real international society" (to use Carr's term) impossible. Consequently, it was essential to place the right of self-determination within a clear framework of international obligation. Carr emphasized the need for "a new conception of obligation." The right of self-determination, he contended, "must carry with it a recognised responsibility to subordinate military and economic policy and resources to the needs of a wider community..."[74] In *The Twenty Years' Crisis* he makes repeated reference to the need to cultivate a spirit of self-sacrifice on the part of privileged groups and privileged classes.[75] The thrust of much of what Woolf had to say about international order involved regulating for the common good the freedom of action of "sovereign" and therefore "irresponsible" states.[76] Despite the shortcomings of the minorities, treaties, he was particularly keen to establish a charter for the rights of minorities the implementation of which would be supervised internationally.[77]

Third, both Carr and Woolf felt that one of the central problems of reconstruction would be how to deal with the "small state." The political and economic weakness of small states had significantly compounded the instability of Europe during the interwar years. Carr argued that small states had become a dangerous anachronism. The great social revolution of the twentieth century, of which the two world wars were the creative birth pangs, demonstrated that the future lay in large-scale economic and political organization. Small states could survive "only as an anomaly and an anachronism in a world which has moved on to other forms of organisation."[78] Carr's rejection of the Wilsonian belief in national self-determination was unequivocal:

> By treating the principle of national self-determination as an absolute and by carrying it further than it had ever been carried before, [Woodrow Wilson and his associates] fostered the disintegration of existing political units, and favoured the creation of a multiplicity of smaller units, at a moment when strategic and economic factors were demanding increased integration and the grouping of the world into fewer and larger units of power.[79]

Accordingly, Carr suggested that small states should pursue their economic and military policies "jointly" with a Great Power. This would involve the pooling of resources and the establishment of some sort of common control.

Woolf's view was that the future of the small state in the "international firmament" would be one of the most crucial and difficult problems of postwar reconstruction. But in contrast to Carr, he emphasized that the status and position of the Great Powers was also a matter of crucial importance. Whilst agreeing with Carr that the sovereignty and independence of small states, both in political and economic terms, would have to be curtailed, Woolf was critical of the notion, strongly implicit in Carr's scheme, that small states would inevitably be reduced to the status of mere satellites around the Great Power in whose orbit they happened to fall. On the contrary, the wings of sovereignty of Powers both small and great had to be clipped. All states would have to consent to some form of international government.[80]

As well as suggesting that it was specifically the sovereignty of small states that would have to be curtailed, Carr, like Woolf, also made a number of assertions about sovereignty *per se*. "The concept of sovereignty," he contended, "is likely to become in the future even more blurred and indistinct than it is at present." The chief task facing the peacemakers was not, therefore, to change the location of frontiers, as had happened disastrously at Versailles, but to change their meaning. Carr further claimed, "The military security and economic well-being of Great Powers, not less than those of smaller countries, is bound up with the acceptance of a new conception of obligation." In doing so he was stepping out onto conceptual ground very similar to that mapped-out by Woolf 25 years earlier.[81]

Fourth, there are pronounced elements of functionalism in both Woolf and Carr. As I argued in chapter 4, Woolf was a pioneer of international functionalism. Carr, as will be further illustrated in my fifth point, was also thinking very much along functionalist lines by the early 1940s. There are numerous allusions to functionalist organization in *Conditions of Peace*. He suggests that "practical international cooperation," such as international public works, could become a "psychological substitute for war." He asserts, "for the control of military and economic policy, the national unit has become visibly too small" and "if a durable international order is to be realised, men must be induced to determine themselves into different units for different purposes." He emphasizes "the psychological importance of introducing at an early stage [in post-war reconstruction] the conception of cooperation in a common task." He talks of "new loyalties arising out of newly felt needs" and the building "new institutions" on the basis of these loyalties. He also talks of forging "regional industrial groupings which cut across national frontiers."[82]

Fifth, both Woolf and Carr contended that the achievement of economic and social equality was an absolute precondition for the future maintenance of international stability, and that this could only be achieved through substantial government intervention. The nineteenth-century idea of the nightwatchman state needed to be replaced by the twentieth-century idea of the social service state. Moreover, this "broadening of national policy" needed to go hand in hand with a "broadening of international policy." The New Europe, as Carr called it, would have to be dedicated to the satisfaction of the interests of the whole and not just, as had happened in the past, the parts. Thus the welfare of Lodz, Lille, and Düsseldorf would have to be taken into account as well as the interests of Oldham and Jarrow.[83] Just as Woolf argued that the pursuit of common interests almost always involved the sacrifice of some "immediate individual interests," so Carr asserted the importance of self-sacrifice. Indeed, in places he gave this an expressly socialist form:

> ... the conflict between nations like the conflict between classes cannot be resolved without real sacrifices, involving in all probability a reduction of consumption by priviledged groups in privileged countries.[84]

Carr went on to advocate international "control" of trade, finance, and production. He argued for production for use rather than production for profit. He asserted that "Employment has become more important than profit, social stability than increased consumption, equitable distribution than maximum production." To ensure full employment he called for a "programme of economically unremunerative expenditure" such as the provision of "free housing, free motor cars, or free clothing." He proposed the establishment of a European Relief Commission, a European Transport Commission, a European Construction and Public Works Commission, and, most radically, a Bank of Europe with "ultimate" control over national currencies. The task of overseeing these bodies would be given to a European Planning Authority, which should, he recommended, "be encouraged to develop into the ultimate authority responsible for vital decisions on European economic policies." Some of these institutions and their areas of competence would be created and assumed immediately, whereas others would be the product of gradual evolution.[85]

Together these bodies have more than a passing resemblance to Woolf's "International Economic Commission" possessing "very extensive powers" and "far-reaching responsibilities."[86] Most significantly, however, Carr's ideas on these matters were similar to the ideas Woolf had been discussing and developing over two decades earlier. No doubt Carr was much more of a "regionalist" than Woolf. He also envisaged a world (certainly a "Europe") with a much greater degree of central planning. Woolf, by contrast, was generally distrustful of extensive centralization (though as we saw in chapters 3 and 4 there are some notable exceptions). Hence his earlier attachment to international Co-operative trade rather than state trading. It is clear, however, that despite certain differences (and it might be added a convenient lack of detail), Carr and Woolf envisaged a world with a very similar economic and political structure. Most importantly, their visions for a new world order were based on very similar assumptions: *laissez faire* was dead; national self-determination was mortally wounded; sovereignty was obsolescent; and the era of mass production and democracy had arrived, and could not be wished away.

Conclusion: Woolf : Carr = Utopianism : Realism?

These similarities in outlook of Woolf and Carr suggest that the conventional view that Woolf was a utopian and Carr a realist is deeply inadequate. By placing Woolf and Carr in opposing schools of thought some of their most important ideas and beliefs have been effectively sidelined. This is especially the case with Carr who, until recently, has been almost invariably characterized in IR on the basis of a one-dimensional interpretation of *The Twenty Years' Crisis*. Yet it is not only realists anxious to co-opt such a great thinker to their cause who stand guilty of this charge. Thinkers of more utopian inclinations do too. Indeed, Woolf was one of the first commentators on *The Twenty Years' Crisis* to misinterpret it as merely a realist tract—a view that regrettably stuck.

Scholars of the "first great debate" have invariably recounted this debate in simplistic terms. No mention of Carr's functionalism, socialism, or collectivism is made, for example, in Bull's "*Twenty Years' Crisis* Thirty Years on." This is significant because it is probably the most widely read article on Carr. By overlooking the socialist, functionalist, and collectivist aspects of Carr's and Woolf's thought, analysts of the idealist–realist debate have omitted a crucial set of factors.[87] Without reference to these factors the thought of Carr, Woolf, and other notable socialist and Left-Liberal thinkers such as Cole, Laski, Brailsford, Mitrany, Hobson, and Keynes, becomes largely inexplicable.

However, given the fact that Woolf was severely critical of the bulk of Carr's thesis, might it not be said that the conventional view is not entirely without merit? The question turns on the meanings of the terms utopianism and realism. Both Woolf and Carr might be considered utopian in the dual sense that they desired radical change of the international system, and that they felt that change was not a wholly predetermined process. Both Woolf and Carr challenged the international system of supposedly sovereign, independent states and argued for its replacement by a more collectivist and functionalist world order.

There is, however, a more pronounced element of historicism in Carr than in Woolf. Carr held that the world was in the throes of a "great social revolution." The task facing both the forward-looking practitioner and the political scientist was to identify the nature of this revolution, assess its ramifications, and alert the body politic as to how social forms and practices could be most efficaciously modified in light of them. While Woolf was fully cognizant of the structural and institutional imperatives issued by industrialism and the communications revolution (see chapter 3), he nonetheless reserved a large degree of scope in his scheme of things for human agency. New needs had been created but this did not mean that the attitudes of mind, the values, and the institutions would necessarily come into being in order to satisfy them. The world could remain for some time, perhaps indefinitely, at odds with itself. Choices based on reason and "the facts" had to be made but there was no guarantee that they would.

In one sense the essence of realism for Carr was the ability to comprehend and adapt to the forces of historical change. These forces were primarily economic. Indeed a central difference between Woolf and Carr is that whereas Carr emphasized the importance of economic substructure over political superstructure, Woolf maintained that substructure and superstructure were interdependent. Carr's principal objection to the League was that it was a blueprint or paper scheme. It sought to rid the world of war by simply acquiring an undertaking from past, present, and potential offenders not to resort to it. This, to Carr, was unforgivably utopian: a form of naïve constitutionalism: a naïve faith in the ability of "rational" laws and institutions to mold behavior.[88] While sharing some of Carr's skepticism, Woolf firmly believed that building a new international system required not only material foundations but also an overall plan or conception. At a minimum, prior agreement on the broad outline of this system was needed if further descent into hostile competition and anarchy was to be avoided.[89] Carr wanted and expected his new world to be built pragmatically, bit by bit, undirected by a grand plan. The founders of the League had given all their attention to its architecture and ignored the foundations. For Woolf, by contrast, the architect was every bit as important as the builder and the structural engineer.

Carr argued that in contrast to Versailles, economic and social questions should have priority over political and territorial questions. Only after social and economic cooperation had been working successfully for some time could the question of a permanent international political framework be addressed. Woolf, by contrast, argued that politics and economics were inextricably linked and that it was a fallacy to suppose that if one looked after the economics, the politics would look after themselves. Concentrating exclusively on social and economic matters—which he doubted was possible—would not solve the problem of nationalism and national self-determination. It was not the case that if Poles, Czechs, and Serbs had enough to live on, they would cease to bother about their nationality. Woolf agreed with Carr that Versailles was a flawed peace. But he considered Carr to be under the illusion that if you reverse what is unequivocally wrong, you get what is right. Economic and social questions were vital and Versailles had largely ignored them. However, if the process was reversed, "we shall do no better with our economics than they did with their politics."[90] In any case, international economic cooperation and control, as advocated by both Woolf and Carr, would immediately and inevitably involve one of the most crucial of all political questions: sovereignty.

CHAPTER 9

Woolf's Legacy: Ideals, Reason, and Historical Change

Given the contentious nature of IR, the nature and significance of Woolf's legacy is bound to vary from observer to observer. Hedley Bull, as we have seen, was of the view that Woolf's *International Government*, along with a number of other early twentieth-century IR works, was "not at all profound" and not worth reading now except for the light it threw on the "preoccupations and presuppositions" of its age. But as we also saw, this judgment rests on a conservative premise: continuity is assumed to be more significant and more revealing of the substance of international politics than change. If the elements of change in international politics, however, are ranked at least as high as the elements of continuity, Bull's judgment becomes far less sound. We saw in chapter 2 that in Bull's view the idealists disparaged the past, seeing it merely as "a series of object lessons" about anarchy and disorder. Moreover present and future possibilities, to the idealist way of thinking, were not limited by the "test of previous experience" but were "deducible from the needs of progress."

These edicts, however, hardly apply to the thought of Leonard Woolf. It is certainly true that for Woolf the past did contain some profound lessons about anarchy and disorder. But more importantly it contained vital clues to the direction of current socioeconomic development. As we saw in chapter 3, the communications revolution of the nineteenth century, in Woolf's view, had given rise to an enormous expansion of international activity, leading to a manifold increase in social, economic, scientific, and cultural interconnectedness, and sparking the growth of a plethora of public and private international organs, bodies, and associations. The problem was that this huge increase in social, economic, scientific, and cultural interdependence, and "every-day" or "practical" international government, had not been matched by corresponding changes in the realm of political organization. Nor had it been accompanied by a sufficiently sizeable shift from "national" to "international communal psychology." It was this dissonance between the socioeconomic and the political organization of mankind, and the tension between a modern, internationalist communal psychology and an atavist, nationalist communal psychology, that was the breeding ground for the terrible conflicts and political ills of the first half of the twentieth century.

Whatever, therefore, we may think of the precise details and overall cogency of Woolf's account of international government—and various problems with it were identified in chapter 4—it is simply not true to say that he believed that future possibilities were not limited by the "test of previous experience" but "deducible from the needs of progress." While Woolf clearly had a vision of the "needs of progress" it was one substantially informed by a reading of past and current trends. Woolf was not calling for a complete break with the past, as Bull's argument implies, but the development of what he regarded as some of its more progressive features. These features had already taken root and were firmly imbedded in socioeconomic reality. The forces that ushered them into being and sustained them—technological innovation and change, scientific and administrative rationality, commercial profit and efficiency—were still powerful forces in society. Their further development had been injured by the catastrophe that was the Great War but not fatally or irreparably. The War stood as a stark and terrifying reminder that if the world wanted to enjoy the fruits of modern, scientific, technologically and economically advanced civilization, it would have to suffer a reduction in the sovereignty and independence of, and individual loyalty toward, its political subunits, and foster the further development of the organs and organisms of international government.

Woolf like Bull, therefore, considered the nineteenth century to be tremendously important from an international point of view. It contained a rich vein of salutary and relevant international experience. But the lessons he drew from it concerning the expansion of the role of international law, organization, and government were very different from those drawn by Bull, whose skepticism toward the role of such methods and devices, particularly the doctrine of the just war and the legal prohibition of war, is well known.[1] Woolf's reading of the nineteenth century is one that put far greater emphasis on what we today call transnational flows and, relatedly, the social, economic, and cultural dimensions of world politics *vis à vis* the strategic and political. It is also one that seems more at home in the more fluid international setting of the post–Cold War period than in the (in many ways) more rigid era of warring modern-industrial states, 1914–1989.

Along with the wishful thinking, the innocence, and the simplemindedness that for over 50 years have been associated with this rather plastic "interwar idealism," must be listed political impotence. It is a sobering thought that Woolf regarded his political career, though worthwhile in many respects, as ultimately a failure. In the final volume of his autobiography, echoing the sentiments of one of his first Fabian mentors, George Bernard Shaw, three decades earlier, Woolf lamented:

> Looking back at the age of eighty-eight over the fifty-seven years of my political work in England, knowing what I aimed at and the results, meditating on the history of Britain and the world since 1914, I see clearly that I achieved practically nothing. The world today and the history of the human anthill during the past fifty-seven years would be exactly the same as it is if I had played pingpong instead of sitting on committees and writing books and memoranda.[2]

But as we have seen in this study, Woolf's achievements in the field of international politics, practical and intellectual, were considerable. His ideas were influential on the creation of the League of Nations. Through his empirical and theoretical work on imperialism, he contributed to the erosion of the intellectual foundations of Empire. His propaganda work for the Fabian Society and Labour Party contributed to the erosion of its political foundations. He played a major part in encouraging the Labour Movement to abandon its traditional indifference to foreign affairs and engage seriously in analysis of and debate on broad issues of international policy. In the process he pioneered international functionalism, and made a substantial contribution to the development of what has been variously called "Fabian," "welfare," or "constructive" internationalism. He also pioneered documentary journalism during his editorship of the *International Review* and the *Contemporary Review*.

Less tangibly, though no less importantly, he was an indefatigable critic, in true dissenting mold, of the "official view" of foreign policy,[3] and a vigilant opponent of all forms of complacency in world politics whether emanating from Left or Right. In doing so he repeatedly challenged the fatalists and dogmatists of his age, as he saw them, to examine and reexamine their assumptions.

It was in this role that he penned a trenchant critique of one of the most important IR texts of the twentieth century. It was this text that, more than any other, established the reputation of the interwar period as the idealist or utopian phase of IR thinking. Paradoxically, its author, E. H. Carr, held many of the beliefs that his acerbic critic, Leonard Woolf, had been advocating for over 20 years.

The considerable common ground between the supposed idealist Woolf and that supposedly paradigmatic mid-twentieth realist, Carr, were explored in chapter 8. They were both men of the Left. Their respective diagnoses of the international crisis of the 1930s both placed considerable emphasis on the obsolescence of liberal democracy, the need for greater social and economic equality, the dangers of an unrestricted right of self-determination, and the potentially destabilizing impact of the proliferation of small states. They both shared a view of the international future that was broadly functionalist and collectivist: though it is important to stress here that at this stage Woolf had not lost faith in Consumers' Co-operation, and Carr had not yet fallen out of love with Soviet-style social and economic planning. The basis and process of collective decision-making at the international level would thus differ. However, both considered the need for such decision-making in the new and radically changed world of the 1940s to be beyond doubt.

In sum it might be said that while they shared much common ground, Woolf provided a necessary antidote to the interwar and wartime materialism and determinism of Carr. Yet he also provided an antidote, rarely taken, to the Cold War conservatism and pessimism of Bull.

That Leonard Woolf should have overlooked his achievements is not surprising in one sense. As I have said elsewhere,[4] Woolf aimed high. He shared the Victorian belief—a product of his middle-class metropolitan upbringing, colonial Ceylon, and the imperial mind-set so prevalent among Englishmen of his generation—that Britain, if not at the pinnacle of civilization, was certainly at its vanguard. But he also shared the Edwardian belief—heightened by *fin de siècle* Cambridge and immersion in the rarefied world of the Apostles—that human emancipation, peace, and genuine civilization were just around the corner. All that was required was the application of a little more human reason.

But Woolf's faith in the efficacy of reason was not blind faith. It did not entail the further belief, as sometimes supposed by critics of "idealism," that human beings will always use and be guided by their reason.[5] In the world of politics, indeed, it was unreason not reason that often prevailed. But this did not mean that through the "intelligent" and "constructive" application of reason great strides could not be made even in this highly complicated world.[6] The basis of Woolf's rationalism was the conviction that reason was not, *pace* Carr's "realism," inevitably the unconscious slave of self-interest.

Nor was it usually so with respect to its employment by the right, that is, carefully trained and tutored, minds. Structure, to use modern social scientific parlance, mattered to Woolf. But it was agency that was in the ascendant. It was not the case that anything was possible. Yet a good deal more was possible than had currently been achieved, or indeed would be achieved during his lifetime.

From the point of view of the development of the study of IR, or today's more circumspect view of what it is possible for any one individual, political party, or pressure group to achieve in the international sphere, Woolf's achievements are impressive. From his Edwardian, Apostolic, Fabian, point of view, however, they were meager.

From International Government to Global Governance

It would no doubt have been a source of sad satisfaction for Woolf to see his ideas once more appear, in a slightly modified form, in the literature on world politics of the late twentieth and early twenty-first century. The idea of globalization, though conceptualizations vary, has much in common with Woolf's idea of internationalization. Both imply or involve the rapid growth of social, economic, and cultural interconnectedness; the blurring of the boundaries between domestic and international society; the emergence of a worldwide "community of fate;" and the development of stronger crossborder interests *vis à vis* national interests.[7] The notion of the emergence of a global civil society has a clear precursor in Woolf's idea of the growth of an international social tissue. It therefore can be doubted whether the phenomenon this notion represents is quite as new as it is claimed to be.[8] The idea of an emerging global rule of law has much in common with Woolf's idea of the growth of cosmopolitan lawmaking. The notion of global consciousness is not far removed from Woolf's concept of international communal psychology.[9] Two leading authorities on the concept of global governance describe their subject matter in the following terms:

> Although world government remains a fanciful idea, there does exist an evolving global governance complex—embracing states, international institutions, transnational networks and agencies (both public and private)—which functions, with variable effect, to promote, regulate, or intervene in, the common affairs of humanity.[10]

The similarities between this formulation and the way Woolf conceived the nature and process of international government 80 years back is striking.

There are also striking similarities between Woolf's work on the nature and evolution of international government and contemporary work on international regimes.[11] Although regimes have been conceptualized in various ways, and the methodological refinement and analytical rigor that have been brought to bear on their study by contemporary students far exceeds that achieved by Woolf, the central idea—that of the almost spontaneous growth of networks of international and transnational cooperation in order to manage ever-greater economic, social, environmental, and technological interdependence—remains essentially the same.[12]

Woolf's sad satisfaction at seeing so many of his ideas reappear, in modern social scientific guise, would no doubt have been accompanied by disappointment at not seeing his works cited as important early contributions, indeed path-breaking contributions, to this important field.[13] The reason for this woeful absence of recognition is undoubtedly his reputation as an idealist and therefore a "flawed" and "inconsequential" thinker.

But as this study has demonstrated the use of this label to characterize Woolf's thought is in many ways deeply inadequate. First, it is important to note that, as we saw in chapter 2, it is extremely difficult to operationalize the concept of idealism. Different authors have different conceptions of it. There is by no means a consensus on its core features. Nor is there a consensus on those shortcomings the prevalence and severity of which, it has been generally assumed, fatally weaken the paradigm and justify it being labeled in such a pejorative way.

Second, if we focus our attention with regard to the shortcomings of idealism on the original and most influential statement of them in *The Twenty Years' Crisis*, we are again confronted with the difficulty of operationalization. Carr makes numerous claims about idealism, most of them, of course, highly critical and dismissive. Indeed, as we saw in chapter 2, Carr defined idealism almost wholly in terms of its defects. Despite the bold claim that he was laying the foundations for a science of international politics, Carr made little attempt to describe the idealist paradigm dispassionately or sympathetically, as an enquiry in the spirit of science would require. Nonetheless, it did prove possible to reduce Carr's many criticisms of "idealism" to three broad objections.

It is true that Woolf's thought contains a number of serious shortcomings, conceptual and empirical, as identified in chapters 4, 6, and 7. Some of these shortcomings—particularly his use of the domestic analogy in his later works, his pronouncements and strictures about disarmament and collective security in the 1930s, and his understanding of the League's mandates system and his proposals for its development in the 1920s—were indeed found to be tantamount to utopianism in two of the three senses alluded to above.

Yet in other areas of his thought—his analysis of the progress of international government, his theory of economic imperialism, even his proposals for the expansion of international Co-operative trade—these charges were found to be largely inaccurate. In these areas it cannot be said that Woolf "ignored facts and paid little attention to analysis of cause and effect." Nor can it be said that he "underestimated the role of power in international relations and overestimated the role of morality, law, and public opinion."

While much of Woolf's vast output was exhortatory and admonitory in nature, his best-known and most substantial books contain a considerable amount of detailed empirical analysis. He was, as pointed out in several chapters, a political publicist in the Radical Dissenting tradition. But he was also a Fabian social investigator with a tremendous faith in reason as revealed by "the facts." Woolf, like Carr, wanted to change the world. But he did not, *pace* Carr, seek to do this by the "elaboration of visionary projects" or by uncritical reference to "*a priori* principles." Few of his proposals for change amount to "projects" in this sense, nor are they based on principles cut-off from their social, economic, and political context.

Woolf's desire to change the world was always informed by an interpretation of that world. Indeed, his most substantial works on the subject can be seen as an attempt, as we have seen, to discern and promote the main currents of modern historical progress. Yet his work on economic imperialism, the rise of militarism and fascism, and the international crisis of the 1930s, demonstrates that he was far from blind, *pace* the strong inference of the term idealist, to currents of a quite different kind. This is why comments to the effect that Woolf was an early "critical liberal internationalist" are not as farfetched as they first seem. It would be foolish to contend that Woolf matched contemporary critical liberal internationalists in rigor and theoretical sophistication. But his approach to the analysis of world politics was essentially the same.

Perhaps the most striking finding of this book, however, concerns the third, and arguably most important, objection to idealism. As with the other two objections, the issues at stake are complex and they involve a high degree of subjectivity. But it would be difficult to construct an argument to the effect that Woolf's thought was, in the ways suggested by Carr, "self-interested," and that his "espousal of universal values," such as peace, "amounted to the unconscious defense and promotion of a particular *status quo*." The reason for this is, at root, quite straightforward.

As seen in chapter 2, and reaffirmed in chapters 4 and 6, *The Twenty Years' Crisis* is essentially a critique of liberalism, particularly the way in which "nineteenth-century liberalism" (meaning classical economics plus utilitarianism plus constitutionalism) was applied to the emerging, twentieth-century field of IR. There are many respects, of course, in which Leonard Woolf can be described as a liberal internationalist. He inherited much, for example, from the Benthamite and Cobdenite radical critique of orthodox foreign policy. But his self-identity was very much wrapped up with the British tradition of reformist socialism: Fabianism in particular. There is a sense in which the former tradition informed his critical faculties whereas the latter tradition educated his creative desires. While he utilized radical liberalism in his critique of protectionism, secret diplomacy, the balance of power, colonialism, national armaments, and so on, his preferred world order, and the one he felt was firmly in the process of becoming, was essentially a socialist world order that differed profoundly from the world envisioned by nineteenth-century liberals. Woolf cannot, therefore, be accused of "unconsciously defending a particular *status quo*" resting on "nineteenth-century" principles since ultimately, like Carr, he rejected these principles. He did not subscribe to the liberal notion of a natural harmony of interests. For Woolf, as for Carr, *laissez faire* in both its economic and political forms was obsolete. The promise of a spontaneous world order arising from the unfettered pursuit of economic interest and the self-determination of free nations was no longer tenable in the heavily armed, industrialized, fiercely nationalistic world of the twentieth century. But this did not mean that some kind of harmony could not rationally and purposefully be *created*. As with other Fabian, welfare, or constructive internationalists, notably G. D. H. Cole, J. A. Hobson, Harold Laski, David Mitrany, and—it is important to stress—E. H. Carr, he firmly believed in the possibility of utilizing modern scientific, administrative, and technical knowledge, to construct a more rational and harmonious world than the one based on the "anarchy" of unfettered capitalism and unregulated interstate competition.

Practical Idealism

Fabians shared at least one thing with Marx: the belief that political blueprints and utopian approaches to socialism were obsolete. For Marx, communism was not utopian but an emergent state of affairs.[14] The Webbs believed that the principles of rational organization and the path of rational social development could be discovered through scientific methods.[15] G. D. H. Cole maintained that guild socialism was not "an imagining of utopia in the clouds, but a giving of form and direction to definite tendencies already at work in society."[16] Woolf shared this conception of the political project and process in which he was engaged. In *International Government* he was at pains to point out that his scheme for international reform was not conjured out of "air or clouds" but, on the contrary, was "a duller and heavier structure placed logically upon the foundations of the existing system." Woolf shared the Fabian horror of having his ideas dismissed as idealistic or utopian. This explains why his responses to the argument of his fellow socialist Carr were so acerbic. In condemning the League and all the ideas associated with it as utopian Carr had committed a cardinal Fabian sin.

Woolf's legacy can be perceived in various ways. Some will point to his path-breaking study of international government. Others will point to his restatement and updating of the radical case against imperialism and colonialism. Still others will point to his attempt to construct a nonstate, nonmarket approach to world economic organization based on an optimistic though not utopian (as argued in chapter 7) reading of the potential for the extension of the principle of consumer Co-operation. Yet there is a sense in which his chief legacy encapsulates all of these things. It is to have shown that not all ideals are impractical ideals. To have ideals in international politics does not mean that one is unrealistic in pursuit of them. This is the implication of the idealist–realist dichotomy: idealists, those with ideals, cannot by definition be realists. This dichotomy has done much damage to the evolution of IR thinking. It is a mental habit and device that Leonard Woolf spent his entire political career seeking to dissolve.

Notes

Preface

1. See Jonathan Haslam's outstanding biography, *The Vices of Integrity: E. H. Carr, 1892–1982* (London, 1999).
2. See Peter Wilson, "Carr and his Early Critics: Responses to *The Twenty Years' Crisis*, 1939–1946," in Michael Cox (ed.), *E. H. Carr: A Critical Appraisal* (London, 2000), 165–97; Lucian M. Ashworth, *Creating International Studies: Angell, Mitrany and the Liberal Tradition* (Aldershot, 1999), 114–15.
3. Ashworth, *Creating International Studies*, 114.
4. Martin Wight, "The Realist's Utopia," *Observer*, 21 July 1946, 3.

Chapter 1 Fabian, Internationalist, and "Interwar Idealist"

1. See Woolf, *Growing: An Autobiography of the Years 1904–1911* (London, 1961), 247; Spotts, *Letters of Leonard Woolf*, (London, 1990) 155; and T. J. Barron, "Before the Deluge: Leonard Woolf in Ceylon," *Journal of Imperial and Commonwealth History*, 6, 1 (1977), 47–63.
2. Woolf, *The Village in the Jungle* (Oxford, 1981 [first published in 1913]).
3. For example, *The Control of Industry by Co-operators and Trade Unionists* (London, 1914); *Education and the Co-operative Movement* (London, 1914); *Co-operation and the War: Co-operative Action in National Crises* (London, 1915).
4. Letter from Sidney Webb to Woolf, quoted in Duncan Wilson, *Leonard Woolf: A Political Biography* (London, 1978), 62. The project was funded by a donation solicited by George Bernard Shaw from the Quaker philanthropist Joseph Rowntree.
5. Wilson, *Leonard Woolf*, 62.
6. See Spotts, *Letters*, 377.
7. Spotts, *Letters*, 161.
8. For an analysis of Woolf's career as a reviewer see Leila Luedeking, "Leonard Woolf and the Book Review," in Luedeking and Edmonds, *Leonard Woolf: A Bibliography*, 284–90. 1,703 items are listed in this outstanding work, around 1,000 of them book reviews.
9. Denis Healey, interview with author, 9 March 2002.

10. Carr used the term utopian. Most writers since, especially American, have used the term idealist. The terms have become largely interchangeable. I use the terms interchangeably throughout this volume. For the most part I use idealist.
11. Hedley Bull, "The Theory of International Politics 1919–1969," in Brian Porter (ed.), *The Aberystwyth Papers: International Politics 1919–1969* (London, 1972), 34.
12. See Peter Wilson, "*The Twenty Years' Crisis* and the Category of 'Idealism' in International Relations," in David Long and Peter Wilson (eds.), *Thinkers of the Twenty Years' Crisis: Inter-War Idealism Reassessed* (Oxford, 1995), 1–24.
13. Martin Wight, *International Theory: The Three Traditions*, Gabriele Wight and Brian Porter (eds.) (London, 1991), 129; J. H. Grainger, *Patriotisms: Britain 1900–1939* (London, 1986), 331; George Modelski, *The Principles of World Politics* (New York, 1972), 320; Craig Murphy, *International Organization and Industrial Change: Global Governance since 1850* (Cambridge, 1994), 25, 268.
14. David Thomson, E. Meyer, and Asa Briggs, *Patterns of Peacemaking* (London, 1945), 149–50, 162–63, 389.
15. Clive Archer, *International Organizations* (London, 1983), 12–13, 68–125.
16. Significantly, Archer puts the former term in inverted commas but not the latter. Ibid., 74.
17. See Hedley Bull, "The Grotian Conception of International Society," in H. Butterfield and M. Wight (eds.), *Diplomatic Investigations* (London, 1966), 51–73.
18. Hidemi Suganami, *The Domestic Analogy and World Order Proposals* (Cambridge, 1989), 94–113, 180–81.

Chapter 2 What is Idealism?

1. Hedley Bull, "The Theory of International Politics, 1919–1969," in Brian Porter (ed.), *The Aberystwyth Papers: International Politics 1919–1969* (London, 1972), 33–36.
2. John Vasquez, *The Power of Power Politics: A Critique* (London, 1983), 13–19.
3. A point also stressed by Ken Booth, "Security in Anarchy: Utopian Realism in Theory and Practice," *International Affairs*, 67, 3 (1991), 538.
4. Trevor Taylor, "Utopianism," in Steve Smith (ed.), *International Relations: British and American Approaches* (London, 1985), 92–107.
5. Michael Joseph Smith, *Realist Thought from Weber to Kissinger* (Baton Rouge, La., 1986), 54–67.
6. Vasquez, *Power of Power Politics*, 13–19; Torbjörn L. Knutsen, *A History of International Relations Theory: An Introduction* (Manchester, 1992), 184–207, 268–70.
7. Charles W. Kegley, Jr., and Eugene R. Wittkopf, *World Politics: Trend and Transformation* (New York, 1989), 12–15.
8. Booth, "Security in Anarchy," 527–45.
9. See e.g., William Olson and A. J. R. Groom, *International Relations Then and Now: Origins and Trends in Interpretation* (London, 1991), 69–92.

10. See e.g., Knutsen, *History of International Relations Theory*, 194.
11. J. E. Dougherty and R. L. Pfaltzgraff, Jr., *Contending Theories of International Relations: A Comprehensive Survey*, 2nd edn., (New York, 1981), 4–6, 84–85.
12. Martin Hollis and Steve Smith, *Explaining and Understanding International Relations* (Oxford, 1990), 10–22, 217.
13. See e.g., the works of Smith, Taylor, and Vasquez cited in notes 2, 4 and 5.
14. Olsen and Groom, *International Relations Then and Now*, 46–134.
15. E. H. Carr, *The Twenty Years' Crisis, 1919–1939: An Introduction to the Study of International Relations* (London, 1939).
16. Ibid., 11.
17. Ibid., 13–14.
18. For further details see my "Carr and his Early Critics," 165–83.
19. Carr, *Twenty Years' Crisis*, 16–17.
20. Ibid., 11–13.
21. Ibid., 28, 96.
22. Ibid., 31–36.
23. Carr, *Twenty Years' Crisis*, 34–36, 43–46.
24. Ibid., 132, 177.
25. Ibid., 56–61.
26. Ibid., 103. I go into this further in "The Myth of the First Great Debate," *Review of International Studies* 24, 5 (1998), 12–13.
27. Carr, *Twenty Years' Crisis*, 8.
28. Ibid., 11–12.
29. Ibid., 16–19.
30. Ibid., 25.
31. Ibid., 68–69.
32. Ibid., 28.
33. Ibid., 87.
34. Ibid., 110–11.
35. Ibid., 80, 118.
36. Ibid., 10–11.
37. Ibid., 187.
38. Ibid., 77.
39. Quoted in ibid., 49.
40. Ibid., 50–51.
41. Ibid., 301.
42. Ibid., 277.

Chapter 3   International Government: An Exposition

1. See Spotts, *Letters*, 371. Woolf describes her as "one of the most eminent women I have known" whose achievements, had she been a man, "would have filled half a page in *Who's Who*." Woolf, *Beginning Again*, 101.

2. Founded in 1913 originally for the purpose of conducting research into the control of industry. Wilson, *Leonard Woolf*, 62.
3. See Woolf's trenchant "Political Thought and the Webbs," in Margaret Cole (ed.), *The Webbs and Their Work* (London, 1949), esp. 259–62.
4. Leonard Woolf, *Beginning Again: An Autobiography of the Years 1911 to 1918* (London, 1964), 183–84.
5. Ibid., 185.
6. Ibid., 187–88.
7. Ibid., 187.
8. A second, American edition with an introduction by Shaw also appeared in 1916. A third edition with an additional chapter on the Danube Commission was published in 1923. French and Swedish editions, and a German-language Swiss edition, were published during the Paris peace negotiations.
9. See John Stevenson, "From Philanthropy to Fabianism," in Ben Pimlott (ed.), *Fabian Essays in Socialist Thought* (London, 1984), 15–26.
10. Bernard Porter, "Fabians, Imperialists and the International Order," in Ben Pimlott (ed.), *Fabian Essays in Socialist Thought* (London, 1984), 54.
11. Patricia Pugh, *Educate, Agitate, Organize: 100 Years of Fabian Socialism* (London, 1984), 72.
12. Whose attitude to the war contrasted sharply with the majority of Fabians. See A. M. McBriar, *Fabian Socialism and English Politics, 1884–1918* (Cambridge, 1966), 136–38.
13. See E. Pease, *The History of the Fabian Society*, 3rd edn. (London, 1963), 131–36; McBriar, *Fabian Socialism*, 121–30; Pugh, *Educate, Agitate, Organize*, 72–81.
14. G. B. Shaw (ed.), *Fabianism and the Empire: A Manifesto* (London, 1900).
15. Porter, "Fabians, Imperialists and the International Order," 59–60.
16. Shaw, *Fabianism and the Empire*, 3.
17. Ibid., 4–5.
18. Ibid., 55.
19. One student has concluded that at the root of Shaw's socialism lay a "collective morality of service toward the community." See Gareth Griffith's valuable, *Socialism and Superior Brains: The Political Thought of Bernhard Shaw* (London, 1993), 5, 233.
20. Shaw, *Fabianism and the Empire*, 23–24.
21. Ibid., 35–37.
22. Ibid., 44–45.
23. Ibid., 44–46.
24. Ibid., 46.
25. Ibid., 47–48.
26. Ibid., 8.
27. Ibid., 50–52.
28. Ibid., 93.
29. Porter, "Fabians, Imperialists and the International Order," 60.

30. See e.g., Woolf, *International Government* (London, 1916), 230.
31. See Kenneth Waltz's classic, *Man, the State, and War: A Theoretical Analysis* (New York, 1959).
32. The emphasis he gives to such factors clearly puts Shaw within the British radical tradition (or "dissenting tradition") of thinking on foreign policy. See A. J. P. Taylor, *The Troublemakers: Dissent over British Foreign Policy, 1789–1939* (Harmondsworth, 1976).
33. See Brian C. Schmidt's important study, *The Political Discourse of Anarchy: A Disciplinary History of International Relations* (New York, 1998).
34. See Gorden K. Lewis, "Fabian Socialism: Some Aspects of Theory and Practice," *Journal of Politics*, XIV, 3 (1952), 442–70. This is an important paper. Note Porter's neat description: "Fabian socialism was fundamentally a statist, interventionist kind. Its main enemy was Liberal individualism... and its highest ideal was the more efficient organisation of society to everyone's benefit, from above." Porter, "Fabians, Imperialists and the International Order," 56. Note also Woolf's brilliant summation of the Webbs's social philosophy: "They were convinced that if the machinery of society was properly constructed and controlled efficiently by intelligent people, if the functions of the various parts of the organisation were scientifically determined and the structure scientifically adapted to the functions, if the round pegs were then fitted into the round holes and the square pegs into the square holes, then we should get an adequately civilised society in which we should all be healthy, wealthy, and wise." Woolf, "Political Thought and the Webbs," 263.
35. Woolf noted two exceptions which he used quite extensively: Paul S. Reinsch, *Public International Unions, Their Work and Organization* (Boston, 1911); and L'Union des Associations Internationales, *Annuaires se la Vie Internationale* (Paris, 1909 and 1911). Reinsch is a much undervalued figure in IR. See Jan-Stefan Fritz, *Regime Theory: A New Theory of International Institutions?* (Ph.D. Thesis, LSE, 2000); and Brian Schmidt, "Paul S. Reinsch and the Study of Colonial Administration," in Brian Schmidt and David Long (eds.), *Imperialism and Internationalism in the Discipline of International Relations* (New York, 2003).
36. Woolf, *Beginning Again*, 187–88.
37. Letter from Webb to Woolf quoted in Wilson, *Leonard Woolf*, 63. Emphasis in original.
38. See Woolf's introduction to his edited book, *The Framework of a Lasting Peace* (London, 1917), 57–58 (subtitled "The Bogey of Utopia"). Woolf also had a term for the billiard ball model of international relations: "the rigid theory of the independence and sovereignty of states." See Woolf, *International Government*, 89–91, 96, 216.
39. Published as the second part to the *New Statesman* Special Supplement. Included in the first two editions but not the third, 1923, edition of *International Government*.
40. J. A. Hobson, *The Nation*, 15 August 1915, 639. See also the debate between Hobson and Woolf in *The Nation*, 7 August 1915, 14, 21.

41. Woolf, *International Government*, 231.
42. Woolf, *Framework of a Lasting Peace*, 13.
43. Woolf, *The Future of International Government* (London, 1940), 3.
44. Woolf, *International Government*, 90.
45. Ibid., 95.
46. Ibid., 96.
47. Ibid., 30–33; *Framework of a Lasting Peace*, 51.
48. Ibid., 30.
49. Ibid., 31.
50. Ibid., 32.
51. Ibid., 34–36.
52. Ibid., 36–37. Interestingly, the act obliged France and Spain to respect the independence of the Sultan of Morocco but entrusted the policing of the country to France and Spain under the auspices of a Swiss Inspector General.
53. Ibid., 23–24.
54. Canning quoted in ibid., 24.
55. Ibid., 24–29. Woolf's analysis suggested to him that a "certain degree of unanimity as to the domestic organisation of states" might be "an absolutely necessary antecedent to any highly developed international organisation" (ibid., 28). In this respect his views mirrored those of Shaw, who maintained that world socialism, a Parliament of Man, or a federation of the world could not come into being until man had become "a much less miscellaneous lot than he is at present." The importance of homogeneity did not extend in Woolf's thought, however, to racial homogeneity, in sharp contrast to Shaw. See Griffith, *Socialism and Superior Brains*, 237.
56. Woolf, *Framework of a Lasting Peace*, 15–22.
57. Woolf, *International Government*, 11–13, 17, 81–82. Emphasis in original.
58. Ibid., 46–47; *Framework of a Lasting Peace*, 20–51.
59. Woolf, *International Government*, 48–51.
60. Ibid., 49.
61. Woolf, *International Government*, 52–55.
62. Ibid., 55.
63. I go into greater detail on this matter in chapter 4.
64. Woolf, *International Government*, 59.
65. Ibid., 96.
66. Ibid., 105.
67. Ibid., 106.
68. To further illustrate the "catholicism of internationalism" Woolf also alludes to the intriguing "International Association for the Rational Destruction of Rats" and the "International Association for the Suppression of Useless Noises." Ibid., 106.
69. Ibid., 108.
70. Ibid., 116–67. These bodies were all established between the years 1865 and 1900.

71. Other examples cited by Woolf include the partial unification of industrial property laws following a convention of 1883; and the partial unification of copyright laws following a convention of 1908. Ibid., 168–95.
72. Ibid., 200.
73. Ibid., 206.
74. This and previous quotation in ibid., 155.
75. Woolf cites a large number of examples. See ibid., 206–11.
76. Ibid., 211–16.
77. See e.g., "Labour's Foreign Policy," *Political Quarterly*, 4, 4 (October–December 1933), 507, 515; *Quack, Quack!* (London, 1935), 42–88, 137–45.
78. See e.g., *Quack, Quack!* 22–24, 41–42.
79. See e.g., "From Geneva to the Next War," *Political Quarterly*, 4, 1 (January–March 1933), 35–40.
80. See e.g., "Meditation on Abyssinia," *Political Quarterly*, 7, 1 (January–March 1936), 16–32; *The League and Abyssinia* (London, 1936), esp. 22–27.
81. See e.g., "From Serajevo to Geneva," *Political Quarterly*, 1, 2 (April 1930), 186–206; "Meditation on Abyssinia," 22–23, 28–30; "The Ideal of the League Remains," *Political Quarterly*, 7, 3 (July–September, 1936), 331–39; "Arms and Peace," *Political Quarterly*, 8, 1 (January–March 1937), 23–24.
82. See e.g., "Labour's Foreign Policy," 509–19; *The League and Abyssinia*, 31–35.
83. See e.g., *The League and Abyssinia*, 12–27; "The Ideal of the League Remains," 341–45; "Arms and Peace," 25–27.
84. See e.g., "From Geneva to the Next War," 41–42; "Meditation on Abyssinia," 31–32; *The League and Abyssinia*, 28–31; "Arms and Peace," 27–31, 34–35.
85. Woolf, "From Serajevo to Geneva," 187.
86. Ibid., 188.
87. Ibid., 188.
88. Ibid., 189–90.
89. Ibid., 190–91.
90. Ibid., 190–94.
91. Ibid., 196–203.
92. Stephen Spender, *World Within World* (London, 1953), 133.
93. Woolf, "From Geneva to the Next War," *Political Quarterly*, 4, 1 (January–March 1933), 30–43.
94. Woolf, *Future of International Government*, 3.
95. "...throughout the last 100 years there has been continual and spontaneous growth of international administration in all kinds of spheres and places, from post offices to prisons." Woolf, *The International Post-War Settlement* (London, 1944), 11. See also 19–21, and "Britain in the Atomic Age," *Political Quarterly*, 18, 1 (January–March 1946), 15–16.
96. "It was not lack of force, but the lack of the will to use it to resist aggression, which made the collective security system of the League ineffective." Ibid., 9. See also 8, 10, and *Foreign Policy: The Labour Party's Dilemma* (London, 1947), 7.

97. "In the relations between states and governments, cooperation must take the place of competitive hostility as the assumed basis of the relationship..." Ibid., 4. See also 5, 8, 14, 18, and *Foreign Policy*, 8, 15, 18, 19–20.
98. "Tory capitalism led in the years between the wars to economic bankruptcy and the international anarchy which gave Fascism and Nazism their opportunity to unloose upon defenceless peoples the most horrible war in human history." Ibid., 3. See also 4, 8.
99. "It is a delusion to believe that states or nations or governments (or even individuals) can remain united and act together generally or in the abstract. They can only do so if they consciously co-operate for a particular and defined common purpose. The reason why Russia, the USA, and ourselves have remained united in the war, despite divergent interests and profound differences in our institutions, traditions, and even some of our aims, is that we have had a clearly defined common purpose which transcends all our differences... Unless after the war we have as clear and compelling a common purpose there is little chance of us remaining united." Ibid., 12. See also 16–17, and Woolf, "The Future of the Small State," 14, 3 (July–September 1943), 221–22.
100. Woolf, *Future of International Government*, 12.
101. Woolf, "Future of the Small State," 209–24; *International Post-War Settlement*, 7–11.
102. Woolf, "The United Nations," *Political Quarterly*, 14, 1 (January–March 1945), 19–20. In 1947 he described the UN as a "dangerous farce" as far as law, order, peace, and collective security were concerned (the "hostile" and "divisive" Soviet Union being mainly to blame). He continued, however, to maintain that "in the long run there is hardly any chance of preventing war unless the UNO is made to work." Woolf, "Foreign Policy," 12–19.
103. The quotation marks are Woolf's.
104. Woolf, "Britain in the Atomic Age," passim, 12–24.

Chapter 4   International Government: Analysis and Assessment
1. Henry Noel Brailsford, *A League of Nations* (London, 1917), 317.
2. Edwin D. Dickinson, "An International Program," *The New Republic*, IX, 112, 23 December 1916, 219.
3. Pitman B. Potter, *An Introduction to the Study of International Organization* (New York, 1922), esp. Part V.
4. C. Howard-Ellis, *The Origin, Structure and Working of the League of Nations* (London, 1928), 85, 301.
5. Edmund C. Mower, *International Government* (New York, 1931), 3.
6. A. C. F. Beales, *The History of Peace: A Short Account of the Organised Movements for International Peace* (London, 1931), 289.
7. Alfred Zimmern, *The League of Nations and the Rule of Law 1918–1935* (London, 1936), 171–72, 40–60.

8. J. L. Brierly, *The Law of Nations: An Introduction to the International Law of Peace*, 3rd edn. (London, 1943), 67.
9. Thomson et al., *Patterns of Peacemaking*, 162–63.
10. "The Week," *The Nation*, 16 August 1917, 182.
11. J. A. Hobson, *A League of Nations* (London, 1915), 19.
12. Waterlow, quoted in Wilson, *Leonard Woolf*, 89.
13. Woolf's ideas on these aspects of international cooperation were also included in another important Foreign Office document, the Zimmern Memorandum of November 1918. See Wilson, *Leonard Woolf*, 82–91; and Philip Noel-Baker's obituary of Woolf, *The Times*, 21 August 1969. There are also significant similarities between the Woolf–Webb plan and Jan Smuts's *The League of Nations: A Practical Suggestion* published in 1918. See F. S. Northedge, *The League of Nations: Its Life and Times* (Leicester, 1986), 33–38.
14. Quoted in Spater and Parsons, *A Marriage of True Minds*, 83.
15. See John Pinder, "Federalism and the British Liberal Tradition," in Andrea Bosco (ed.), *The Federal Idea: The History of Federalism from the Enlightenment to 1945* (London, 1991), 104.
16. Northedge, *League of Nations*, 12–16.
17. See Woolf's introduction to *The Intelligent Man's Way to Prevent War* (London, 1933), esp. 9–10.
18. *International Government* was one of the first books the late Professor Joseph Frankel read when he arrived in Britain in the 1930s. He later said that he found it "astonishing" since he had not previously realised the extent to which government had already been applied to the relations between states. Interview with author, December 1989.
19. K. J. Holsti, "Governance without Government: Polyarchy in Nineteenth-Century European International Politics," in James N. Rosenau and Ernst-Otto Czempiel (eds.), *Governance Without Government: Order and Change in World Politics* (Cambridge, 1992), 50.
20. Robert Jervis, "From Balance to Concert: A Study of International Security Cooperation," *World Politics*, 38, 1, (October 1985), 58–59.
21. Holsti, "Governance without Government," 50–51. Cf. Martin Ceadel's view that the concert was not "an embryonic form of supranationalism" but "merely a self-selecting group of major states which took action only when it was their particular interest to do so" (Ceadel, "Supranationalism in the British Peace Movement during the Early Twentieth Century," in Bosco, *The Federal Idea*, 170); and also Northedge's view that at least until the first Hague conference, the concert, "even if dignified with the name 'system,'" could not be described as a legislative body since its meetings were "all highly intermittent and *ad hoc*" (Northedge, *League of Nations*, 9–10).
22. See esp. Holsti, "Governance without Government," 30–57; Ian Clark, *The Hierarchy of States* (Cambridge, 1989).
23. For Woolf's clearest statements on interdependence see *International Government*, 82–83, 115–16, 140–44, 157–58.

24. Few postwar scholars have acknowledged Woolf's importance in this respect. Three exceptions are: George Modelski, *Principles of World Politics* (New York, 1972), 320; Craig Murphy, *International Organization*, 17, 25, 285; Clive Archer, *International Organizations* (London, 1983), 83. Andreas Osiander has recently interpreted Woolf as an "industrial modernist": someone who saw growing interdependence as rendering traditional realist ways of thinking "obsolete and harmful." See his excellent, "Rereading Early Twentieth-Century IR Theory," *International Studies Quarterly*, 42 (1998), 409–32. See also Akira Iriye's elegant study, *Cultural Internationalism and World Order* (Baltimore, 1997), 29, 54, 84.
25. See Ernst Haas, *Beyond the Nation State: Functionalism and International Organization* (Stanford, 1964), 8; Paul Taylor, *International Co-operation Today* (London, 1972), 50–51; Paul Taylor, "Functionalism: The Theory of David Mitrany," in Paul Taylor and A. J. R. Groom (eds.), *International Organization: A Conceptual Approach* (London, 1978), 237.
26. In his "Memoir" Mitrany mentions but does not give any special weight to Woolf's contribution to the evolution of his thought. See David Mitrany, *The Functional Theory of Politics* (London, 1975), 3–82.
27. For example, in many of his writings Mitrany cites the Danubian Commission as a highly significant early case of functionalist cooperation. The importance of the Commission was first highlighted by Woolf in his *The Future of Constantinople* (London, 1917), 36–80.
28. Analyzed in Cornelia Navari, "David Mitrany and International Functionalism," in David Long and Peter Wilson (eds.), *Thinkers of the Twenty Years' Crisis: Inter-War Idealism Reassessed* (Oxford, 1995), 214–46; and David Long, "International Functionalism and the Politics of Forgetting," *International Journal*, XLVIII, 2 (1993), 355–79.
29. Woolf, *International Government*, 196.
30. Ibid., 65, 220–24.
31. Ibid., 168–69.
32. Ibid., 113–15. (See also Woolf, *The War for Peace* (London, 1940), 70–71.)
33. Ibid., 92, 99. See also 96, 120, 222.
34. Ibid., 221.
35. Ibid., 109.
36. Ibid., 221.
37. Ibid., 190–92. In true Fabian fashion Woolf also put much emphasis on the role of the "expert." See e.g., *International Co-operative Trade*, Fabian Tract No. 201, (London, 1922), 16.
38. Etherington, *Theories of Imperialism: War, Conquest and Capital* (Beckenham, 1984), 182–83.
39. Woolf, *International Government*, 60.
40. Ibid., 104. Emphasis added.
41. There are numerous purple passages of dissent in Woolf's work. See e.g., ibid., 22, 50, 70, 81; and *War for Peace*, 17–27.

42. Woolf, *The Future of Constantinople* (London, 1917), 82–83. See also *International Government*, 65; "Meditation on Abyssinia," *Political Quarterly*, 7, 1 (January–March 1936), 18–19.
43. Woolf, *Future of International Government*, 9–10.
44. Woolf, *The International Post-War Settlement* (London, 1944), 17. Emphasis added.
45. Carr, *Twenty Years' Crisis*, ix.
46. On which see Hans Morgenthau's penetrating analysis of "pure disputes," "disputes with the substance of a tension," and "disputes representing a tension," in *Politics Among Nations: The Struggle for Power and Peace*, 5th edn., revised (New York, 1978), 430–39.
47. See Woolf, *Framework of a Lasting Peace*, 30–40; *Imperialism and Civilisation* (London, 1928), 115–35.
48. Woolf, *International Government*, 57.
49. Ibid., 75–76.
50. See Andrew Hurrell's excellent recent analysis, "Collective Security and International Order Revisited," *International Relations*, XI, 1 (1992), 37–55.
51. L. Oppenheim, *International Law*, 2nd edn. (London, 1912). Oppenheim read the manuscript of *International Government* and made "several valuable suggestions." See Woolf, "Preface" and "Select Bibliography," *International Government*, 3, 256.
52. Woolf, *International Government*, 12–13, 16–17. See also *Framework of a Lasting Peace*, 20–23.
53. See C. A. W. Manning, "The Legal Framework in a World of Change," in Porter, *Aberystwyth Papers*, 301–35; Hedley Bull, "Hans Kelsen and International Law," in Richard Tur and William Twining (eds.), *Essays on Kelsen* (Oxford, 1986), 321–36.
54. Woolf, *International Government*, 64.
55. See ibid., 74, 91.
56. I know of only one instance: *International Post-War Settlement*, 5.
57. Woolf, *International Government*, 101.
58. Woolf, "From Serajevo to Geneva," *Political Quarterly*, 1, 2 (April 1930), 188–94.
59. Woolf, "From Geneva to the Next War," *Political Quarterly*, 4, 1 (January–March 1933), 30–35; "Meditation on Abyssinia," *Political Quarterly*, 7, 1 (January–March 1936), 18–19, 22–23, 27.
60. Woolf drops the occasional hint (e.g., "From Serajevo to Geneva," 189; "The Resurrection of the League," *Political Quarterly*, 8, 3 (July–September 1937), 340, fn. 1).
61. Woolf, "From Geneva to the Next War," 30–43.
62. Woolf sees no problem in regarding crime organized across boundaries as a form of international government, though there is more than a hint of irony in the way he discusses the issue. See his account of a "congress" of white slave traffickers held in Warsaw in 1913, in *International Government*, 166–67.

63. Ibid., 207.
64. As discussed in the writings of various contemporary thinkers, e.g., Richard Falk, David Held, Robert Keohane, and Robert Jackson.
65. Margaret Cole's "Preface" to Beatrice Potter, *The Co-operative Movement in Great Britain* (Aldershot, 1987), xxxiii.
66. M. J. Weiner, "Graham Wallas (1858–1932): Fabian Socialist and Political Psychologist," in J. M. Bellamy and J. Saville (eds.), *Dictionary of Labour Biography* (London, 1979), 227.
67. The more radical aspects of Carr's thought are discussed in Hidemi Suganami, *The Domestic Analogy and World Order Proposals* (Cambridge, 1989), 101–05; Peter Wilson, "The Myth of the First Great Debate," *Review of International Studies*, 24, 5 (1998); and Charles Jones, *E. H. Carr and International Relations* (Cambridge, 1998), esp. chs. 4–6.
68. Woolf's wartime *International Post-War Settlement* made a number of more or less detailed proposals for a new international order, but it is no more of a blueprint than Carr's *Conditions of Peace*. Woolf explicitly rejects the drawing up of blueprints in *International Co-operative Trade*, 5, 21.
69. Other striking examples include his introduction to *Intelligent Man's Way to Prevent War*, and *Quack, Quack!* (London, 1935), 108–17 (and 22–27, where he conceives history, equally sweepingly, as a struggle between "minorities" and "majorities").
70. An extended note is perhaps justified here. Victor Gollancz and his fellow directors of the Club, John Strachey and Harold Laski, whose sentiments were much more pro-Soviet than Woolf's, refused initially to publish the book. Although it reads today like a Soviet *apologia*, to them it was disturbingly *anti*-Soviet and they feared it would be used as propaganda by "reactionaries and fascists." They also feared it would prompt the resignation of 10,000 Club members and jeopardize the Anglo-Soviet negotiations then under way. Woolf replied that to prohibit *all* criticism of the Soviet Union was in itself a more pernicious, if unconscious, form of anti-Sovietism; that it was a wild exaggeration to suggest that publication would result in mass resignations (as it turned out, it was not); and that it was fanciful to think that the book would have any effect whatsoever on the Anglo-Soviet negotiations (as it turned out, it was). See Luedeking and Edmonds, *Leonard Woolf*, 49–51; Wilson, *Leonard Woolf*, 197–98; Woolf, *Letters*, 415–22 [and my review in *Millennium*, 20, 3 (1991)]. Throughout his political career Woolf was bitterly critical of but not entirely unsympathetic to the Soviet experiment. He felt, e.g., that the Soviet Union had had much success in building "economic democracy" but that its record on "political democracy" was nothing short of disastrous. See Woolf, "Democracy in the Soviet Union—II," Anglo Soviet Public Relations Association, Leaflet 3 (n.d. 1942?), 5–8; and also *Foreign Policy: The Labour Party's Dilemma* (London, 1947), 10–16.
71. Woolf, "From Geneva to the Next War," 32–40.

72. See ibid., 42; Woolf, *The League and Abyssinia* (London, 1936), 28–31.
73. While he joined Woolf in castigating the pacifists, Shaw had no such difficulties with the problem of opposing aggression. In the absence of an effective international military policy, he said in 1931, even socialist governments should prepare for the worst. "An army and navy in the hand," he continued, "is worth ten League of Nations in the bush." Quoted in Griffith, *Socialism and Superior Brains*, 228.
74. Woolf, *Foreign Policy*, 16–25. Subsequently these issues were decisively tackled by Hedley Bull in *Control of the Arms Race* (London, 1961).
75. Woolf, "Arms and Peace," *Political Quarterly*, 8, 1 (January–March 1937), 22–23, 26–27, 33.
76. Woolf, *International Post-War Settlement*, 2–3, 8–10; and *Foreign Policy*, 7, 10, 15, 18.
77. A position that he also adopted, despite his formal denunciations of "Tory appeasement," in the late 1940s ("At the present moment in framing a foreign policy everything should be subordinated to an attempt to secure peace.") Woolf, *Foreign Policy*, 15.
78. Woolf, "Labour's Foreign Policy," *Political Quarterly*, 4, 4 (October–December 1933), 510–12, 523–24.
79. At least until 1937. At this point, for the first time in his career, Woolf began to cautiously lend his support to the idea of a "peace front" of non-fascist states to "resist" fascist aggression. Although such a "front" ran the risk of precipitating war—by tempting Germany and Italy to strike their first blow before the balance of power turned against them—he nonetheless saw it as the best out of a set of undesirable alternatives—including imperial isolation, defensive/nonoffensive isolation, and appeasement—none of which offered any real hope of peace. See "Arms and Peace"; "The Resurrection of the League," 342–52. For denunciations of alliances see "Labour's Foreign Policy," 510, 521–22; "From Serajevo to Geneva," 203–04.
80. Woolf, "From Geneva to the Next War," 42.
81. Woolf, "Meditation on Abyssinia," 19, 23, 26.
82. Ibid., 29–32.
83. Woolf, "Meditation on Abyssinia," 26; *League and Abyssinia*, 18, 26.
84. Woolf, "Meditation on Abyssinia," 31.
85. Woolf, *League and Abyssinia*, 30.
86. Ibid., 29–31; Woolf, "The Ideal of the League Remains," *Political Quarterly*, 7, 3 (July–September 1936), 333–34.
87. Woolf, *League and Abyssinia*, 30.
88. See ibid., 16, 19; "Meditation on Abyssinia," 27.
89. "From Serajevo to Geneva," 195; "From Geneva to the Next War," 40–42; "Meditation on Abyssinia," 17–19, 22–23.
90. Woolf, "The Ideal of the League Remains," 335; "From Geneva to the Next War," 39; "Arms and Peace," 23.

91. Woolf, "From Geneva to the Next War," 35–43. He later argued that it was "not true that the League of Nations or the Allied nations had not adequate armed forces... to resist the preparations for aggression and the actual aggressions by Japan, Mussolini, and Hitler." He went on to provide some justification for this contention with respect to Mussolini and Hitler but remained ominously silent on Japan. Woolf, *International Post-War Settlement*, 9.
92. Indeed, Woolf's argument for a *working* system of collective security in "The Ideal of the League Remains" (the title is ironic) is a model example of one of Carr's "abstractly neat and accurate solutions obtained by leaving out of account the vital strategic factor." Woolf's argument is lucid and logical but no account is taken of British or French preparedness for war either in the Far East, the Mediterranean, Africa, or in Europe (nor, indeed, of the tremendous financial difficulties that constrained them). His radical proposals for British foreign policy in *Foreign Policy: The Labour Party's Dilemma* provide another good example.
93. Woolf, *International Government*, 7.
94. Woolf, *International Government*, 219.
95. Woolf, *Framework of a Lasting Peace*, 51.
96. Woolf, *International Government*, 68–69.
97. Ibid., 78. See also 61–62, 236–45.
98. Woolf, *Foreign Policy*, 8–10.
99. See ibid., 8–26.
100. Meinecke quoted by Carr, *Twenty Years' Crisis*, 111–12.
101. Woolf, *International Government*, 55–56. See also 14–15, 26–27; *Framework of a Lasting Peace*, 48–51.
102. Carr, *Twenty Years' Crisis*, 247–54.
103. In Carr's words "dissolving politics into law." Ibid., 260–61.
104. Compare Woolf's international conference, deciding disputes in accordance with "equity" (*International Government*, 56–57), with Carr's process of "give and take" in which both morality and power are indispensable components (*Twenty Years' Crisis*, 264–84).
105. Suganami, *Domestic Analogy*, 1.
106. Ibid., 95–96, 179–81.
107. Ibid., 165–96.
108. Woolf, *The Future of International Government* (London, 1940), 3.
109. Woolf, *The War for Peace*, 79–80. See also 105, 156–57; and *The Intelligent Man's Way to Prevent War*, 11–12.
110. Woolf, *Future of International Government*, 5–6.
111. Woolf, *International Government*, 22, 31. See also 25, 40, 100, 232.
112. Woolf, *International Government*, 46–48.
113. Ibid., 98. See also 196–200.
114. In this respect Woolf adopted, in Suganami's terms, the "cosmopolitanist" version of the domestic analogy and argued on very similar lines to "welfare internationalists." See Suganami, *Domestic Analogy*, 35–39, 100–11, 191–94.

115. See especially Hedley Bull, "Society and Anarchy in International Relations" in H. Butterfield and M. Wight (eds.), *Diplomatic Investigations: Essays in the Theory of International Politics* (London, 1966), 35–50; *The Anarchical Society: A Study of Order in World Politics* (London, 1977); and "The State's Positive Role in World Affairs," *Daedalus*, 108, 4 (1979), 111–23.
116. "W. H. F.," review of Woolf's *Principia Politica: A Study of Communal Psychology*, in *International Affairs*, XXX, 2 (1954), 196–97.

Chapter 5 Imperialism: An Exposition

1. Woolf, *Downhill All The Way* (London, 1967), 195–96.
2. See Lewis S. Feuer, *Imperialism and the Anti-Imperialist Mind* (New Brunswick, 1989), 154; L. H. Gann and Peter Duignan, *Burden of Empire: An Appraisal of Western Colonialism in Africa South of the Sahara* (London, 1968), 76.
3. Feuer, *Imperialism and the Anti-Imperialist Mind*, 157; Norman Etherington, *Theories of Imperialism: War, Conquest and Capital* (Beckenham, 1984), 177; Richard Koebner, "The Concept of Economic Imperialism," *Economic History Review*, 2nd Series, 2, 1 (1949), 4.
4. See Francis Lee, *Fabianism and Colonialism: The Life and Political Thought of Lord Sydney Olivier* (London, 1988).
5. The Labour Party, *The Empire in Africa: Labour's Policy* (London, 1920). The document was not adopted until 1926 when it was republished with minor revisions (by Woolf and Norman Leys) as *Labour and the Empire: Africa* (London, 1926). See Penelope Hetherington, *British Paternalism and Africa, 1920–1940* (London, 1978), 16; Luedeking and Edmonds, *Leonard Woolf*, 73, 76; Woolf, Letter to the Editor, *New Statesman*, 10 January 1969, 48.
6. Woolf, *The Village in the Jungle* (Oxford, 1981 [1913]).
7. T. J. Barron, "Before the Deluge: Leonard Woolf in Ceylon," *Journal of Imperial and Commonwealth History*, vi (1977), 57–58.
8. Woolf, *Growing: An Autobiography of the Years 1904–1911* (London, 1961). Alec Waugh concludes a fascinating letter to Woolf in 1965 with the words: "You have done what I did not think it was possible for a Westerner to do—got inside the mind and heart of the Far East. It is a unique achievement." Quoted in Spater and Parsons, *A Marriage of True Minds*, 76–81. See also Spotts, *Letters*, 61–62.
9. Woolf, *Stories from the East* (London, 1924), later reprinted in his *Diaries in Ceylon* (London, 1962).
10. Woolf, *Empire and Commerce in Africa: A Study of Economic Imperialism* (London, 1920); *Economic Imperialism* (London, 1920).
11. Woolf meticulously recorded his daily literary output. He began *Empire and Commerce in Africa* on 23 November 1917 and finished it on 26 February 1919. He wrote between 300 and 500 words every day except on exceptionally good or bad days. Leonard Woolf Papers, IL6.

12. Luedeking and Edwards, *Leonard Woolf*, 22–23; Etherington, *Theories of Imperialism*, 182.
13. Woolf, *Imperialism and Civilization* (London, 1928); Hedley Bull and Adam Watson (eds.), *The Expansion of International Society* (Oxford, 1984).
14. Woolf, *Empire and Commerce in Africa*, 4–5.
15. Ibid., 8–9.
16. Ibid., 6.
17. Ibid., 15.
18. Ibid., 19.
19. Ibid., 25.
20. Woolf, *Economic Imperialism*, 44.
21. Ibid., 43.
22. Woolf, *Empire and Commerce in Africa*, 36.
23. English statesman, 1836–1914. Social reforming Mayor of Birmingham, 1873–1875. President of the Board of Trade, 1880–1885. Colonial Secretary, 1895–1903. Advocate of imperial union and imperial preference in trade.
24. Soldier and colonial administrator, 1858–1945. High Commissioner, Northern Nigeria, 1900–1906. Governor, Hong Kong, 1907–1912. Governor General, Nigeria, 1914–1919. Developed the system of indirect rule. Member, League of Nations Permanent Mandates Commission, 1922–1936.
25. Woolf, *Empire and Commerce in Africa*, 18.
26. Ibid., 7.
27. Ibid., 26.
28. Ibid., 24, 57–58.
29. Ibid., 38–45.
30. Ibid., 36.
31. Ibid., 46–47.
32. Ibid., 58.
33. Ibid., 58.
34. Ibid., 18, 22, 44, 58, 323–24.
35. At this Congress the Powers pledged to "watch over the preservation of the native tribes...care for the improvement of the conditions of their moral and material well-being...instructing the natives and bringing home to them the blessings of civilization." For Woolf the subsequent history of imperialism was the history of how this pledge was broken. Ibid., 43–45; *Imperialism and Civilization*, 78–79.
36. Woolf, *Economic Imperialism*, 18.
37. Ibid., 20–23.
38. Ibid., 24.
39. Woolf, *Mandates and Empire* (London, 1920), 5.
40. Woolf, *Imperialism and Civilization*, 9–11.
41. Ibid., 32–38.
42. Ibid., 40–47.
43. Ibid., 63. Emphasis added.

44. Ibid., 71. Emphasis added.
45. Woolf, *Empire and Commerce in Africa*, 352. Except where otherwise stated the following account is abstracted from ibid., 315–351 and *Economic Imperialism*, 40–73, 92–99.
46. Woolf, *Empire and Commerce in Africa*, 30.
47. Ibid., 38.
48. The figure is an annual average for the period 1909–1913. Ibid., 334.
49. Ibid., 333. Woolf failed to mention that the absolute value of trade between Britain and British East Africa was much greater than that between Britain and German East Africa [the relevant figures are recorded in one of his tables (p. 322)]. Between the years 1909–1913, British imports from the former were 8.8 times greater than from the latter. British exports were 7.9 times greater.
50. Woolf, *Economic Imperialism*, 59.
51. Woolf, *Empire and Commerce in Africa*, 330.
52. Ibid., 336–37.
53. Woolf, *Economic Imperialism*, 65.
54. Labour Party, *Labour and the Empire*, 15.
55. Woolf, "The League and the Tropics," *The Covenant*, 1/1 (1919), 28–32; *Mandates and Empire*, 8–11; Labour Party, *Labour and the Empire*, 12–16.
56. Woolf, *Empire and Commerce in Africa*, 356.
57. Ibid., 357.
58. Woolf, *Empire and Commerce in Africa*, 358. A point, incidentally, stressed by Shaw in *Fabianism and the Empire*, 15.
59. From Article 22. A favourite phrase of Woolf's.
60. Woolf, *Empire and Commerce in Africa*, 358.
61. Ibid., 358.
62. Ibid., 359.
63. Ibid., 360–61.
64. Ibid., 362–63.
65. Woolf, *Empire and Commerce in Africa*, 364.
66. Ibid., 365–66.
67. Ibid., 366.
68. Ibid., 366–67.
69. See Woolf, *Mandates and Empire*, 7; *Imperialism and Civilization*, 115–34.
70. Woolf, *Mandates and Empire*, 15.
71. Woolf, *Scope of the Mandates under the League of Nations* (London, 1921), 5–16.
72. Woolf, *Mandates and Empire*, 15–17.
73. Ibid., 5–10; "Article XXII," *The New Statesman*, 1 May 1920, 94–95.
74. Woolf, *Imperialism and Civilization*, 66–70.
75. Ibid., 121–26.
76. Etherington, *Theories of Imperialism*, 183.
77. "Lenin and Kenya," *The New Statesman*, 10 September 1922, 615–16.

78. Woolf, *Empire and Commerce in Africa*, 340–43; *Economic Imperialism*, 71; "Native Labour in Africa," *The New Statesman*, 10 April 1920, 7–8; *Imperialism and Civilization*, 90–91.
79. Currency manipulation in Kenya Colony e.g. See Woolf, "Sacred Trust," 151.
80. Woolf, *Empire and Commerce in Africa*, 340, 347–49.
81. Woolf, "Lenin and Kenya," 615–16. The intriguing title of this article refers to the propaganda efforts of white groups campaigning for greater autonomy in Kenya Colony. They claimed that Indian opposition to their plans was instigated from Moscow.
82. Woolf, *Empire and Commerce in Africa*, 367; "Lenin and Africa," 615.
83. Woolf, *Imperialism and Civilization*, 90–92.
84. Woolf, "Something New Out of Africa," *Political Quarterly*, 23, 4 (October–December 1952), 322–31.
85. Paul Rich, *Race and Empire in British Politics* (Cambridge, 1986), 77–78.
86. Labour Party, *Labour and the Empire*, 26.
87. Ibid., 25.
88. Woolf, "A Challenge to All of Us: Two Views on the Responsibilities of Colonial Empire," Part I, *The Listener*, 12 August 1943, 180; Woolf, "The Political Advance of Backward Peoples," in Rita Hinden (ed.), *Fabian Colonial Essays* (London, 1945), 94–95.
89. Woolf, *Mandates and Empire*, 14.
90. Woolf, "Challenge to All of Us," 180.
91. Woolf, "Political Advance of Backward Peoples," 94–98.
92. Ibid., 87–88.
93. Ibid., 89–90.
94. Ibid., 90.
95. Ibid., 91–92, 97–98.
96. Ibid., 92–93.
97. Ibid., 93–94, 97. Emphasis added.
98. The beginnings of such an examination can be found in Barron, "Before the Deluge," 52–54.
99. Woolf, *Growing*, 158.
100. Ibid., 156–57.
101. Ibid., 159–63.
102. Ibid., 54.
103. Ibid., 24–25.
104. Ibid., 157.

Chapter 6 Imperialism: Analysis and Assessment

1. The NFRB was set up by G. D. H. Cole in 1931, with Clement Attlee as chairman, in order to counteract the increasing inactivity of the still Webb-dominated Fabian Research Bureau. After protracted negotiations it remerged

with the mainstream Fabian Society in 1940. The Committee for International Affairs became the International Section of the Fabian and New Fabian Research Bureau, metamorphosing into the Fabian International Bureau (again under Woolf's chairmanship) in 1942. Patricia Pugh has skilfully unravelled the tortuous history in her valuable *Educate, Agitate, Organise*, 173–99. For Woolf's account see *Downhill All the Way*, 219–20.
2. John Stevenson, "From Philanthropy to Fabianism," in Ben Pimlott (ed.), *Fabian Essays in Socialist Thought* (London, 1984), 24.
3. See Bernard Porter, "Fabians, Imperialists and the International Order," in Ben Pimlott (ed.), *Fabian Essays*, 62–67; Woolf, *The Journey Not the Arrival Matters*, 161–62.
4. Rita Hinden (ed.), *Fabian Colonial Essays* (London, 1945).
5. *Common Sense* (the official journal of the Union of Democratic Control), 31 January 1920.
6. *Common Sense*, 27 March 1920.
7. *Commonwealth*, August 1921.
8. *Daily Herald*, 4 February 1920.
9. H. E. Barnes in *Journal of International Relations*, July 1921.
10. *Nation*, 6 March 1920.
11. *Glasgow Herald*, 3 February 1920.
12. *Daily Mail*, 16 January 1920. For further favorable reviews see *Cambridge Magazine*, 17 January 1920; *Co-operative News*, 24 January 1920; *Saturday Westminster Gazette*, 14 February 1920; *Ceylon Daily News*, 21 July 1920; W. E. Burghardt Du Bois, "Eternal Africa," *Nation* (New York), 111, 2882, 25 September 1920.
13. *New Statesman*, 15 January 1921.
14. *European Press* (Breman), 16 December 1920.
15. *New Leader*, 16 May 1928; Lewis S. Gannett, "Analysis and Mush," *Nation* (New York), 25 April 1928.
16. *Economist*, 31 January 1920.
17. *Manchester Guardian*, 27 January 1920.
18. *Times Literary Supplement*, 9 February 1920.
19. "The Ethics of Imperialism," *New Statesman*, 19 June 1920.
20. Review of *Economic Imperialism*, *Nation*, 1 January 1921.
21. Review of *Imperialism and Civilization*, *Manchester Guardian*, 30 May 1928.
22. See D. K. Fieldhouse, *Economics and Empire 1830–1914* (London, 1984), 30–32, 63–76, 365 ff; R. J. Hammond, "Economic Imperialism: Sidelights on a Stereotype," *Journal of Economic History*, 22, 4 (1961), 582–98; Anver Offer, "The British Empire, 1870–1914: A Waste of Money?" *Economic History Review*, 46, 2 (1993), 215–38.
23. See D. K. Fieldhouse (ed.), *The Theory of Capitalist Imperialism*; Fieldhouse, *Economics and Empire 1830–1914*, esp. Part III; C. C. Eldridge (ed.), *British Imperialism in the Nineteenth Century* (London, 1984).

24. See R. E. Robinson and J. A. Gallagher, "The Imperialism of Free Trade," *Economic History Review*, 2nd Series, 6, 1 (1953), 1–15; R. E. Robinson and J. A. Gallagher, *Africa and the Victorians* (London, 1961); D. K. Fieldhouse, "'Imperialism': An Historiographical Revision," *Economic History Review*, 2nd Series, 14, 2 (1961), 187–209; Fieldhouse, *Economics and Empire*, 3–84.
25. Fieldhouse, *Economics and Empire*, 3–38.
26. Ibid., 3–87, 459–77.
27. See *Empire and Commerce in Africa*, 21, 24, 27, 37, 55; Etherington, *Theories of Imperialism*, 180. Although it is not strictly relevant to the argument, I should perhaps briefly add here that I do not agree with Etherington's claim that Woolf set in motion, with his conservative definition of imperialism as the acquisition and control of colonial territory, a "monumental misunderstanding" of the meaning and significance of imperialism as a sociopolitical phenomenon. Etherington criticizes Woolf for his ignorance of prewar debates, and for not considering the classical theories of Hobson, Hilferding, Lenin, and Luxemburg. Etherington is clearly right to argue that the classical theorists were looking to the future rather than trying to explain the past, and that therefore to test their theories of imperialism *exclusively* against the colonial experience of the late nineteenth century is to commit an error of anachronism. But he underestimates the extent to which these writers employed "imperialism" as a convenient term of rhetoric that enabled them to castigate all sorts of things—protectionism, monopoly, capitalism, militarism, war, as well as colonialism—which they disliked. In other words I do not think it would be as gross a misreading as Etherington suggests to say that by "imperialism" Hobson, Lenin, et al. by and large meant the acquisition of colonial territories. While imperialism involved lots of things, colonialism is at its hub. In any event it is somewhat dogmatic of Etherington to imply that Woolf's narrower definition was somehow an incorrect or misleading one. It has the great merit of clarity. In addition, although conservative, the Woolf definition is perhaps not quite as conservative as Etherington suggests since it does allow for informal means of domination and control, e.g., spheres of influence.
28. Robinson and Gallagher, "The Imperialism of Free Trade," 1–15.
29. W. L. Langer, *The Diplomacy of Imperialism* (New York, 1935); Fieldhouse, *Economics and Empire*, 63–69, 459–77.
30. Northedge, *League of Nations*, 37–38.
31. Inis L. Claude, Jr., *Swords into Plowshares: The Problems and Progress of International Organization*, 3rd edn. (London, 1965), 329.
32. Quoted in Northedge, *League of Nations*, 193.
33. Although, as we saw in chapter 5, he was deeply suspicious of the Allies' intentions before the article was coined.
34. Northedge, *League of Nations*, 64; Claude, *Swords into Plowshares*, 328–29.
35. See Northedge, *League of Nations*, 201.
36. Woolf frequently, and emphatically, claimed it was the latter. See e.g., "The League and the Tropics," 29; *The Scope of Mandates*, 6. Claude uses the

word "influence" (*Swords into Plowshares*, 328). "Accountability" seems more precise.
37. Perhaps with the exception of the Trusteeship Agreement for Italian Somaliland, which, as well as appointing an International Advisory Council to assist in its administration, also required the administering authority, Italy, to adhere to a Declaration of Constitutional Principles. See Claude, *Swords into Plowshares*, 340–41.
38. Ibid., 327.
39. See ibid., 322–23.
40. Woolf, "Article XXII," 94–95; "A Sacred Trust," *The New Statesman*, 14 May 1921, 151–52; *Scope of Mandates*, 9–10; *Imperialism and Civilization*, 115–35.
41. Woolf in Lord Perth et al., "The Future of the Mandates: A Symposium," *African Affairs*, 43 (October 1944), 168.
42. See Northedge, *League of Nations*, 65, 219–20; Claude, *Swords into Plowshares*, 341–43.
43. Penelope Hetherington, *British Paternalism and Africa, 1920–1940* (London, 1978), 19–20, 90–104, 154–58; Ronald Robinson, "The Moral Disarmament of African Empire, 1919–1947," *Journal of Imperial and Commonwealth History*, 8, 1 (1979), 86–104.
44. Northedge, *League of Nations*, 196–98, 217–18.
45. Claude, *Swords into Plowshares*, 329.
46. Notably Kenya Colony governor, Edward Grigg, the governor of Northern Rhodesia, Herbert Stanley, and colonial secretaries, Churchill and Amery. See Robinson, "Moral Disarmament," 92–97.
47. Ibid., 98–102.
48. Woolf, *Imperialism and Civilization*, 70.
49. Noel Annan, *Our Age: The Generation that made Post-War Britain* (London, 1991), 482.
50. Ibid., 17.
51. Woolf maintained in *Empire and Commerce in Africa* (p. 8) that "in history there is no logic of events and no logic of facts, there is only a logic of men's beliefs and ideals."
52. Woolf, *Imperialism and Civilization*, 34–35.
53. As pointed out by James Joll, *Europe Since 1870* (London, 1973), 78–79.
54. Though not always. Amanullah Khan and Kemal Attaturk, e.g., "deliberately westernized the organization and framework" of their governments and societies. "They ... used Western civilization in order to be strong enough to throw off the economic and political domination of Western civilization." Woolf, *Imperialism and Civilization*, 67.
55. Woolf, "Challenge to All of Us," Part I, 179–80.
56. Huxley, "Challenge to All of Us," Part II, 180–81.
57. Labour Party, *Labour and the Empire*, 8.
58. "Challenge to All of Us," 180. See also *Imperialism and Civilization*, 85; "Political Advance of Backward Peoples," 93–95.

59. Hetherington, *British Paternalism and Africa*, 104.
60. Woolf, "Political Advance of Backward Peoples," 85.
61. Paul Kennedy, *The Realities Behind Diplomacy* (London, 1981), 333.
62. Though his position was considerably more pragmatic and less romantic than the received wisdom suggests. See Ronald Hyam, "Churchill and the British Empire," in Robert Blake and Wm. Roger Louis, *Churchill* (Oxford, 1993), 167–85.
63. Although, interestingly, by the time of the Creech Jones era most officials within the Colonial Office had embraced the "new morality." Robinson, "*Moral Disarmament*," 100–01.
64. Denis Healey, *The Time of My Life* (New York, 1990), 222.
65. Kennedy, *Realities*, 332–33.
66. Quoted in Annan, *Our Age*, 482.
67. David Mitrany, *A Working Peace System*, 2nd edn. (Chicago, 1966; first edn. pub. 1943), 13.
68. Gupta, *Imperialism and the British Labour Movement*, 126, 276–78.
69. See Woolf, *Imperialism and Civilization*, 104–05; Woolf, "Challenge to All of Us," 180; "Political Advance of Backward Peoples," 89–94; Hetherington, *British Paternalism and Africa*, 76–89.
70. The essence of which—a strict dichotomy between a superior "us" and an inferior "them," with corresponding sense of *noblesse oblige*—is discussed by Barron, "Before the Deluge," 49.
71. The leading lights in the functionalist school were Bronislaw Malinowski, A. R. Radcliffe-Browne, and Lucy Mair. They stressed the importance of detailed fieldwork and replaced the heavily teleological search for universally valid "stages" of development with a search for universal characteristics of *all* societies regardless of their geographical or historical location. See Hetherington, *British Paternalism and Africa*, 62–75.
72. See e.g., *Empire and Commerce in Africa*, 337, 352, 354, 356–57, 360, 365–67.
73. See "Empire, Subject Peoples," in H. B. Lees-Smith (ed.), *The Encyclopedia of the Labour Movement*, Vol. I (London, 1928), 258, 261; *Imperialism and Civilization*, 72.
74. "Challenge to All of Us," 179–80; "Political Advance of Backward Peoples," 85–98.
75. A. J. P. Taylor, *The Troublemakers: Dissent over Foreign Policy, 1792–1939* (Harmondsworth, 1985 [1957]).
76. Woolf, *Empire and Commerce in Africa*, 53–54.
77. Ibid., 352–53.
78. Woolf, *Imperialism and Civilization*, 12–13.
79. Woolf, *Empire and Commerce in Africa*, 349.
80. See Rodney Barker, "The Fabian State," in Pimlott, *Fabian Essays*, 28–31.
81. Quoted in Peter Beilharz's fascinating study, *Labour's Utopias: Bolshevism, Fabianism, Social Democracy* (London, 1992), 62.

82. Woolf, *Mandates and Empire*, 12.
83. Woolf, *Imperialism and Civilization*, 131.
84. Woolf, "Challenge to All of Us," 180.

Chapter 7 Liberal Internationalism, Anticapitalism, and Consumers' Co-operation: Toward a Nonstate, Nonmarket Approach to International Economic Organization

1. See Spotts, *Letters of Leonard Woolf*, 4.
2. See J. M. Keynes, "My Early Beliefs" in *Essays in Biography* (Cambridge, 1972), 433–50; Bertrand Russell, Leonard Woolf, Morton White, and John Wisdom, "The Influence and Thought of G. E. Moore: A Symposium," *The Listener*, 30 April 1959, 755–62. Papers read by Woolf to meetings of the Apostles included: "What is Style?" "Othello or Lord Byron?" and "Embryos or abortions?" Leonard Woolf Papers, II, O, 2.
3. Woolf, *Growing*, 180–81.
4. Ibid., 181.
5. In this chapter I use "Co-operation" to distinguish the Co-operative Movement and the Co-operative system of economic organization from cooperation in general.
6. Woolf, *Education and the Co-operative Movement* (London, 1914), 13.
7. Margaret Cole, "Woolf, Leonard Sidney (1880–1969): Author, Publisher and Socialist," in J. M. Bellamy and J. Saville (eds.), *Dictionary of Labour Biography* (London, 1979).
8. Woolf, "The Co-operative Movement and Socialism: Better Than the State or Municipality?" *The New Leader*, 7 February 1927.
9. G. B. Shaw (ed.), *Fabian Essays in Socialism* (London, 1889).
10. Rodney Barker, "The Fabian State," in Ben Pimlott (ed.), *Fabian Essays in Socialist Thought* (London, 1984), 28.
11. Ibid., 29–30, 34–38.
12. G. W. Shepherd, *The Theory and Practice of Internationalism in the British Labour Party with Special Reference to the Inter-War Period*, University of London Ph.D. Thesis, 1952, 371.
13. See Woolf, *Taxation* (London, 1916), 29.
14. Woolf, *International Economic Policy*, 1–2.
15. Ibid., 2.
16. Woolf, "Way of Peace," 12–13.
17. Ibid., 3.
18. Ibid., 3.
19. Ibid., 4.
20. As recommended by the Royal Commission on Supply of Food and Raw Materials in Time of War. Cited by Woolf, ibid., 4.
21. Ibid., 4–5.

22. Ibid., 5.
23. Ibid., 6–8.
24. Excluding the small band of capitalists who gain from international hostility. Woolf's repeated references to this small group of capitalists suggests that not all capitalists were implicated. This further confirms the influence of liberal internationalism on his thought since the liberals consistently sought to make a distinction between good and bad capitalists. See Shepherd, *Theory and Practice of Internationalism*, 40–44.
25. Woolf, "Way of Peace," 28.
26. See Independent Commission on International Development Issues (Brandt Commission), *North–South: A Programme for Survival* (London, 1980).
27. Woolf, *International Economic Policy*, 8. See also *Empire and Commerce in Africa*, 355–56; *International Co-operative Trade*, 13–15.
28. See Robert Heilbroner, *The Worldly Philosophers*, (London, 1980), 53.
29. See Woolf, *Socialism and Co-operation*, 44–55, 76–87.
30. Woolf, *Education and the Co-operative Movement*, 3; *Co-operation and the War II: Co-operative Action in National Crises* (London, 1915), 2–4.
31. Woolf, *Socialism and Co-operation*, 47. See also Robert Owen, *A New View of Society and Other Writings* (London, 1991).
32. Woolf, *Socialism and Co-operation*, 40.
33. Woolf, *The Control of Industry by the People* (London, 1915), 5–6; *Co-operation and the War*, 5–6.
34. Woolf, *Control of Industry by the People*, 3; *Co-operation and the Future of Industry*, 10–11.
35. Woolf, *Socialism and Co-operation*, 11.
36. Woolf, *The Control of Industry by Co-operators and Trade Unionists* (London, 1914), 4.
37. Woolf, *Socialism and Co-operation*, 9.
38. Ibid., 47, 81–82; *Co-operation and the War*, 3–4.
39. See Paddy Maguire, "Co-operation and Crisis: Government, Co-operation, and Politics, 1917–1922," in Stephen Yeo (ed.), *New Views of Co-operation* (London, 1988), 192–96.
40. Woolf, *Socialism and Co-operation*, 9–10, 26–30.
41. Ibid., 32–34.
42. Woolf, "Way of Peace," 11.
43. Woolf, *Socialism and Co-operation*, 43, 47–48.
44. Ibid., 12–13, 51, 55, 74.
45. Woolf, "Way of Peace," 6–7.
46. See Woolf, *Control of Industry by the People*, 5–6.
47. Woolf, *Socialism and Co-operation*, 14, 59.
48. See Woolf, *The Control of Industry by Co-operators and Trade Unionists*, 2; "Way of Peace," 5.
49. Woolf, *The Control of Industry by Co-operators and Trade Unionists*, 11; *Socialism and Co-operation*, 90.

50. See Woolf, *The Control of Industry by the People*, passim, 1–16.
51. See Annan, *Our Age*, 453–85.
52. Woolf, *Co-operation and the Future of Industry*, 36.
53. Woolf, *International Co-operative Trade*, 4–5.
54. Woolf, *The Control of Industry by the People*, 12.
55. Woolf, "Can Democracy Survive?" in Mary Adams (ed.), *The Modern State* (London, 1933), 42, 24–25.
56. Beilharz, *Labour's Utopias*, 91.
57. Woolf, "Can Democracy Survive?" 7–12; *Co-operation and the Future of Industry*, 50–55.
58. Woolf, *The Control of Industry by the People*, 8.
59. Ibid., 11–12.
60. Woolf, *Co-operation and the Future of Industry*, 122–38; *Socialism and Co-operation*, 65–110.
61. See Peter Guerney, "George Jacob Holyoake: Socialism, Association, and Cooperation in Nineteenth Century England," in Yeo *New Views*, 52–72. Holyoake was one of the founders of the Co-operative Movement and its first historian.
62. See Beilharz, *Labour's Utopias*, 9–10, 41–48.
63. In fairness, Woolf was not unaware of the problem. In *Socialism and Co-operation* (98–100) he accepts that compulsion is an "evil" but then rationalizes it by saying that it is impossible to conceive of an economic system that entirely does away with the need for it. While Woolf was right to point out that capitalism employed many different types of coercion at many different levels he never embarked on the detailed examination of the nature and extent of "socialist" *vis à vis* "capitalist" compulsion that his theory requires.
64. Woolf, "Way of Peace," 18.
65. Ibid., 7.
66. See Woolf, *The Control of Industry by Co-operators and Trade Unionists*, passim, 1–16.
67. Woolf, "Way of Peace," 14.
68. Ibid., 14.
69. See chapter 5; and Woolf, *Empire and Commerce in Africa*, 365–68.
70. Woolf, *International Economic Policy*, 8–10.
71. Ibid., 9–10.
72. See Suganami, *Domestic Analogy*, 100–11; David Long, *Towards a New Liberal Internationalism: The International Theory of J. A. Hobson*, University of London Ph.D. Thesis, 1991; Craig Murphy, *International Organization and Industrial Change* (Oxford, 1994), 153–87; Peter Wilson, "The New Europe Debate in Wartime Britain," in Philomema Murray and Paul Rich (eds.), *Visions of European Unity* (Boulder, Colo., 1996).
73. See Martin Wight, *International Theory: The Three Traditions*, Brian Porter and Gabrielle Wight (eds.) (Leicester, 1991).
74. Woolf, *International Economic Policy*, 9–10. Woolf's frequent use of the word "control" with respect to commerce and industry arguably implies a static

conception of these activities. He never talks of "encouraging" efficiency or "stimulating" innovation or "attracting" investment.

75. See Alan James, *Sovereign Statehood: The Basis of International Society* (London, 1986).
76. Woolf, *The International Post-War Settlement* (London, 1944), 6–7.
77. Ibid., 7.
78. Ibid., 7.
79. Ibid., 8–9.
80. Ibid., 3, 7.
81. Ibid., 6–8.
82. Most explicitly stated in *International Co-operative Trade*, 5, 21, 24.
83. Beatrice Potter, *The Co-operative Movement in Great Britain* (Aldershot, 1987 [1891]), xxxiii. It is doubtful, however, that he went as far as Owen (and Miss Potter) in regarding the elimination of profit, and the substitution of the model civil servant for the profit-maker, as vital for the future of humanity. See Beilharz, *Labour's Utopias*, 69–70.
84. Margaret Cole, "Preface," in Potter, *The Co-operative Movement*, xxiii.
85. M. J. Weiner, "Wallas, Graham (1858–1932): Fabian Socialist and Political Psychologist," in Bellamy and Saville, *Dictionary of Labour Biography*, 227.
86. See E. H. Carr, *Conditions of Peace* (London, 1942), 236–75; chapter 8, below. On the solidarity of international society see Hedley Bull, "The Grotian Conception of International Society," in Herbert Butterfield and Martin Wight (eds.), *Diplomatic Investigations* (London, 1966), 51–73.
87. Woolf, "The Development of the C.W.S.," 441.
88. Woolf, *International Co-operative Trade*, 24.
89. Woolf, "The Development of the C.W.S.," 440–41; Paddy Maguire, "Co-operation and Crisis: Government, Co-operation, and Politics, 1917–1922," in Yeo, *New Visions*, 194.
90. Woolf, "The Development of the C.W.S.," 440–41.
91. Ibid., 440–41.
92. Ibid., 440–41; *International Co-operative Trade*, 8.
93. Stephen Yeo, "Rival Clusters of Potential: Ways of Seeing Co-operation," in Yeo, *New Views*, 5; Maguire, "Co-operation and Crisis," 192; Neil Killingback, "Limits to Mutuality: Economic and Political Attacks on Co-operation During the 1920s and 1930s," in Yeo, *New Views*, 213, 216.
94. Maguire, "Co-operation and Crisis," 191–92.
95. J. B. Jeffreys, *Retail Trading in Britain 1850–1950* (Cambridge, 1954), quoted in Killingback, "Limits to Mutuality," 211.
96. See Neil Killingback's excellent, "Limits to Mutuality," 207–28.
97. Ibid., 211, 217.
98. Woolf, *International Co-operative Trade*, 4, 9.
99. Ibid., 9, 24. Co-operators were frequently condemned as utopian. See Killingback, "Limits to Mutuality," 218–19.

Chapter 8 The Idealist Counterattack: Mr. Woolf versus Professor Carr

1. One small exception is Moorhead Wright, Ieuan John, and John Garnett, "International Politics at Aberystwyth, 1919–1969," in Brian Porter (ed.), *The Aberystwyth Papers* (London, 1972), 94–95, which notes Woolf's response.
2. As expertly analyzed by Charles Jones, *E. H. Carr and International Relations: A Duty to Lie* (Cambridge, 1998), 46–65.
3. See Peter Wilson, "Carr and his Early Critics: Responses to *The Twenty Years' Crisis*," in Michael Cox (ed.), *E. H. Carr: A Critical Appraisal* (London, 2000).
4. Morgenthau, "The Political Science of E. H. Carr," *World Politics*, 1,1 (1948–1949).
5. Carr, *Twenty Years' Crisis*, 21–22.
6. Woolf, "Utopia and Reality," *Political Quarterly*, 11, 2 (April–June 1940); *The War for Peace* (London, 1940).
7. Woolf, "Unheard of Adventures," Review of *Michael Bakunin* by E. H. Carr, *New Statesman and Nation*, 2 December 1937.
8. Woolf first set out his objections to the "attack on reason" in *Quack, Quack!* (London, 1935).
9. Woolf, "Utopia and Reality," 172; *War for Peace*, 117, 178.
10. Of the many marginal comments expressing puzzlement, disbelief, and consternation in Woolf's review copy of *Twenty Years' Crisis*, only one expresses approval: on p. 279 where Carr discusses the role of morality in peaceful change and argues that a procedure of peaceful negotiation requires "not merely an acute perception on both sides of the strength and weakness of their respective positions at any given time, but also a certain measure of common feeling as to what is just and reasonable in their mutual relations, a spirit of give-and-take and even of potential self-sacrifice, so that a basis, however imperfect, exists for discussing demands on grounds of justice recognised by both." Leonard's book collection is housed in the library of Washington State University.
11. For a striking interpretation of this aspect of Carr's thought see R. H. S. Crossman, "Illusions of Power—E. H. Carr," in R. H. S. Crossman, *The Charm of Politics and Other Essays in Political Criticism* (London, 1958), 93.
12. Woolf, "Utopia and Reality," 172.
13. Woolf, *War for Peace*, 114.
14. Ibid., 77. A good example of the utopian propensity to "couch optative propositions in the indicative mood." See Carr, *Twenty Years' Crisis*, 17.
15. Woolf, "Utopia and Reality," 168.
16. Woolf, *War for Peace*, 59.
17. Ibid., 120.
18. Ibid., 119.
19. Woolf, "Utopia and Reality," 177.
20. Ibid., 176.
21. Ibid., 178–79.

22. Quoted in Michael Howard, "The United Nations and International Security," in Adam Roberts and Benedict Kingsbury (eds.), *United Nations, Divided World: The United Nations' Roles in International Relations* (Oxford, 1988), 31.
23. This aspect of Woolf's analysis of world politics—his belief in the futility of traditional, realist, methods of foreign policy in an age of interdependence—is highlighted in Andreas Osiander's recent article, "Rereading Early Twentieth-Century IR Theory: Idealism Revisited," *International Studies Quarterly*, 42, 3 (1998).
24. Woolf, *War for Peace*, 124–26.
25. Ibid., 129.
26. Ibid., 98.
27. Ibid., 142.
28. See C. A. W. Manning, *The Nature of International Society* (London, 1962); Hidemi Suganami, "C. A. W. Manning and the Study of International Relations," *Review of International Studies*, 27, 1 (2001); Peter Wilson, "Manning's Quasi-Masterpiece: *The Nature of International Society* Revisited," unpublished paper.
29. Ibid., 161.
30. Ibid., 164–75; "Utopia and Reality," 180–81.
31. Woolf, "Utopia and Reality," 180.
32. Woolf, *War for Peace*, 200–01.
33. Ibid., 176. This assumption also underlies Carr's view of "peaceful change," i.e. self-sacrifice by the "haves" in order to appease the "have-nots." See *Twenty Years' Crisis*, ch. 13, 264–84.
34. Woolf, "Utopia and Reality," 176.
35. For a clear example of this ("unsophisticated realism" in Manning's terms) see *War for Peace*, 147–49.
36. See Fred Halliday, "State and Society in International Relations: A Second Agenda," *Millennium: Journal of International Studies*, 16, 2 (1987); and Hidemi Suganami, "Halliday's Two Concepts of State," *Millennium: Journal of International Studies*, 17, 1, (1988).
37. Woolf, "Utopia and Reality," 170.
38. Ibid., 174.
39. Ibid., 170–71, 181–82. Woolf was not alone among Carr's critics in conceding his brilliance. See Wilson, "Carr and his Early Critics," 165–83.
40. Bull, "*The Twenty Years' Crisis* Thirty Years On," 627–28.
41. Carr, *Twenty Years' Crisis*, 26, 86, 88, 113–19, 148–49, 289–92.
42. Ibid., 8–11.
43. Ibid., 33.
44. Ibid., 34. Carr held Benthamism and "nineteenth century liberalism" to be largely synonymous.
45. Ibid., 37.
46. Ibid., 36.

47. Ibid., 35–36.
48. Ibid., 50–53.
49. See, further, chapter 2 and my "Myth of the First Great Debate," 8–13.
50. See Carr, *Twenty Years' Crisis*, 113.
51. Ibid., 13–15, 113–19, 282–84, 287–307.
52. This has since become firmly established in the secondary literature on Carr. See L. Susan Stebbing, *Ideals and Illusions* (London, 1941), 6–26; Morgenthau, "The Political Science of E. H. Carr," 134; Bull, "*Twenty Years' Crisis* Thirty Years On," 637–38.
53. Carr, *Twenty Years' Crisis*, 16–19, 24–25, 39, 87, 110–11, 123–30.
54. Ibid., 14–15, 87–91.
55. Ibid., 91–96. Count Walewski was the French foreign minister during 1855–1860.
56. Ibid., 81–112.
57. Ibid., 110–11.
58. See e.g., Trevor Taylor, "Power Politics" in Trevor Taylor (ed.), *Approaches and Theory in International Relations* (Harlow, 1978), 122–31; Robert Gilpin, "The Richness of the Tradition of Political Realism," *International Organization*, 30, 2 (1984); Gene M. Lyons, "The Study of International Relations in Great Britain: Further Connections," *World Politics*, 38, 4 (1986), 627–28; Steve Smith, "Paradigm Dominance in International Relations: The Development of International Relations as a Social Science," *Millennium: Journal of International Studies*, 16, 2 (1987), 193. The recent crop of literature on Carr has succeeded in putting the record straight. See especially Ken Booth, "Security in Anarchy: Utopian Realism in Theory and Practice," *International Affairs*, 67, 3 (1991); Paul Howe, "The Utopian Realism of E. H. Carr," *Review of International Studies*, 20, 3 (1994); Jones, *E. H. Carr and International Relations*; and Peter Wilson, "Radicalism for a Conservative Purpose: The Peculiar Realism of E. H. Carr," *Millennium: Journal of International Studies*, 30, 1 (2001).
59. Carr, *Twenty Years' Crisis*, 14–15, 113–19.
60. Ibid., 68.
61. Ibid., 69.
62. Ibid., 69–77.
63. Stebbing, *Ideals and Illusions*, 9. A point voiced also by Woolf, *War for Peace*, 60 (Carr "contradicts in the latter part of his book almost everything that he says in the first part").
64. Stebbing, *Ideals and Illusions*, 13–14.
65. Ibid., 17. William Pfaff made the same observation of *The Twilight of Comintern*: "Carr sought to demonstrate, tautologically, that those who were successful were right, as is proved by their success." Quoted in W. T. R. Fox, "E. H. Carr and Political Realism: Vision and Revision," *Review of International Studies*, XI, 1 (1985), 6.
66. Woolf, *War for Peace*, 125.

67. Carr, *Twenty Years' Crisis*, 81–86. Morgenthau argued that Carr's relativistic and instrumentalist conception of ethics made him a "utopian of power"—superior power being the necessary repository of superior morality. Morgenthau, "Political Science of E. H. Carr," 136. See also Whittle Johnston, "E. H. Carr's Theory of International Relations: A Critique," *Journal of Politics*, 29 (1967), 874–84.
68. Crossman, "Illusions of Power," 91.
69. Carr, *Twenty Years' Crisis*, 278; W. T. R. Fox, "Vision and Revision," 4. Also note Carr's remark in the first edition (p. 277), substantially modified in the second (p. 215), that yielding to threats of force "is a normal part of the process of peaceful change." For a comprehensive survey of the, *pace* Carr, quite significant revisions to the first edition see Michael Cox, "From the First to the Second Editions of *The Twenty Years' Crisis*: A Case of Self-Censorship," in the 3rd edition of the book (London, 2001).
70. See chapters 3 and 4.
71. Woolf, review of E. H. Carr, *Conditions of Peace, Political Quarterly*, 13, 3 (July–September 1942).
72. Ibid., 330. Norman Angell reached much the same conclusion in "Who are the 'Utopians,' and Who the 'Realists'?" *Headway*, 4 (January 1940).
73. Carr, *Conditions of Peace*, 36; Woolf, "Can Democracy Survive?" in Mary Adams (ed.), *The Modern State* (London, 1933), 42–45. See also E. H. Carr and S. de Madariaga, *The Future of International Government* (London, 1941), where Carr asserts (p. 3) that if liberty is to be "effective in the modern world" it must be defined as "something like 'maximum social and economic opportunity.'"
74. Carr, *Conditions of Peace*, 62–66.
75. Carr, *Twenty Years' Crisis*, 213–15, 304, 306–07.
76. See Wilson, "The New Europe Debate in War Time Britain," 45–47.
77. Woolf, "The Future of the Small State," *Political Quarterly*, 14, 3 (July–September 1943), 218.
78. Carr, *Nationalism and After* (London, 1945), 37.
79. Carr, *Conditions of Peace*, 49. See also *Nationalism and After*, 54–55.
80. Woolf, "Future of the Small State," 209, 221–24.
81. Carr, *Twenty Years' Crisis*, 295–97; *Conditions of Peace*, 65, 241. Carr's views on sovereignty brought a stinging response from Charles Manning. See his review of *Conditions of Peace* in *International Affairs*, XIX, 8 (1942), 443–44.
82. Carr, *Conditions of Peace*, 252, 261, 274. See also *Nationalism and After*, 47–51.
83. Carr, *Twenty Years' Crisis*, 306–07.
84. Ibid., 304.
85. Ibid., 302–7; *Conditions of Peace*, 236–75. See also *The New Society* (London, 1951), 98–99. Hayek was not impressed. See *The Road to Serfdom* (London, 1986 [1944]), 138–41.
86. Woolf, "How to Make the Peace," 374. Chapter 7, in this book.
87. See W. Olson and N. Onuf, "The Growth of the Discipline: Reviewed," in Steve Smith (ed.), *International Relations: British and American Perspectives*

(Oxford, 1985), 24; John Vasquez, *The Power of Power Politics* (London, 1983), 13–16. Not all writers have ignored these factors: see the works of Hayek and Johnston cited above; Suganami, *Domestic Analogy*, 100–05; K. W. Thompson, *Masters of International Thought* (London, 1980), 67–78. Woolf recognized them, as mentioned, in his *Conditions* review.
88. Carr (*Twenty Years' Crisis*, 239) dismissed proposals for world federation or a "more perfect" League of Nations as "elegant superstructures" devoid of foundations. His emphasis on substructure led R. W. Seton-Watson to conclude that he had "succumbed to onesided materialism." See "Politics and Power," *The Listener*, Supplement No. 48, 7 December 1939.
89. Woolf, "How to Make the Peace," 376.
90. Ibid., 370.

Chapter 9   Woolf's Legacy: Ideals, Reason, and Historical Change

1. See Kai Alderson and Andrew Hurrell (eds.), *Hedley Bull on International Society* (London, 2000), esp. chs. II, IV, and VI.
2. Woolf, *The Journey Not the Arrival Matters*, 158. Griffith, *Socialism and Superior Brains*, 12.
3. The term "official view" is from Taylor, *The Troublemakers*. It is what we would broadly call today realism. Woolf's terms for it, including "the rigid theory of the sovereignty and independence of states" are recounted in chapter 3.
4. Wilson, "Leonard Woolf and International Government," 122–23.
5. Lucian Ashworth has reached the same conclusions with regard to Angell and Mitrany. See *Creating International Studies*, 114–15.
6. As Woolf neatly sums up in *Downhill All the Way*, 198–99.
7. See David Held et al., *Global Transformations: Politics, Economics and Culture* (Cambridge, 1999), 1–10.
8. See e.g., Helmut Anheir, Marlies Glasius, and Mary Kaldor (eds.), *Global Civil Society Yearbook, 2001* (London, 2001), iii, 20.
9. For an introduction to these "new" concepts see ibid., 3–22.
10. David Held and Anthony McGrew, *Governing Globalization: Power, Authority and Global Governance* (Cambridge, 2002).
11. A detailed analysis is conducted by Jan-Stefan Fritz in *Regime Theory: A New Theory of International Institutions?* (Ph.D. Thesis, London School of Economics, 2000), ch. 1.
12. A helpful introduction is provided by Peter Mayer and Volker Rittberger (eds.), *Regime Theory and International Relations* (Oxford, 1996).
13. Though judging by his unsentimental attitude, in sharp contrast to Virginia's, toward the reception and fate of his books, any disappointment would not have been prolonged. See *Downhill all the Way*, 204–06.
14. Beilharz, *Labour's Utopias*, 94.
15. Ibid., 55–56.
16. Ibid., 77.

Bibliography

Primary Sources: Works by Leonard Woolf
Books
The Village in the Jungle, Oxford, Oxford University Press, 1981 (first published 1913).
International Government: Two Reports, London, George Allen and Unwin, 1916.
The Framework of a Lasting Peace (Woolf ed.), London, George Allen and Unwin, 1917.
The Future of Constantinople, London, George Allen and Unwin, 1917.
Co-operation and the Future of Industry, London, George Allen and Unwin, 1919.
Empire and Commerce in Africa: A Study of Economic Imperialism, London, Labour Party Research Dept. and George Allen and Unwin, 1920.
Economic Imperialism, London, Swarthmore Press, 1920.
Socialism and Co-operation, London, George Allen and Unwin, 1921.
Stories from the East, London, Hogarth Press, 1924.
Essays on Literature, History, Politics, Etc., London, Hogarth Press, 1928.
Imperialism and Civilization, London, Hogarth Press, 1928.
After the Deluge: A Study of Communal Psychology, Harmondsworth, Penguin, 1937 (first published 1931).
The Intelligent Man's Way to Prevent War (Woolf ed.), London, Gollancz, 1933.
Quack, quack! London, Hogarth Press, 1935.
After the Deluge: A Study of Communal Psychology, Vol. II, London, Hogarth Press, 1953 (first published 1939).
Barbarians at the Gate (Left Book Club Edition), London, Gollancz, 1939 (also published in the United States under the title *Barbarians Within and Without*).
The War for Peace, London, George Routledge, 1940.
Principia Politica: A Study of Communal Psychology, Vol. III, London, Hogarth Press, 1953.
Sowing: An Autobiography of the Years 1880–1904, London, Hogarth Press, 1960.
Growing: An Autobiography of the Years 1904–1911, London, Hogarth Press, 1961.
Diaries in Ceylon, 1908–11: Records of a Colonial Administrator, London, Hogarth Press in association with the Ceylon Historical Journal, 1962.

252 • Bibliography

Beginning Again: An Autobiography of the Years 1911–1919, London, Hogarth Press, 1964.
Downhill all the Way: An Autobiography of the Years 1919–1939, London, Hogarth Press, 1967.
The Journey Not the Arrival Matters: An Autobiography of the Years 1939–1969, London, Hogarth Press, 1969.
Letters of Leonard Woolf (Frederic Spotts ed.), London, Weidenfeld and Nicolson, 1990.

Pamphlets

Education and the Co-operative Movement, London, Women's Co-operative Guild, 1914.
The Control of Industry by Co-operators and Trade Unionists, London, Women's Co-operative Guild, 1914.
The Control of Industry by the People, London, Women's Co-operative Guild, 1915.
Co-operation and the War I: Effects of War on Commerce and Industry, London, Women's Co-operative Guild, 1915.
Co-operation and the War II: Co-operative Action in National Crises, London, Women's Co-operative Guild, 1915.
Taxation, London, Women's Co-operative Guild, 1916.
The Control of Industry by the People through the Co-operative Movement, New York, Co-operative League of America, 1920.
Mandates and Empire, London, League of Nations Union, 1920.
Scope of the Mandates under the League of Nations, London, C. F. Roworth, 1921.
International Co-operative Trade, Fabian Tract No. 201, London, Fabian Society, 1922.
International Economic Policy, London, Labour Party, 1923.
Fear and Politics: A Debate at the Zoo, London, Hogarth Press, 1925.
Hunting the Highbrow, London, Hogarth Press (Hogarth Essays, Second Series), 1927.
The Future of International Government, London, Labour Party, 1940.
Democracy in the Soviet Union—Part 2, London, Anglo-Soviet Public Relations Association, 1942.
The International Post-War Settlement, London, Fabian Publications (Research Series No. 85), 1944.
Foreign Policy: The Labour Party's Dilemma (with a Critical Comment by W. N. Ewer and Foreword by Harold Laski), London, Fabian Publications in association with Gollancz (Research Series No. 121), 1947.

Articles and Chapters in Books

"Perpetual Peace" (Review of Kant, *Perpetual Peace*), *New Statesman*, 31 July 1915.
"The International Mind" (Review of Hobson, *Towards International Government*), *The Nation*, 7 August 1915.

"Crowds and their Leaders," *New Statesman*, 29 January 1916.
"The Inhuman Herd," *New Statesman*, 8 July 1916.
"The Gentleness of Nature," *New Statesman*, 6 January 1917.
"The Two Kings of Jerusalem," *New Statesman*, 28 April 1917.
"Hazlitt," *New Statesman*, 15 December 1917.
"Winged and Unwinged Words," *New Statesman*, 6 July 1918.
"The League and the Tropics," *The Covenant*, Vol. 1, No. 1, October 1919.
"Native Labour in Africa," *New Statesman*, 10 April 1920.
"Article XXII," *New Statesman*, 1 May 1920.
"The Development of the C.W.S.," *New Statesman*, 15 January 1921.
"A Sacred Trust," *New Statesman*, 14 May 1921.
"Lenin and Kenya," *New Statesman*, 10 September 1922.
"Labour and Foreign Affairs," in Richard W. Hogue (ed.), *British Labour Speaks*, New York, Boni and Liveright, 1924.
"Empire, Subject Peoples," in H. B. Lees-Smith (ed.), *The Encyclopaedia of the Labour Movement, Vol. I*, London, Caxton Publishing, 1928.
"The Way of Peace," in Percy Redfern (ed.), *Self and Society: Social and Economic Problems from the Hitherto Neglected Point of View of the Consumer*, Manchester, Co-operative Wholesale Society, 1930.
"From Serajevo to Geneva," *Political Quarterly*, 1, 2, April 1930.
"The Future of British Broadcasting," *Political Quarterly*, 2, 2, April–June 1931.
"Educating the Listener-in," *New Statesman and Nation*, 5 September 1931.
"Reflections on the Crisis: A Constitutional Revolution," *Political Quarterly*, 2, 4, October–December 1931.
"From Geneva to the Next War," *Political Quarterly*, 4, 1, January–March 1933.
"Labour's Foreign Policy," *Political Quarterly*, 4, 4, October–December 1933.
"Can Democracy Survive?" in Mary Adams (ed.), *The Modern State*, London, George Allen and Unwin, 1933.
"Rousseau: A Modern Man in the Ancient World," *The Listener*, 22 February 1933.
"Muddle, Muddle, Toil and Trouble," *New Statesman and Nation*, 10 March 1934.
"Up and Up or Down and Down," *New Statesman and Nation*, 29 June 1935.
"Meditation on Abyssinia," *Political Quarterly*, 7, 1, January–March 1936.
"The Ideal of the League Remains," *Political Quarterly*, 7, 3, July–September 1936.
"Arms and Peace," *Political Quarterly*, 8, 1, January–March 1937.
"The Resurrection of the League," *Political Quarterly*, 8, 3, July–September 1937.
"Does Education Neutralise Thought?" *The Listener*, 22 December 1937.
"De Profundis," *Political Quarterly*, 10, 4, October–December 1939.
"Utopia and Reality," *Political Quarterly*, 11, 2, April–July 1940.
"The Politician and the Intellectual," *New Statesman and Nation*, 20 July 1940.
"Democracy at Bay," *Political Quarterly*, 11, 4, October–December 1940.
"The Future of Imperialism," *New Statesman and Nation*, 25 January 1941.
"How to Make the Peace," *Political Quarterly*, 12, 4, October–December 1941.
"Hitler's Psychology," *Political Quarterly*, 13, 4, October–December 1942.

"A Challenge to All of Us: Two Views on the Responsibilities of Colonial Empire," I, *The Listener*, 12 August 1943.
"The Future of the Small State," *Political Quarterly*, 14, 3, July–September 1943.
"The United Nations," *Political Quarterly*, 16, 1, January–March 1945.
"The Political Advance of Backward Peoples," in Rita Hinden (ed.), *Fabian Colonial Essays*, London, George Allen and Unwin, 1945.
"Britain in the Atomic Age," *Political Quarterly*, 18, 1, January–March 1946.
"The Man of Munich," *Political Quarterly*, 18, 3, July–September 1947.
"Music in Moscow," *Political Quarterly*, 20, 3, July–September 1949.
"Political Thought and the Webbs," in M. Cole (ed.), *The Webbs and Their Work*, London, Muller, 1949.
"Something New Out of Africa," *Political Quarterly*, 23, 4, October–December 1952.
"The Influence of G. E. Moore—II," *The Listener*, 30 April 1955.
"What is History?" *Political Quarterly*, 26, 3, July–September 1955.
"Thou Shalt Not Kill," *New Statesman and Nation*, 12 November 1955.
"Espionage, Security, and Liberty," *Political Quarterly*, 27, 2, April–June 1956.
"The Prehistoric 'NS & N,'" *New Statesman and Nation*, 12 May 1956.
"The Nemisis of Being Too Late," *New Statesman*, 4 January 1958.
"Kingsley Martin," *Political Quarterly*, 40, 3, July–September 1969.

Primary Sources: Personal Papers

Leonard Woolf Papers, University of Sussex, Sussex, England.
Library of Leonard and Virginia Woolf, Washington State University, Pullman, Washington, USA.
Norman Angell Papers, Ball State University, Muncie, Indiana, USA.

Primary Sources: Interviews

Professor Joseph Frankel, December 1989.
Lord Healey, March 2002.

Secondary Sources: Books and Articles on Leonard Woolf

Alexander, Peter F., *Leonard and Virginia Woolf: A Literary Partnership*, London, Harvester Wheatsheaf, 1992.
Annan, Noel, "Leonard Woolf's Autobiography," *Political Quarterly*, 41, 1, 1970.
—— "The Best of Bloomsbury" (Review of *Letters of Leonard Woolf*), *New York Review of Books*, 29 March 1990.
Bell, Quentin, *Elders and Betters*, London, Pimlico, 1997.
Barron, T. J., "Before the Deluge: Leonard Woolf in Ceylon," *Journal of Imperial and Commonwealth History*, 6, 1977.

Brogan, Denis, "The Last of Bloomsbury," *The Spectator*, 23 August 1969.
Cole, Margaret, "Leonard Sidney Woolf (1880–1969): Author, Publisher and Socialist," in J. M. Bellamy and J. Saville (eds.), *Dictionary of Labour Biography*, London, Macmillan, 1979.
Lehmann, John, "Bloomsbury Sage," *The Sunday Telegraph*, 17 August 1969.
Leventhal, F. M., "Leonard Woolf and Kingsley Martin: Creative Tension on the Left," *Albion*, 24, 2, 1992.
Luedeking, Leila, and Edmonds, Michael, *Leonard Woolf: A Bibliography*, Winchester, St Paul's Bibliographies, 1992.
Nicolson, Nigel, "Precious Mettle" (Review of *Letters of Leonard Woolf*), *The Sunday Times*, 4 March 1990.
Noel-Baker, Philip, "Mr. Leonard Woolf: Vision of International Co-operation," *The Times*, 21 August 1969.
Robson, William, "Leonard Woolf," *New Statesman*, 22 August 1969.
Rosenbaum, S. P., "At Last—Something New about the Woolfs" (Review of *Letters of Leonard Woolf*), *The Toronto Globe and Mail*, 6 January 1990.
Rosenfeld, Natania, *Outsiders Together: Virginia and Leonard Woolf*, Princeton, NJ, Princeton University Press, 2000.
Plomer, William, "Leonard Woolf and his Autobiography," *The Listener*, 4 July 1969.
Spater, George, and Parsons, Ian, *A Marriage of True Minds: An Intimate Portrait of Leonard and Virginia Woolf*, London, Jonathan Cape, 1977.
Wilson, Duncan, *Leonard Woolf: A Political Biography*, London, Hogarth Press, 1978.
Wilson, Jean Moorcroft, *Leonard Woolf: Pivot or Outsider of Bloomsbury?* London, Cecil Woolf, 1994.
Wilson, Peter, Review of *Letters of Leonard Woolf*, *Millennium: Journal of International Studies*, 20, 3, 1991.

Secondary Sources: General

Books

Alderson, Kai, and Hurrell, Andrew (eds.), *Hedley Bull on International Society*, London, Macmillan, 2000.
Angell, Norman, *The Great Illusion 1933*, London, Heinemann, 1933.
Annan, Noel, *Our Age: The Generation that Made Post-War Britain*, London, Fontana, 1991.
Anheir, Helmut, Glasius, Marlies, and Kaldor, Mary (eds.), *Global Civil Society Yearbook, 2001*, Oxford, Oxford University Press, 2001.
Archer, Clive, *International Organization*, London, George Allen and Unwin, 1983.
Ashworth, Lucian, *Creating International Studies: Angell, Mitrany, and the Liberal Tradition*, Aldershot, Ashgate, 1999.
Beales, A. C. F., *The History of Peace: A Short Account of the Organised Movements for International Peace*, London, Bell, 1931.
Beilharz, Peter, *Labour's Utopias: Bolshevism, Fabianism, Social Democracy*, London, Routledge, 1992.

Blake, Robert, and Louis, Wm. Roger (eds.), *Churchill*, Oxford, Oxford University Press, 1993.
Blythe, R., *The Age of Illusion: England in the Twenties and Thirties*, London, Hamish Hamilton, 1963.
Brailsford, H. N., *A League of Nations*, London, Headley, 1917.
Briar, A. M., *Fabian Socialism and English Politics 1884–1918*, Cambridge, Cambridge University Press, 1966.
Brierly, J. L., *The Law of Nations: An Introduction to the International Law of Peace*, 3rd edn., London, Oxford University Press, 1943.
Bull, Hedley, *The Control of the Arms Race*, London, Weidenfeld and Nicolson, 1961.
—— *The Anarchical Society: A Study of Order in World Politics*, London, Macmillan, 1977.
Carr, E. H., *The Twenty Years' Crisis: An Introduction to the Study of International Relations*, London, Macmillan, 1939.
—— *The Future of Nations: Independence or Interdependence*, London, Kegan Paul, 1941.
—— *Conditions of Peace*, London, Macmillan, 1942.
—— *Nationalism and After*, London, Macmillan, 1945.
—— *The Twenty Years' Crisis: An Introduction to the Study of International Relations*, 2nd edn., London, Macmillan, 1946.
—— *The New Society*, London, Macmillan, 1951.
—— *International Relations Between the Two World Wars, 1919–1939*, London, Macmillan, 1965 (first published 1947).
Ceadel, Martin, *Thinking about Peace and War*, Oxford, Oxford University Press, 1987.
Clark, Ian, *The Hierarchy of States: Reform and Resistance in the International Order*, Cambridge, Cambridge University Press, 1989.
Claude, Inis L., Jr., *Swords into Plowshares: The Problems and Progress of International Organization*, London, University of London Press, 1965.
Cox, Michael (ed.), *E. H. Carr: A Critical Appraisal*, London, Palgrave, 2000.
Dougherty, J. E. and Pfaltzgraff, R. L., Jr., *Contending Theories of International Relations: A Comprehensive Survey*, 2nd edn., New York, Harper Row, 1981.
Edel, Leon, *Bloomsbury: A House of Lions*, London, Penguin, 1981.
Egerton, George W., *Great Britain and the Creation of the League of Nations: Strategy, Politics and International Organisation, 1914–19*, London, Scolar Press, 1979.
Eldridge, C. C. (ed.), *British Imperialism in the Nineteenth Century*, London, Macmillan, 1984.
Etherington, Norman, *Theories of Imperialism: War, Conquest and Capital*, Beckenham, Croom Helm, 1984.
Feuer, Lewis S., *Imperialism and the Anti-Imperialist Mind*, New Brunswick, Transaction Publishers, 1989.
Fieldhouse, D. K. (ed.), *The Theory of Capitalist Imperialism*, London, Longman, 1967.
—— *Economics and Empire 1830–1914*, London, Macmillan, 1984.

Gann, L. H., and Duigan, Peter, *Burden of Empire: An Appraisal of Western Colonialism in Africa South of the Sahara*, London, Pall Mall Press, 1968.
Griffith, Gareth, *Socialism and Superior Brains: The Political Thought of Bernard Shaw*, London, Routledge, 1993.
Gupta, P. S., *Imperialism and the British Labour Movement, 1914–1964*, London, Macmillan, 1975.
Haas, Ernst, *Beyond the Nation State: Functionalism and International Organization*, Stanford, Stanford University Press, 1964.
Haslam, Jonathan, *The Vices of Integrity: E. H. Carr, 1892–1982*, London, Verso, 1999.
Hayek, F. A., *The Road to Serfdom*, Routledge and Kegan Paul, 1986 [1944].
Healey, Denis, *The Time of My Life*, New York, Norton, 1990.
Held, David et al., *Global Transformations: Politics, Economics and Culture*, Cambridge, Polity Press, 1999.
Held, David and McGrew, Andrew, *Governing Globalization: Power, Authority and Global Governance*, Cambridge, Polity Press, 2002.
Hetherington, Penelope, *British Paternalism and Africa 1920–1940*, London, Frank Cass, 1978.
Hinden, Rita (ed.), *Fabian Colonial Essays*, London, Allen and Unwin, 1945.
Hobson, J. A., *A League of Nations*, London, George Allen and Unwin, 1915.
Hollis, Martin, and Smith, Steve, *Explaining and Understanding International Relations*, Oxford, Clarendon Press, 1990.
Howard, Michael, *War and the Liberal Conscience*, Oxford, Oxford University Press, 1981.
Howard-Ellis, C., *The Origin, Structure and Working of the League of Nations*, London, 1928.
Independent Commission on International Development Issues (Brandt Commission), *North–South: A Programme for Survival*, London, Pan, 1980.
Iriye, Akira, *Cultural Internationalism and World Order*, Baltimore, Johns Hopkins University Press, 1997.
James, Alan, *Sovereign Statehood: The Basis of International Society*, London, George Allen and Unwin, 1986.
Jones, Charles, *E. H. Carr and International Relations: A Duty to Lie*, Cambridge, Cambridge University Press, 1998.
Kegley, Charles W., Jr., and Wittkopf, Eugene R., *World Politics: Trend and Transformation*, New York, St. Martins, 1989.
Kennedy, Paul, *The Realities Behind Diplomacy: Background Influences on British Foreign Policy 1865–1980*, London, Fontana, 1981.
Keynes, J. M., *Essays in Biography*, London, Macmillan for the Royal Economic Society, 1972.
Knutsen, Torbjörn L., *A History of International Relations Theory: An Introduction*, Manchester, Manchester University Press, 1992.
Kramnick, Isaac, and Sheerman, Barry, *Harold Laski: A Life on the Left*, London, Hamish Hamilton, 1993.
Langer, W. L., *The Diplomacy of Imperialism: 1890–1902*, New York, Knopf, 1935.

Long, David, *Towards a New Liberal Internationalism: The International Theory of J. A. Hobson*, Cambridge, Cambridge University Press and the London School of Economics, 1996.
—— and Wilson, Peter (eds.), *Thinkers of the Twenty Years' Crisis: Inter-War Idealism Reassessed*, Oxford, Clarendon Press, 1995.
Lee, Francis, *Fabianism and Colonialism: The Life and Political Thought of Lord Sydney Olivier*, London, Defiant Books, 1988.
Manning, C. A. W., *The Nature of International Society*, London, Macmillan and the London School of Economics, 1975.
Mayer, Peter, and Rittberger, Volker (eds.), *Regime Theory and International Relations*, Oxford, Clarendon Press, 1986.
Morgenthau, Hans J., *Politics Among Nations: The Struggle for Power and Peace*, 5th edn. revised, New York, Alfred A. Knopf, 1978.
Miller, J. D. B., *Norman Angell and the Futility of War*, London, Macmillan, 1986.
Mitrany, David, *Towards International Government*, London, 1933.
—— *The Functional Theory of Politics*, London, Martin Robinson in association with the London School of Economics, 1975.
Modelski, George, *Principles of World Politics*, New York, Free Press, 1972.
Mower, Edmund C., *International Government*, New York, 1931.
Murphy, Craig N., *International Organization and Industrial Change: Global Governance since 1850*, Cambridge, Polity, 1994.
Noel-Baker, P. J., *The League of Nations at Work*, London, Nisbit, 1926.
Northedge, F. S., *The League of Nations: Its Life and Times 1920–1946*, Leicester, Leicester University Press, 1988.
Olson, William, and Groom, A. J. R., *International Relations Then and Now: Origins and Trends in Interpretation*, London, Harper Collins, 1991.
Pimlott, Ben, *Labour and the Left in the 1930s*, London, Allen and Unwin, 1986.
—— (ed.), *Fabian Essays in Socialist Thought*, London, Heinemann, 1984.
Potter, Pitman B., *An Introduction to the Study of International Organization*, New York, Appelton-Century, 1922.
Pugh, Patricia, *Educate, Agitate, Organise: 100 Years of Fabian Socialism*, London, Methuen, 1984.
Reynolds, P. A., *British Foreign Policy in the Inter-War Years*, London, Longman, 1954.
Robson, William A., *The Political Quarterly in the Thirties*, London, Allen Lane and Penguin, 1971.
Rich, Paul, *Race and Empire in British Politics*, Cambridge, Cambridge University Press, 1986.
Robbins, Keith, *The Abolition of War: The "Peace Movement" in Britain, 1914–1919*, Cardiff, University of Wales Press, 1976.
Robinson, R. E. and Gallagher, J. A., *Africa and the Victorians: The Official Mind of Imperialism*, London, Macmillan, 1961.
Roberts, Adam and Kingsbury, Benedict, *United Nations, Divided World*, Oxford, Clarendon Press, 1988.

Shaw, George Bernard (ed.), *Fabian Essays in Socialism*, London, Fabian Society, 1889.
—— (ed.), *Fabianism and the Empire: A Manifesto*, London, Grant Richards, 1900.
Schmidt, Brian, *The Political Discourse of Anarchy: A Disciplinary History of International Relations*, Albany, State University of New York Press, 1998.
Smith, Michael Joseph, *Realist Thought from Weber to Kissinger*, Baton Rouge, La., Louisiana University Press, 1986.
Spender, Stephen, *World Within World*, London, Readers Union, 1953.
Stebbing, Susan L., *Ideals and Illusions*, London, Watts, 1941.
Suganami, Hidemi, *The Domestic Analogy and World Order Proposals*, Cambridge, Cambridge University Press, 1989.
Taylor, A. J. P., *The Trouble Makers: Dissent Over Foreign Policy, 1792–1939*, Harmondsworth, Penguin, 1985.
Taylor, Paul, *International Co-operation Today: The European and the Universal Pattern*, London, Elek, 1971.
Thomson, David, Meyer, E., and Briggs, Asa, *Patterns of Peacemaking*, London, Kegan Paul, 1945.
Vasquez, John, *The Power of Power Politics: A Critique*, London, Frances Pinter, 1983.
Waltz, Kenneth, *Man, the State, and War: A Theoretical Analysis*, New York, Columbia University Press, 1959.
Wight Martin, *International Theory: The Three Traditions* (ed. Brian Porter and Gabrielle Wight), Leicester, Leicester University Press, 1991.
Yeo, Stephen (ed.), *New Views of Co-operation*, London, Routledge, 1978.
Zimmern, Alfred, *The League of Nations and the Rule of Law 1918–1935*, London, Macmillan, 1936.

Pamphlets

Carr, E. H., and Madariaga, S. de, *The Future of International Government* (Peace Aims Pamphlet No. 4), London, National Peace Council, 1941.
Terrins, Deirdre, and Whitehead, Phillip, *100 Years of Fabian Socialism*, London, Fabian Society, 1984.

Articles and Chapters in Books

Angell, Norman, "Who are the 'Utopians'? And who the 'Realists'?" *Headway*, January 1940.
Banks, Michael, "The Evolution of International Relations Theory," in Michael Banks (ed.), *Conflict in World Society*, London, Wheatsheaf, 1984.
Birn, D. S., "The League of Nations Union and Collective Security," *Journal of Contemporary History*, 9, 3, 1974.
Booth, Ken, "Security in Anarchy: Utopian Realism in Theory and Practice," *International Affairs*, 67, 3, 1991.
Bull, Hedley, "Society and Anarchy in International Relations," in H. Butterfield and M. Wight (eds.), *Diplomatic Investigations*, London, George Allen and Unwin, 1966.

Bull, Hedley "The Grotian Conception of International Society," in H. Butterfied and M. Wight (eds.), *Diplomatic Investigations*, London, George Allen and Unwin, 1966.

—— "*The Twenty Years' Crisis* Thirty Years On," *International Journal*, 24, 4, 1969.

—— "The Theory of International Politics, 1919–1969," in Brian Porter (ed.), *The Aberystwyth Papers: International Politics 1919–1969*, London, Oxford University Press, 1972.

—— "The State's Positive Role in World Affairs," *Daedalus*, 108, 4, 1979.

—— "Hans Kelsen and International Law," in Richard Tur and William Twining (eds.), *Essays on Kelsen*, Oxford, Clarendon Press, 1986.

Ceadel, Martin, "Supranationalism in the British Peace Movement during the Early Twentieth Century," in Andrea Bosco (ed.), *The Federal Idea: The History of Federalism from the Enlightenment to 1945*, London, Lothian Foundation Press, 1991.

Cole, Margaret, "The Fabian Society," *Political Quarterly*, 15, 3, 1944.

—— "Preface," Beatrice Potter, *The Co-operative Movement in Great Britain*, Aldershot, Croom Helm in association with the London School of Economics and Political Science, 1987.

Crossman, R. H. S., "Illusions of Power—E. H. Carr," in R. H. S. Crossman, *The Charm of Politics and Other Essays in Political Criticism*, London, Hamish Hamilton, 1958.

Dickinson, Edwin D., "An International Program," *New Republic*, 9, 112, 23 December 1916.

Earle, Edward Mead, "H. G. Wells, British Patriot in Search of a World State," *World Politics*, 2, 2, 1950.

Etherington, Norman, "Reconsidering Theories of Imperialism," *History and Theory*, 21, 1, 1982.

Evans, Graham, "Some Problems with a History of Thought in International Relations," *International Relations*, 4, 6, 1974.

—— "E. H. Carr and International Relations," *British Journal of International Studies*, 1, 2, 1975.

Fieldhouse, D. K., " 'Imperialism': An Historiographical Revision," *Economic History Review*, Second Series, 14, 2, 1961.

Fox, W. T. R., "E. H. Carr and Political Realism: Vision and Revision," *Review of International Studies*, 11, 1, 1985.

Gallagher, John, and Robinson, Ronald, "The Imperialism of Free Trade," *Economic History Review*, Second Series, 6, 1, 1953.

Gilpin, Robert, "The Richness of the Tradition of Political Realism," *International Organization*, 30, 2, 1984.

Grantham, J. T., "Hugh Dalton and the International Post-War Settlement: Labour Party Foreign Policy Formulation, 1943–44," *Journal of Contemporary History*, 14, 4, 1979.

Halliday, Fred, "State and Society in International Relations: A Second Agenda," *Millennium: Journal of International Studies*, 16, 2, 1987.

—— "Three Concepts of Internationalism," *International Affairs*, 64, 2, 1988.
Hammond, R. J., "Economic Imperialism: Sidelights on a Stereotype," *Journal of Economic History*, 21, 4, 1961.
Healey, Denis, "Collective Security after Fifty Years," *LSE Quarterly*, 1, 1, 1987.
Himmelfarb, Gertrude, "The Intellectual in Politics: The Case of the Webbs," *Journal of Contemporary History*, 6, 3, 1971.
Holsti, K. J., "Governance without Government: Polyarchy in Nineteenth-Century European International Politics," in James N. Rosenau and Ernst-Otto Czempiel (eds.), *Governance without Government: Order and Change in World Politics*, Cambridge, Cambridge University Press, 1992.
Howard, Michael, "The United Nations and International Security," in Adam Roberts and Benedict Kingsbury (eds.), *United Nations, Divided World: The United Nations' Roles in International Relations*, Oxford, Clarendon Press, 1988.
Hurrell, Andrew, "Collective Security and International Order Revisited," *International Relations*, 11, 1, 1992.
James, Alan, "The Realism of Realism: The State and the Study of International Relations," *Review of International Studies*, 15, 3, 1989.
Jervis, Robert, "From Balance to Concert: A Study of International Security Cooperation," *World Politics*, 38, 1, 1985.
John, Ieuan, Wright, Moorhead, and Garnett, John, "International Politics at Aberystwyth," in Brian Porter (ed.), *The Aberystwyth Papers: International Politics 1919–69*, London, Oxford University Press, 1972.
Johnston, Whittle, "E. H. Carr's Theory of International Relations: A Critique," *Journal of Politics*, 29, 1967.
Kegley, Charles W., Jr., "The Neoidealist Moment in International Studies? Realist Myths and the New International Realities," *International Studies Quarterly*, 37, 2, 1993.
Koebner, Richard, "The Concept of Economic Imperialism," *Economic History Review*, Second Series, 2, 1, 1949.
Leventhal, F. M., "H. N. Brailsford and the *New Leader*," *Journal of Contemporary History*, 9, 1, 1974.
Lewis, Gordon K., "Fabian Socialism: Some Aspects of Theory and Practice," *Journal of Politics*, 14, 3, 1952.
Long, David, "J. A. Hobson and Idealism in International Relations," *Review of International Studies*, 17, 3 1991.
—— "International Functionalism and the Politics of Forgetting," *International Journal*, 48, 2, 1993.
Lukowitz, D. C., "British Pacifists and Appeasement: The Peace Pledge Union," *Journal of Contemporary History*, 9, 1, 1974.
Manning, C. A. W., "The Legal Framework in a World of Change," in Brian Porter (ed.), *The Aberystwyth Papers: International Politics 1919–69*, London, Oxford University Press, 1972.
Markwell, D. J., "Sir Alfred Zimmern Revisited: Fifty Years On," *Review of International Studies*, 12, 4, 1986.

Marwick, Arthur, "The Impact of the First World War on British Society," *Journal of Contemporary History*, 3, 1, 1968.
Morel, E. D., "The Union of Democratic Control," *Contemporary Review*, 108, 1915.
Morgan, I, "Theories of Imperialism: A Bibliographical Sketch," *Journal of Area Studies*, 6, 1, 1982.
Morgenthau, Hans J., "The Political Science of E. H. Carr," *World Politics*, 1, 1, 1948–1949.
Navari, Cornelia, "The Great Illusion Revisited: The International Theory of Norman Angell," *Review of International Studies*, 15, 4, 1989.
—— "David Mitrany and International Functionalism," in David Long and Peter Wilson, (eds.), *Thinkers of the Twenty Years" Crisis: Inter-War Idealism Reassessed*, Oxford, Clarendon Press, 1995.
Offer, Anver, "The British Empire, 1870–1914: A Waste of Money?" *Economic History Review*, 46, 2, 1993.
Olson, W., and Onuf, N., "The Growth of the Discipline: Reviewed," in Steve Smith (ed.), *International Relations: British and American Perspectives*, Oxford, Basil Blackwell, 1985.
Osiander, Andreas, "Rereading Early Twentieth Century IR Theory: Idealism Revisited," *International Studies Quarterly*, 42, 3, 1998.
Peretz, Martin, "Laski Redivivus," *Journal of Contemporary History*, 1, 2, 1966.
Pinder, John, "Federalism and the British Liberal Tradition," in Andrea Bosco (ed.), *The Federal Idea: The History of Federalism from the Enlightenment to 1945*, London, Lothian Foundation Press, 1991.
Porter, Brian, "David Davies: A Hunter after Peace," *Review of International Studies*, 15, 1, 1989.
Robinson, Ronald, "The Moral Disarmament of African Empire 1919–1947," *Journal of Imperial and Commonwealth History*, 8, 1, 1979.
Samuels, Stuart, "The Left Book Club," *Journal of Contemporary History*, 1, 2, 1966.
Schmidt, Brian, "Lessons from the Past: Reassessing the Interwar Disciplinary History of International Relations," *International Studies Quarterly*, 42, 3, 1998.
Schneer, Jonathan, "Hopes Defeated or Shattered: The British Labour Left and the Third Force Movement, 1945–49," *Journal of Modern History*, 56, 2, 1984.
Seton-Watson, R. W., "Politics and Power," *The Listener*, Supplement No. 48, 7 December 1939.
Smith, Steve, "Paradigm Dominance in International Relations: The Development of International Relations as a Social Science," *Millennium: Journal of International Relations*, 16, 2, 1987.
Stokes, Eric, "Late Nineteenth-Century Colonial Expansion and the Attack on the Theory of Economic Imperialism: A Case of Mistaken Identity?" *Historical Journal*, 12, 2, 1969.
Suganami, Hidemi, "Halliday's Two Concepts of State," *Millennium: Journal of International Studies*, 17, 1, 1988.
—— "C. A. W. Manning and the Study of IR," *Review of International Studies*, 27, 1, 2001.

Taylor, Paul, "Functionalism: The Theory of David Mitrany," in Paul Taylor and A. J. R. Groom (eds.), *International Organization: A Conceptual Approach*, London, Frances Pinter, 1978.

Taylor, Trevor, "Power Politics," in Trevor Taylor (ed.), *Approaches and Theory in International Relations*, Harlow, Longman, 1978.

—— "Utopianism," in Steve Smith (ed.), *International Relations: British and American Approaches*, Oxford, Basil Blackwell, 1985.

Weiner, Martin J., "Graham Wallas (1858–1932): Fabian Socialist and Political Psychologist," in J. M. Bellamy and J. Saville (eds.), *Dictionary of Labour Biography*, London, Macmillan, 1979.

Winkler, Henry R., "The Development of the League Idea in Great Britain, 1914–1919," *Journal of Modern History*, 20, 2, 1948.

—— "The Emergence of a Labor Foreign Policy in Great Britain, 1918–1929," *Journal of Modern History*, 28, 3, 1956.

Wilson, Peter, "The New Europe Debate in Wartime Britain," in P. Murray and P. Rich (eds.), *Visions of European Unity*, Boulder, Colo., Westview Press, 1996.

—— "The Myth of the First Great Debate," *Review of International Studies*, 24, 5, 1998.

—— "Radicalism for a Conservative Purpose: The Peculiar Realism of E. H. Carr," *Millennium: Journal of International Studies*, 30, 1, 2001.

Winter, J. M., "The Webbs and the Non-White World: A Case of Socialist Racialism," *Journal of Contemporary History*, 9, 1, 1974.

Theses

Fritz, Jan-Stefan, *Regime Theory: A New Theory of International Institutions?* London School of Economics and Political Science Ph.D. Thesis, 2000.

Long, David, *Towards a New Internationalism: J. A. Hobson and International Relations*, London School of Economics and Political Science Ph.D. Thesis, 1991.

Markwell, D. J., *John Maynard Keynes and International Relations: Idealism, Economic Paths to War and Peace, and Post-war Reconstruction*, University of Oxford D.Phil. Thesis, 1995.

Shepherd, G. W., *The Theory and Practice of Internationalism in the British Labour Party with Special Reference to the Inter-War Period*, University of London Ph.D. Thesis, 1952.

Index

Africa, 89–90, 91–2, 95–8, 108–12, 127, 128–9, 131
  African nationalism, 108, 129
  relationship to Europe, 100–1, 151
America, 74, 121
Angell, Norman, 16, 57, 166, 178, 190, 193
anticapitalism, *see* capitalism
Apostles, the, 1, 143
arbitration, 37–8, 76, 78, 148
Archer, Clive, 7–8, 10
armament, 72, 147
arms control, 50–1, 61, 69
Asia, 105–6, 138
atomic power, 49–51, 61
atomic weapons, 49–51, 74

balance of power, 13, 56, 57, 69, 70
Balkans, the, 34–5, 184
Benthamites, 17, 56, 190, 191
Bismarck, Otto von, 90–1
Boer War, the, 25–7
Borchard, Edwin, 8–9
Brailsford, Henry Noel, 15, 53, 86, 205
Britain, 74, 121, 184–5
British Empire, the, 25, 26–7, 29, 36, 47, 127, 133–4, 150
  Woolf's role in, ix, 2, 84, 144
Bull, Hedley, 4, 12, 15, 53, 80, 85, 205, 209

capitalism and capitalists, 145–6, 148–9, 151–7
anticapitalism, 155–7
capitalist psychology, 153, 154, 155
Carr, Edward Hallett, vii, 4–5, 9, 15–21, 67, 68, 76, 177ff, 212, 214, 216, 247n, 248n, 249n
  his determinism, 179,198
  The Twenty Years' Crisis, ix, 15, 18, 178, 196, 199, 200, 216, 245n
  Woolf's critique of, 179ff
Ceylon, 84, 112–13, 131
Chamberlain, Joseph, 89, 92, 96, 118
China, 27–8, 95, 99
Churchill, Winston, 20, 133
Cobden, Richard, 137, 147, 149
Cold War, the, 74
Cole, George Douglas Howard, vii, 143, 147, 166, 175, 205, 216, 236n
Cole, Margaret, 116, 145
collective security, 9, 49, 50, 68, 69–72, 232n
colonialism, 88, 89, 91, 93, 95, 107, 124, 128–9
  Colonial Development and Welfare Act, 133
  decolonisation, ix
  education and colonial peoples, 109–11, 130–4, 136
  indirect rule, 111, 132
  self-government, 110, 111–12, 125–6, 127, 130–1, 132–3, 140–1
  white settlers, 85, 106–8, 128–30, 133, 138–9, 236n

colonialism—*Continued*
  see also British Empire, the;
    imperialism
commerce and industry, 43, 87, 152, 158, 162, 243–4n
common interests, 185–6, 194, 197
communications revolution, the, 40, 57, 66, 209
conflicting interests, 182, 184, 185, 194, 197
consumers, 146, 148, 152, 153, 158, 163–4
Co-operation, 145, 147, 158–64, 172–5
  Co-operative societies, 158, 172–3
  nonCo-operative economic organization, 165–9
  see also Women's Co-operative Guild
Co-operative Movement, the, 144, 147, 172–4
Creech Jones, Arthur, 116, 133
cultural relativism, 63, 110, 112
CWS, 158, 172–3

democracy, 87–8, 157, 159–62, 201
  federation of democracies, 61–2
disarmament, 32, 49, 69, 195
dissent, radical, 137–9
domestic analogy, the, 76–9

economic factors, 145
economic imperialism, 85, 86ff, 120–3, 135
economics, 144ff
ECOSOC, 49
education, role of, *see under* colonialism
Europe, viii, 34–6, 94–5, 204
  its states as "instrument[s] of exploitation", 88, 94, 99–100
  relationship to Africa, 100–1, 151
  see also France; Germany

Fabian Society, the, 2, 24–6
  Fabian Colonial Bureau, 116

Fabian Draft Treaty, 24, 32
Fabian paternalism, 139–41
Fabian Research Bureau, 23, 236–7n
Fabian socialism, 27, 146–7, 223n
Fabianism, 30–1
New Fabian Research Bureau, 116, 236–7n
facts, 30, 139, 140, 180–1, 192
First World War, vi, 12, 45, 61, 71, 148, 154, 210
France, 97, 121, 184–5
free trade, 19, 27–8, 146, 147–8, 150, 151, 170, 189, 190
  see also trade
functionalism, anthropological, 135, 240n
functionalism, international, 7, 58–60, 67, 203, 228n

Germany, 97, 121
globalisation, 81, 213
governance, 81, 213
government, domestic, 77, 79
government, international, 24, 31, 33ff, 53ff, 102, 167, 214
  feasibility of, 55–6
  see also "*International Government*" under Woolf, Leonard Sidney
Great Powers, the, 26–7, 30, 34–7, 54, 56, 94
  Britain as a, 26–7
  quasi-legislative role of, 35–6, 37, 56
Great War, the, *see* First World War

Hague conferences, the, 38–40
harmony of interests, 17–18, 19, 170, 183, 194, 195
Hobson, John Atkinson, vii, 15, 54, 57, 83, 86, 120, 143, 149, 166, 205, 216, 238n
Hogarth Press, the, 3, 144
Home Rule question, the, 36, 38, 78
Huxley, Elspeth, 130–2

idealism and idealists, vi, vii, 5, 11–21, 79, 209, 214, 217, 220n
  as a pejorative or ambiguous term, 11, 214
  institutions and, 13
  see also utopianism
ILO, 42
imperialism and imperialists, 83ff, 115ff, 150, 234n, 238n
  decolonisation, ix
  imperial institutes, 28
  "new imperialism", 120, 121, 130
  see also British Empire, the; colonialism; economic imperialism
indirect rule, *see under* colonialism
individualism, 17, 30, 154
industrialism, 87–8, 155, 157
industry, *see* commerce and industry
interdependence theory, 57–8
interests, *see* common interests; conflicting interests; national interests
international adjudication, 37–40, 75–6
  see also international law
international anarchy, 11, 12, 59, 191
international economic organization, 147, 154, 157, 165–75
  see also Co-operation; Co-operative Movement, the
international law, 37–40, 62–4, 75
  and power, 73
  harmonization of international laws, 42–3
  see also international adjudication
international organization, 7, 30, 40–4, 45, 61–2
  functional approaches to, viii
  international associations as agents of, 41–2
international trade, *see* trade
internationalism, 17–18, 29, 44, 45–7, 65, 101–2, 103, 166, 210, 211

liberal internationalism, ix, 15, 145, 147–51, 215, 242n
new internationalism, the, 15
interpretivism, 122
ITU, 41

Keynes, John Maynard, 1, 3, 143, 166, 205

labor, 148–9, 151, 152
Labour Party, the, 2–3, 115
Laski, Harold, vii, 205, 216, 230n
League of Nations, the, 5, 6, 9, 12, 17, 46–7, 54–5, 70, 71–2, 102–3, 104, 106, 119, 128, 148, 186, 201, 225n
  League Covenant, the, 54–5, 72, 100, 104–5, 123–6
  Permanent Mandates Commission of, 125, 128
  "reformed League idea", 9, 70
Left Book Club, the, 68, 230n
Lenin, Vladimir Ilych, 86, 120, 238n
liberal internationalism, *see under* internationalism
Lugard, Frederick, 89–90, 92, 127

mandates, 99–106, 119, 120, 123–30, 136
military sanctions, *see under* sanctions
Mitrany, David, vii, 7, 58–60, 134, 166, 168, 205, 216
modern interdependence theory, *see* interdependence theory
Moore, George Edward, 1, 136, 143
morality, 17, 19, 27, 119
Morel, Edmund Dene, 86, 117–18, 137
Morris, William, 152, 155

national interests, 182–3, 184–6, 195
nationalism, 17–18, 29, 36, 44–7, 87–8, 210
  African nationalism, 108, 129
natural harmony of interests, *see* harmony of interests

268 • Index

"new imperialism", *see under* imperialism
new internationalism, the, *see under* internationalism
nonCo-operative economic organization, *see under* Co-operation

Owen, Robert, 152, 171

peace, 8, 9, 75, 77, 148, 163–4, 196–7
"peace through law", 8
power and power politics, 20, 73–4, 123, 126, 129, 147, 180, 182, 183, 184
and international law, 73
producer socialism, *see under* socialism
profit, 152, 153, 244n
progress, 12
protectionism, 148–51, 195
public opinion, 17, 19–20, 190, 191

realism and realists, 5–6, 9, 16, 32, 51, 179, 180–2, 184, 188–9, 192–4, 195–6, 198, 205
Marx as a realist, 188
rearmament, 69
reason, 12–13, 17, 80, 191, 212–13
Ruskin, John, 152, 155

sanctions, 7, 63, 70–1
military sanctions, 70
Second World War, 9, 47, 226n
self-determination, 59, 130, 201–2
self-government, *see under* colonialism
semi-utopianism, *see under* utopianism
Shaw, George Bernard, 23, 26–9, 140, 223n, 224n, 231n
Fabianism and the Empire, 26–30
socialism and socialists, 31, 146, 154, 155, 157–8, 160, 168–9, 183, 204
international socialism, 25
producer socialism, 157–8, 159
South Africa, 26–7, 108, 128

see also Africa; Boer War, the
sovereignty, 66, 167, 203
Soviet Russia, 68, 74, 154, 157, 230n
state, the, 87–8, 94, 146–7, 186
small state, the, 202
strategic considerations, 72, 93, 123, 150
Suganami, Hidemi, 8–10, 76–7

tariffs, 149, 150, 195
Toynbee, Arnold, 16, 178, 193
trade, 28, 42, 148, 149, 151, 158–9, 163–4
see also free trade

UN, viii, 49–51, 69, 74, 125, 226n
UPU, 41, 42
utopianism and utopians, 5–6, 9, 12, 13, 15, 16–20, 32, 51, 67–8, 177, 180–1, 186–91, 192, 193, 195, 205, 220n, 245n
Carr's critique of, vii, 18–21, 67, 179–80, 187–91
Marx as a utopian, 188
semi-utopianism, 6
see also Carr, Edward Hallett; idealism

Versailles Conference, the, 45–6, 55, 203, 206–7

war, 7, 9, 13–14, 17, 26, 30, 32, 55–6, 62, 71, 75, 77, 145, 150, 180–1, 190–1
laws of, 78
weapons manufacturers and other "sinister interests" in, 13, 154, 242n
see also Boer War, the; First World War; Second World War
Webb, Beatrice, 3, 23, 140, 147, 223n
Webb, Sidney James, 2, 24, 140, 146, 147, 223n
Wells, Herbert George, 15, 137, 147

white settlers, *see under* colonialism
Wilson, Woodrow, 123, 178, 193, 202
Women's Co-operative Guild, 2, 23, 144
Woolf, Leonard Sidney, vii, viii–ix, 1–4, 23–4, 112–13, 122, 143–4, 211, 212, 233n
   as advocate of international government, 7
   as idealist or utopian, ix, 4, 7, 11, 119–20, 122–3, 125, 126, 128, 135–6, 139, 170–5, 214
   as anti-imperialist thinker, 2–3, 80, 84
   as radical dissenter, 137–9
   concept of government, 32–3

Empire and Commerce in Africa, 85, 93, 116–17
International Government, 2, 6–7, 23–6, 29–33, 53–4, 55, 65, 67, 72–3, 217
   racial categories in his thinking, 134
   role in the British Empire, ix, 2, 84, 144
Woolf, Virginia, 47, 144, 249n
Woolf-Webb plan, the, 54–5, 68
workers, 148, 153, 154
world government, 29, 49, 62, 213
World War One, *see* First World War
World War Two, *see* Second World War

Zimmern, Alfred, 15, 16, 54